High Praise f(

MY VIETNAM, YOUR VIETNAM
by Christina Vo and Nghia M. Vo

A STUNNING, PRISMATIC MEMOIR about Vietnam's past and present as experienced by two generations.

FOREWORD REVIEWS

COMBINES THE FRAUGHT TENSION of Ava Chin's *Mott Street* and the tenderness of Elliot Tiber's *Taking Woodstock* . . . A nuanced contribution to the literature of the Vietnamese diaspora.

KIRKUS REVIEWS

MY VIETNAM, YOUR VIETNAM crosses borders and generations to give a panoramic view of a people. With heartfelt honesty, both Christina and Nghia grapple with displacement and identity in the long aftermath of war. A more extraordinary duet has never been written.

ERIC NGUYEN, author, *Things We Lost to the Water*

WRITTEN BY A DAUGHTER and her father, *My Vietnam, Your Vietnam* is a search for home, belonging and reconciliation. It is an unforgettable read for anyone who has been affected by trauma and who needs to find healing for themselves and for those they love.

NGUYEN PHAN QUE MAI, author, *Dust Child*

AN ENGROSSING DUAL MEMOIR of two generations steeped in loss and forged in trust. Beautifully written and a triumphant homage to one's homeland.

AMY M. LE, author, *Snow in Vietnam*; CEO, Quill Hawk Publishing

THIS BOOK IS MANY THINGS: an illustration of Vietnam seen through the prism of a father-daughter duo; a history of a country in upheaval; a diligent search for understanding; a contemplation of identity; a longing for belonging; a detailed, multifaceted look into the life of an immigrant family and the barriers children of immigrants face in connecting with their parents' culture, legacy, and heritage; a powerful narrative of the forces that shape how we define ourselves.

ALLISON HONG MERRILL, author, *Ninety-Nine Fire Hoops*

NGHIA M. VO AND CHRISTINA VO have composed a beautifully written story.

ROGER CANFIELD, author, *Hawks on the Other Side: Vietnam Peace Movement 1963-1967*

MY VIETNAM, YOUR VIETNAM

MY VIETNAM, YOUR VIETNAM

A FATHER FLEES. A DAUGHTER RETURNS. A DUAL MEMOIR.

CHRISTINA VO & NGHIA M. VO

THREE ROOMS PRESS
New York, NY

My Vietnam, Your Vietnam
by Christina Vo & Nghia M. Vo

© 2024 by Christina Vo & Nghia M. Vo

All rights reserved. No part of this book may be reproduced in any form or by any electronic or mechanical means, including information storage and retrieval systems, without permission in writing from the publisher, except by a reviewer, who may quote brief passages in a review. For permissions, please write to the address below or email editor@threeroomspress.com. Any members of education institutions wishing to photocopy or electronically reproduce part or all of the work for classroom use, or publishers who would like to obtain permission to include the work in an anthology, should send their inquiries to Three Rooms Press, 243 Bleecker Street #3, New York, NY 10014.

This is a work of creative nonfiction. The events are portrayed to the best of the author's memory. Some names have been changed to protect the identities of those involved. In addition, some parts of this book, including dialogue, characters and their characteristics, locations and time, may not be entirely factual.

ISBN 978-1-953103-46-8 (trade paperback original)
ISBN 978-1-953103-47-5 (Epub)
Library of Congress Control Number: 2023949977

TRP-111

First edition.
Publication Date: April 16, 2024

BISAC category codes
BIO002020 BIOGRAPHY & AUTOBIOGRAPHY / Cultural, Ethnic & Regional / Asian & Asian American
BIO026000 BIOGRAPHY & AUTOBIOGRAPHY / Personal Memoirs
HIS048000 HISTORY / Asia / Southeast Asia
SOC066000 SOCIAL SCIENCE / Refugees

COVER AND INTERIOR DESIGN:
KG Design International, www.katgeorges.com

COVER ILLUSTRATION:
Xuan Loc Xuan
behance.net/xuanlocxuan | instagram.com/xuanlocxuan

DISTRIBUTED INTERNATIONALLY BY:
Publishers Group West: www.pgw.com

Three Rooms Press
New York, NY
www.threeroomspress.com
info@threeroomspress.com

To Thủy for your love, support, and compassion.

How can you ever understand?

You've never lost and left your land.

All peoples share the human shape,

but human hearts don't beat alike.

—Du Tử Lê—

TABLE OF CONTENTS

FOREWORD

Nghĩa 3

Christina 5

DEPARTURE/ARRIVAL

Christina: North Carolina | 2002 11

Nghĩa: Connecticut | 1975 17

Christina: North Carolina | 2002 24

Nghĩa: Connecticut | 1975 28

Christina: Indiana | 2002 31

THE JOURNEY

Nghĩa: Việt Nam | 1974 39

Christina: Virginia | 1998 44

Nghĩa: South Việt Nam | 1974-1975 49

Christina: Hà Nội | 2002 53

Nghĩa: Phú Quốc | 1975 60

Christina: Hà Nội | 2002 66

Nghĩa: The Vast Ocean | 1975 74

Christina: Hà Nội | 2002 79

Nghĩa: Guam & Fort Indiantown Gap, Pennsylvania | 1975 85

TWO WORLDS

Christina: Hà Nội | 2002 95

Nghĩa: South Việt Nam | 1940s 104

Christina: South Việt Nam | 2003 109

Nghĩa: Vũng Tàu | 1950s 117

Christina: Vũng Tàu & Phú Quốc Island | 2003 126

Nghĩa: Vũng Tàu | 1950s 130

Christina: Hà Nội | 2003 134

Nghĩa: Vũng Tàu | 1950s 138

Christina: Hà Nội | 2003 144

THE SEDUCTRESS OF THE SOUTH

Nghĩa: Sài Gòn | 1950s 149

Christina: Hà Nội | 2003 155
Nghĩa: Sài Gòn | 1960s 159
Christina: Sài Gòn | 2003 163
Nghĩa: Sài Gòn | 1960s-70s 167
Christina: Sài Gòn | 2003 172
Nghĩa: Sài Gòn | 1975 176
Christina: Sài Gòn | 2003 179
Nghĩa: Sài Gòn | 1980s 183
Christina: Sài Gòn | 2003 187

REEDUCATION | REPATRIATION
Christina: Virginia | 2004 193
Nghĩa: Hartford, Connecticut | 1977-1988 196
Christina: San Francisco | 2005 201
Nghĩa: Sài Gòn | Late 1970s 205
Christina: Hà Nội | 2006 212
Nghĩa: Connecticut | 1980 219
Christina: Hà Nội | 2006 222
Nghĩa: Tennessee | 1985-1991 229

A CHILD OF VIỆT NAM
Christina: Virginia | 2008 235
Nghĩa: Indiana | 1991 246
Christina: Hà Nội | 2010 250
Nghĩa: Indiana | 1993 258
Christina: Hà Nội | 2010 264
Nghĩa: Orange County, CA | 1970s-Today 270
Christina: Hà Nội | 2011 273
Nghĩa: Everywhere, U.S.A. | 1970s-2000s 277
Christina: Virginia | 2011 283

EPILOGUE
Nghĩa: Virginia | 2023 293
Christina: Texas | 2023 295

AFTERWORD 299

ABOUT THE AUTHORS 303

MY VIETNAM, YOUR VIETNAM

FOREWORD

NGHĨA

ONCE UPON A TIME IN VIỆT Nam—a country steeped in mythology and history—I was born into a world torn apart by war. According to one legend, the Vietnamese people were the descendants of Lạc Long Quân and the Fairy Âu Cơ; eventually, the couple split and the children they bore went on to form two different groups: the highlanders and the lowlanders. This division—the first recorded divorce in history—would shape the fate of Việt Nam for centuries to come.

Between 1600 and 1802, for more than 200 years, Việt Nam was divided into two states whose boundaries roughly correspond to the 1960s North and South Vietnam. The North was ruled by the Lê King with the support of the northern Trịnh lords while the South was governed by the Nguyễn lords. Without connection between the two states, northerners and southerners evolved apart while fighting each other for the next fifty years. The arrival of the French in 1859 brought about a new division in Việt Nam: the South was made a colony of France while the center and North became a protectorate governed by local kings. After World War II, for the third time, the country was split again—this time into a communist north and a democratic south. The north was more disciplined and cautious, while the south was more individualistic and entrepreneurial.

This divided land was my home, where I witnessed the horrors of war and revolution. Despite the uncertainty and devastation, I struggled through school and college, amidst the background of war. I finished medical school and was eventually drafted into the military to serve my country in the South Vietnamese Army as a physician.

But when the war ended with the collapse of my homeland, I, like so many others, had to flee the communist regime. I set off on a journey across the sea to a new land.

I drifted on a small boat toward the unknown, and then, after two months in refugee camps, I found myself in the United States—a vast, modern, and foreign country. Through many years of retraining, I settled down in a small town, trying to make sense of my life. I was not alone, as thousands of my former countrymen had gone through similar struggles and hardships.

This tale of my story, woven with the rich history of a divided country, is a testament to the human spirit's unwavering determination to overcome obstacles in order to find peace.

To know our past helps shape who we become. For those of us who call Việt Nam home, our motherland is built on a history of divisions and wars that impacted all Vietnamese people, including our families and ourselves. Like the bloodstains on a soldier's uniform, our history reminds us of the sorrow of war. Perhaps, the division of our country, extending back to the legend of Lạc Long Quân and the Fairy Âu Cơ, remains within each of us, as we struggle to find wholeness from our history.

On my journey to the United States, I often found myself staring at the waves of the vast ocean, searching for a sense of peace, only to one day recognize that I could find that peace in another country, while still holding a deep abiding love and longing for my motherland. That was a deep division that remained within me for my entire life.

CHRISTINA

I NEVER IMAGINED THAT VIỆT NAM would play such a prominent role in my story. It was a distant land, foreign and unfamiliar. Growing up in small towns in the Southeast and Midwest, with a less than one percent Asian population, I hadn't entertained the idea of visiting, let alone living there. It was easy to deny my Vietnamese heritage in a sea of white faces.

My parents kept their history hidden away, never sharing it with my sister and me. They spoke Vietnamese to each other but didn't teach us a single word—not even hello. They kept us at arm's length, distancing us from their world—withholding a past they seemed so desperate to keep locked up. There were hints, mostly old black and white photos I found in a box in the basement, reflecting another place and time where they existed together. I only knew fragments of the story and yearned to reconstruct their narrative.

Throughout my childhood, there were moments when I was exposed to Vietnamese culture. We'd visit my father's family, who lived in Vietnamese communities, such as Orange County, California and New Orleans East, where hundreds of thousands of Vietnamese people created a version of little Việt Nam in the States. My uncle once took us to eat phở for breakfast. I asked him how people could eat such heavy meals—noodles and rare beef—for breakfast. He responded, "If you go to Việt Nam, you will understand." Our family had a Sunday night tradition of eating what my sister and I coined "noodle on the table," where we made summer rolls together—yet another tiny glimpse of my cultural background. Just as my parents seemed to withhold their history, I wanted to hide anything that identified me as being Vietnamese. I loathed my middle name, Tuyết, because it looked so unusual. Whenever friends came over to my house, I'd put away anything that looked foreign—like fish sauce and sriracha—not wanting to appear different from them.

It wasn't until my mother was diagnosed with cancer that I learned more about her family. She'd been estranged from them for twenty years, since she left Việt Nam, and only months after her terminal diagnosis, when her brother in Louisiana contacted my father's brother in New Orleans, were they reunited. My mother's sisters and grandmother, who lived in Europe, visited and shared their refugee stories and how they rebuilt their lives, finding new homelands in Switzerland and France. Their stories opened my eyes to the significance of Vietnam in my family's past. Only then did I hear that I had a brother who passed away in Việt Nam. Many years after that I learned his name was Thắng.

In college, race began to rise in my consciousness, as I began to explore my identity as a Vietnamese American. During my junior year, I waited tables at a Japanese restaurant and befriended other women who worked there—a Korean woman, a Japanese woman, and a Chinese American woman, born in Việt Nam. I started to develop an understanding of a certain kinship that I could have with other Asians, in particular, a friendship—a sisterhood—which I'd never experienced before.

There was a turning point when my college boyfriend and I broke up, and he asked me why we never spoke about being a mixed-race couple on a Southern campus. "Didn't you ever notice that people would look at us?" I realized that my identity was not something I had explored or given much thought to. In retrospect, there were opportunities to be involved with Vietnamese communities on campus and even study Vietnamese, but I was not interested, keeping my cultural heritage at bay.

And so, about a year after college, a desire suddenly burned deep within me to be someplace else, to know another country, and more importantly, to know myself better. I finally made the journey to Việt Nam. There I learned to understand my family history on a deeper level. I discovered my own identity as a Vietnamese American. I identified as being Việt Kiều, an overseas Vietnamese, and I finally came to know my father. Stepping foot on the soil of my motherland, Việt Nam became so much more than a distant land. It became a place that would forever be intertwined with my story.

DEPARTURE | ARRIVAL

CHRISTINA
North Carolina | 2002

THE FLUORESCENT LIGHTING. THE CUBICLE. THE campus with manicured lawns that housed our global headquarters. Everything about corporate America felt constraining as a recent college graduate. My tiny space was the only aspect of my job and life that I felt I could control. I tacked up a card featuring a Buddhist monk gazing at a stream, a black and white picture of the Eiffel Tower, and a bright pink note card with my favorite Eleanor Roosevelt quote, "Life was meant to be lived," emblazoned upon it. Despite these reminders of life outside the confines of those tiny four walls, I knew that I was too young to feel so suffocated, so restricted by my environment.

One morning, I logged into my personal email account while at work and discovered an email from the United Nations Development Programme in Hà Nội. They informed me that I'd been accepted for a six-month internship. A mixture of excitement, relief, and fear overwhelmed me as I skimmed the main points: the internship would begin in the fall, and I would be working with the social and poverty development cluster on an HIV/AIDS project.

I darted to the desk of a colleague, another intern who had become one of my close friends and told him the news. "I'm going to Việt Nam—I'm really going!" I crowed, as if I had won the only winning ticket out of the office.

SIX WEEKS PRIOR AT AN OFFSITE retreat for our marketing department, I realized that I needed to leave corporate life behind, or else I

CHRISTINA VÕ & NGHĨA M. VÕ

might always feel trapped in a life I didn't really want. I arrived a few minutes late to the retreat. I wanted to plunge into one of the plush sofas and spend the day in the lobby. Instead, I grabbed a cup of cheap, lukewarm coffee from the large stainless-steel dispenser in the lobby, snuck as quietly as I could into the auditorium-style room where the day's activities were scheduled to take place, and settled into a seat in the back.

A corporate coach had flown in from California to lead the retreat. With his bright yellow polo shirt and sunny disposition, the coach oozed optimism. He belted a loud "Good morning!" as he paced the front of the stage. I thought to myself, *This must be what all Californians are like.*

"I want us to get to know each other today in a way that you don't normally know your colleagues," he began, "so we're going to go around the room and each of you will share with us one thing your colleagues don't know about you. That's what we'll use to remember each other throughout the rest of the day."

I listened to my colleagues, most of them approaching middle age or older, announce their accomplishments, one after the other. Many recounted events in college or spoke longingly about the years before they entered their corporate job. They mentioned being in a band, their most exciting international travel, and impressive sports records. None of them said anything memorable about their current existence.

I thought to myself: *Is this what I have to look forward to? Is this time in my life actually going to be the most interesting? If it is, then what am I doing here?*

I was twenty-two years old and had been working as a marketing associate for the HIV/AIDS marketing department of a large pharmaceutical company for nine months. I'd started as an intern in the patient relations department but had found the marketing department to be much more exciting. I networked with one of the managers and landed a job on the team with one of the largest budgets. Still, it was ironic to me that our team was called the "HIV/AIDS marketing department." We were not marketing HIV/AIDS but rather the company had developed and launched the first single and combination HIV medications.

When I started college, my father desperately wanted me to pursue medicine—to become a doctor like him. I understood that his fundamental desire was for me to have a sense of stability and security. From his refugee perspective, only doctors, lawyers, and engineers were successful in the world. Instead, I chose to study public health. Not because I felt passionate about it, but rather because it would give me more options than simply studying medicine, and I assumed my father would be pleased that I was at least in the healthcare field.

From the outside, my first professional job looked great. I had a good salary and benefits. A corporate trajectory dangled in front of me. But truthfully, everything about it was underwhelming. I woke up dreading the twenty-minute drive from my home in Chapel Hill to the corporate campus in Research Triangle Park.

Older friends reminded me that the job would be a great resume builder. But I couldn't satiate the feeling of wanting more—not in the material sense, but spiritually. I wanted to create a deeply meaningful and purposeful life, not simply own a two-story home with a white picket fence in a nice suburban neighborhood.

During my nine months at the pharmaceutical company, I'd done my due diligence. I'd asked some of the more senior colleagues about their trajectory and—more importantly to me—if they were satisfied with their life paths. One responded that she wished she had pursued medicine instead. Another colleague on my team, sensing my ambivalence, assured me that I would have a solid future at the company. "You could become a pharmaceutical sales rep anywhere in the country," she told me. "You can go anywhere you want to." I was sent to San Diego to shadow one of the sales reps there, but his day bored me even more than my own. He shuffled from doctor's office to doctor's office, dragging along a small suitcase packed with pharmaceuticals and offering compliments to the assistants in order to increase his chances of meeting with the doctors. After two hours,

I knew that even if it meant I could live in a place as beautiful as San Diego, I didn't want his job.

The future didn't seem as bright as my colleagues insisted it would be.

"WHAT DID YOU SAY?" MY COLLEAGUE asked.

Absorbed in thought, I'd lost track of the conversation at hand. I realized it was my turn to answer the question.

"I am going to live and work in Việt Nam," I blurted out again.

Going to Việt Nam was not something I'd consciously thought about. Yet once I said it out loud, I knew I had to make it happen. It must have been an untapped dream, a desire rooted inside me—maybe it had been there for many years—that had never risen to the surface of my awareness until this second. But the moment the words left my mouth, I knew I would somehow find my way there.

A more interesting life would await me in Việt Nam. An unknown country and people, a personal history I was ready to explore.

A few weeks after the retreat, I sat at a local Starbucks on the main street of my college town. At the table next to me, a man in his early thirties chatted with a woman who I assumed was around the same age.

My ears perked up as I overheard the man say something about his friend Thomas who worked for the Asia Foundation office in Hà Nội.

"He's doing great there," he said. "He loves living in Việt Nam."

I scribbled down *Thomas, Asia Foundation* on a notepad. I believed that hearing this conversation was a serendipitous encounter, and that somehow this Thomas guy must be linked to my future life in Hà Nội.

While I pondered my new future in Việt Nam, I neither discussed details with my father, nor sought advice from him. I'd already chosen Hà Nội as my first choice of location in Việt Nam—even over Sài Gòn, where my parents had met in medical school. In the travel section of *The New York Times*, I'd seen a feature on Northern Việt

Nam, and I'd fallen in love with Hà Nội, which looked charming and quaint with its tree-lined streets, historical French architecture, and lakes dotted throughout town. All the international NGOs and development organizations were located there, so I figured I could parlay my public health degree into an internship in Hà Nội.

I only had a faint idea that in my father's eyes, Hà Nội unequivocally represented northern Việt Nam and therefore communism. I couldn't even begin to understand then that this would seem like a betrayal to him: choosing to venture to Hà Nội over Sài Gòn, the city he'd grown up in, the city he so deeply loved. I was too naive to consider anything but my own adventure.

I purchased cheap international prepaid calling cards from a local Asian market down the street and started reaching out to development organizations located in Hà Nội. I could only call just before bed each night, since Việt Nam's time zone was ten hours ahead of North Carolina. Whenever someone picked up, I didn't know what to expect. I wondered if anyone would agree to take me on.

One evening, I called the Asia Foundation. The executive director picked up the phone, and I quickly gave him my spiel, which by that point I could confidently articulate.

"I recently graduated from UNC Chapel Hill and I'm looking for an internship in Hà Nội," I said with as much confidence as I could muster.

"I'm busy right now but I have another Carolina alumni here that you could speak to," he said to me.

I knew he meant Thomas. I smiled.

Thomas's warm voice and sweet southern accent comforted me. "How can I help you?" he asked me.

"I want to work in Việt Nam," I said. "I'd love to get an internship related to public health. That's what I studied as an undergrad. If I could work on an HIV/AIDS project, that would be even better."

"I know who you can talk to," he assured me. "I'm going to email my boss's wife, Laura; she's a staff member in the United Nations Resident Coordinator's office. Maybe they will have something there for you."

"And when you get here," he added, "we can meet for dinner. Let me know if you need anything before then."

"Thank you so much!" I said, amazed by my good luck. Over the next few months, I made other Việt Nam connections. In that period, they all seemed to converge. A professor at Columbia University who had been doing research on the development of Việt Nam told me that two of his former students were in Việt Nam and he would reach out to them. It turned out those two students were Thomas's boss and his wife. So, when Laura received word of me from both her husband *and* her former professor, she was doubly motivated to fashion an internship that would work for me.

I was shocked at how quickly everything had fallen into place. It felt like a sign that it was all meant to be.

THE EVENING I RECEIVED CONFIRMATION OF my internship, still elated from the news, I ran into a Vietnamese American classmate of mine who had been involved with the Vietnamese Student Association throughout college.

I proudly told her about the internship and that I would be moving to Việt Nam.

"That's so funny," she exclaimed. "I remember when I called you at the beginning of our freshman year and asked if you wanted to join the Vietnamese Student Association. You said that you didn't really do the Vietnamese thing. And now you're going to Việt Nam."

I laughed. She was right. But so much had changed since then. For most of my life, aside from knowing my parents were from Việt Nam, I'd felt little connection to the place. In many ways, I'd rejected the Vietnamese part of myself. The country itself, and its people, had not at all been part of my consciousness. Now I felt a yearning to learn about my roots—about the place where my family, where I, came from.

I had no idea that one day, I would look back at my time in Việt Nam as some of the best years of my life.

NGHĨA
Connecticut | 1975

THE SLEEK, ELEGANT AMTRAK TRAIN SLIPPED slowly into the New London, Connecticut, train station on the western bank of the Thames River and stopped long enough to disgorge some of its customers. It was the end of June 1975, and I stood in front of the train station, pondering my future. I imagined that the Brits probably landed there first and named this town New London by the Thames to remind them of their cosmopolitan London city nestled by the Thames River. Had it been the French, perhaps they would have baptized it Nouveau Paris sur Seine; had it been the Germans, it could've been called New Frankfurt by the Rhine. Like these pilgrims from centuries past, I, too, would soon long for reminders of my homeland.

I couldn't help but think to myself that how I ended up in this country was nothing short of a miracle. My arrival marked the end of a two-month-long journey that had begun in my war-torn and shattered South Việt Nam. I'd escaped by boat from Phú Quốc Island, eventually landed in Guam, and then continued to Fort Indiantown Gap, a refugee camp outside of Harrisburg, Pennsylvania.

Only two months prior—on April 30, 1975—a bloody and tumultuous twenty-one-year war had ended with the communist takeover of Sài Gòn, forcing more than a hundred thousand Vietnamese people to abandon our beloved motherland, South Việt Nam. After seeing the ferocity and violence of the long war, I knew instinctively that I had to escape, or I would be imprisoned and maybe even killed. The communists had blatantly invaded South Việt Nam—they'd sent their

17

sixteen divisions to conquer our country with only eleven divisions. I saw only two possible futures in South Việt Nam: either I could follow the communists' strict rules, or I would die in their jails.

Now, after being so suddenly transplanted to America from Việt Nam, it struck me that I, along with my fellow Vietnamese refugees, knew nothing about America and its culture. I barely even spoke the language. Although America had been involved in the Việt Nam War for almost two decades, the relationship had been strictly about the war—fighting communism, killing, celebrating wins, and mourning losses. It hadn't been about an exchange of culture or historiography. I had no idea how I would integrate into this country.

By the end of the war, a total of 130,000 out of seventeen million people (less than one percent of the population) were able to leave as refugees—looking for freedom and survival, a shelter from retribution from a victorious communist regime. Years later, three million more escaped from South Việt Nam as "boat people," although only two million arrived safely in the shanty camps of Southeast Asia. Approximately one million people perished at sea from storms, winds, pirate attacks, power failures, or lack of food and water.

The sudden transition from war to peace bore down heavily on my mind. Yet here I was, standing on the streets of a small and peaceful town in an apparently serene country. It was this peace that the South Vietnamese had been searching frantically for over two decades without any luck. Now, strangely enough, many of us were finding it—not in our palm-covered country dotted with golden rice fields but in a foreign land called America.

Why America? Why 10,000 miles away from home? I was too confused at that moment to formulate an adequate answer. But at least, I thought to myself, there would be no more gunshots, artillery shelling, airplane bombings, grenade explosions, disfigured bodies, or crying and wailing mothers, daughters, and other relatives.

FOR A MONTH, I WANDERED AROUND the Indiantown Gap camp waiting for a sponsor. One day, I heard news that a hospital in

Connecticut was looking for someone who'd passed the equivalency test, and the interviewer would drop by in a few days to see potential candidates. I knew that I wanted to be interviewed, but because I was a refugee, stranded in a camp, I couldn't afford to get dressed adequately. I didn't have fancy shoes; I didn't even have a coat.

I went to the interview anyway.

The hospital was looking to recruit house officers because it had lost accreditation for its residency program. I had no idea what accreditation meant. All I wanted was a job. A few weeks later, I heard the news that my friend and I would be sponsored by that small hospital in Connecticut. I was relieved; I thought to myself, This is what makes America so great—the opportunities afforded to people, even refugees.

The next day, he, his wife, their seven children, and I boarded the train in Harrisburg, Pennsylvania to our unknown future.

We were on safe terrain, but my thoughts turned to economic survival. Could refugees—modern pilgrims from a small and defunct country the size of an elongated Washington State—forge a future in a foreign land? Could we survive in America? I thought about all the issues I would face: political safety, medical training, finding a job, raising a family, the language barrier, my future, and the loss of homeland and personal property. These thoughts popped up in no specific order and clashed wildly in my worried mind. Peace, I now understood, brought with it a flurry of new issues and unique problems. I wondered where we would be if the strangers we were barreling toward did not open their arms to welcome us.

WE ARRIVED AT OUR DESTINATION IN New London, Connecticut, and exited the train doors. A cool sea breeze blew gently past me, bringing me back to my present reality and away from my concerns, as I disembarked. Although it was almost July, the weather was cool, if not cold, for someone arriving straight from the tropics. I looked around me; the town, with its beachfront and shoreline, reminded me of Vũng Tàu, where my grandmother lived and where I'd spent a few years of my childhood. The only difference was that New London, with its characteristic Cape Cod houses (this was the first time I had seen anything like them) and its busy lifestyle, lay in a temperate region, while Vũng Tàu, with its palm trees and provincial atmosphere, was perpetually bathed in a sweltering tropical heat. I couldn't have known then that these comparisons were the first of many to come; I would forever make references and find connections to Việt Nam over the course of my years in America. No matter how well I integrated into my new life, a certain nostalgia would linger with me.

Disconnected from our families and friends and still reeling from the biggest loss of all—the loss of South Việt Nam—I tentatively put my feet down on this new land and cast my eyes toward my unknown future.

On the train ride, I'd learned more about my new friend and colleague, Tùng: he was in his mid-forties, and had practiced medicine for twelve years in Việt Nam. I noticed he was restless, getting up frequently while on the train. At each stop, he would stand up and ask if we had arrived; then he would double-check the names of the stations, referring back to his map. I understood the uncertainty he was feeling. The map in his hand was the only tangible thing he could hold on to as we moved toward an uncertain future.

During the war and the period of turmoil, families were often divided. Some—mostly middle-aged men who had stayed close to home during the war—were able to escape with their families intact. Most young men, like myself, were forced to leave the country by themselves, because we were serving in the military and were free to escape only when our units disbanded. I'd left alone after my unit disbanded, and it was only later that I'd received notification from my wife's family that she and my two-year-old son had remained in South Việt Nam.

I waited for Tùng and his family to gather their belongings before heading to town, where we were greeted by the local press. I imagined they'd been notified by the local hospital. I was surprised and overwhelmed by the wild reception and would have preferred a much more low-key first hour in my new home, but I knew that I didn't have a say in the matter.

A handful of photographers snapped pictures, particularly of Tùng and his large family. We were told that there would be a press conference after the photos. As I understood it, we were the talk of the small town.

Tùng did most of the talking at the press conference. He spoke about his past experiences, his escape, and his family. He told the reporters how he was born in North Việt Nam and had lived in an area that was previously controlled by communists. In 1954, just before the armistice that divided the country into two states, he'd migrated south with his family. His family had established themselves in Sài Gòn and now, twenty-one years later, after the fall of Sài Gòn, they'd escaped the communists one more time.

"All my life, I was haunted by the communists," he said. "I have always tried to put distance between them, myself and my family."

Exhausted from the journey, I didn't talk much myself. I only wanted to rest after such a long trip.

When the interview ended, I went to the cafeteria, hoping for a hot meal, and discovered that it was closed. On my first night of real freedom—my first night outside of a refugee camp in the U.S.—I went to bed hungry.

THE NEXT DAY, I WENT TO Tùng's house and he informed me that he had inquired with the hospital's chief of surgery about the accreditation of the program. We needed one accredited internship year in order to be allowed to sit for the state board license exam. Once we had the license, we would be able to practice. But this program was not accredited, which meant that the internship would not help us get licensed. Tùng thought he and his family should leave so that he could join an accredited program elsewhere.

A few days later, he told me that his friend had lined up a transitional year for him at a hospital in New Jersey, and he and his family were heading there. Within a week, they had packed up and left. I believed it was the right decision for him and his large family; I didn't begrudge his choice. But now my one friend was gone. The agency administrator should have explained to me the importance of accreditation before sending me to New London; if I'd understood the situation better, I would have stayed in the camp longer to look for another position.

As I became familiar with the small town and adjusted to my new life in this country, I noticed that the publication of the interview Tùng had given on our first day in town drew a lot of attention and strange reactions. At the grocery store, someone asked me if I was the man with seven children. At the local barbershop, I received the same question. I was glad that people mistook me for Tùng, making me feel that I could hide under the radar. There were so few Vietnamese in the town that I suppose it was easy for the people to confuse the two of us.

A FEW WEEKS INTO MY TIME in New London, the head of the local nursing school asked me if I could give a talk on Việt Nam to the students. I didn't know what to say, but she was so insistent that I finally agreed. I looked around town at the local library and bookstores for materials about Việt Nam to bring to the talk, but I couldn't find any. So, I improvised and spoke about Việt Nam's history, geography, and schooling, and Vietnamese ways of thinking.

During the talk, someone asked me, "How do people meet in Việt Nam? In bars?"

"Certainly not," I responded. "Vietnamese society is rather segregated, and it is not widely accepted for men and women to meet in the streets—especially not in bars, which carry a pejorative meaning in Việt Nam."

Not long after giving this talk, I received a call from a Japanese woman who was married to an American seaman, Ed. She told me that she hadn't met an Asian person for quite some time, so she was eager to meet me. Eventually, the two of us became close friends and a source of support for me—which I desperately needed, with how far away from my family I was.

A lady whose church had sponsored a group of Vietnamese refugees called me one day and asked if she could introduce me to the group. This I welcomed, because I longed to have Vietnamese friends. I discovered that in my small town, there were four Vietnamese people, all between the ages of twenty-one and twenty-five years old, and all single except for one. The local churches who had sponsored them placed them together in an apartment complex downtown. They were in the armed forces and had somehow found a way to leave Việt Nam. Now, they worked in factories and studied English at night.

Connecting with these other Vietnamese immigrants helped me adjust to my life in New London; it was comforting to have a reminder of my homeland, to have some anchors to my past. Still, I knew that I had no choice but to forge ahead, to find my footing on this new terrain.

CHRISTINA

North Carolina | 2002

IN THE MONTHS AFTER I RECEIVED confirmation about my internship, my plans to venture to Việt Nam began to crystallize. I reached out to Lara, a Vietnamese American doctoral candidate from California, who I'd met during my senior year in college at a public health conference. She had mentioned to me that she was planning to spend a few months in Hà Nội to conduct her dissertation research. I sent her an email, and discovered that she'd be there at the same time. She offered to let me stay at her aunt's place in Hà Nội for a few months while I settled in, and I knew she'd be a lifeline for me as I navigated a foreign land.

Lara introduced me to another Vietnamese American, Thi, who had also spent time in Việt Nam and was moving to Chapel Hill to start a doctoral program in public health. Her arrival in Chapel Hill coincided with the last two months I would be there, and during that time, we grew close.

In many ways, Thi was like an older sister to me: she was intelligent and savvy, and always seemed to be in control. As I prepared for my departure, she advised me on how to pack my suitcase to maximize the items that I could bring with me. Spending time with her made me realize how much I longed to be more connected to Việt Nam, and even more specifically to family. My real older sister, who was two years older than me, and I were not close. While I was venturing to Việt Nam, she had just given birth to her first child. Our paths were dramatically different, and I didn't feel a kinship to her in the same way as I did with Thi. Mostly, though, I wished my father was more present in helping me navigate these next steps. Yet, the words "help me" seemed to be lodged somewhere in my throat.

One evening, Thi brought out her old photo album and told me stories of her time in Việt Nam.

"I wished I could've stayed longer in Hà Nội," she said to me. "A few days before I left, I saw a posting for a position at the United Nations. Before I knew it, I was sliding an envelope with my cover letter and resume under the gate."

I tilted my head in surprise. "You would've lived there longer?"

"Yes, I think I would have if things had worked out with that job," she responded.

I joked that maybe I would meet a boyfriend there. "Maybe Thomas will be my boyfriend!" I exclaimed with a laugh. "Wouldn't that be interesting—if I ended up being with the man who helped me get to Việt Nam?"

While I was kidding, I knew that I was clutching for something tangible to hold on to—someone to help anchor me. I wondered how long I would be in Việt Nam, and if I, like Thi, would hope to stay as my time there ended. In Thi's photos, I recognized the French architecture of some of the buildings in Hà Nội that I'd seen in images online. One photo—a man smoking a cigarette, relaxing in a cyclo, awaiting his next customer—looked as if it had been taken decades earlier. It seemed so romantic; magical, even.

Hà Nội was beginning to feel very real to me—and frightening. It looked so different from where I was currently living, and I was acutely aware that Việt Nam was still technically a developing country. Was I ready for the challenges living there would present?

During my last weeks in the States, I wondered what I was doing, and if I could actually survive in a developing country or if I would miss the comforts I was so accustomed to.

I NEVER ASKED MY FATHER WHAT he thought about me going to Việt Nam, and he didn't offer his opinion, but I yearned to know: Did he disapprove? Did he support my adventure? Did he think I was brave for venturing there?

Instead, there was silence.

There had never been much dialogue between my father and me. My mother, while she was alive, had been the primary line of communication between us. If my sister or I needed something, my mother asked him; we never spoke directly to him about anything, really. I wasn't comfortable asking him questions, and if I did, I didn't receive much of an answer, often just a mumble. I feared my father. When my mother passed away when I was fourteen years old, I didn't know how to engage with him.

I knew implicitly that he loved Việt Nam, although he never spoke about it. I'm not sure how I understood this as a kid, but after my mother passed away—which seemed to be a trigger for him to explore his own history and wounds—he started writing about the history of Việt Nam and also curated anthologies of stories of other Vietnamese refugees. I knew that nobody could spend that much time writing about something if they didn't love it.

His first book, *The Pink Lotus*, was a fictionalized account of the story of his life. When he published it, I was still a teenager and, truth be told, uninterested in the story. I didn't even read it in its entirety. I simply skimmed the parts that were most interesting to me—namely, the parts about my mother and his escape from Việt Nam. I knew the highlights: he was a doctor in the South Vietnamese Army stationed in the Mekong Delta, and then transferred to Phú Quốc Island, and it was from there that he escaped when Sài Gòn fell to the communists. But I did not know, nor did I care to understand, the essence of his story and his deep love of South Việt Nam.

So much remained unspoken in my family about our history. In my adolescence, I didn't have the consciousness to understand how hurtful my lack of interest might be to my parents.

DURING MY JUNIOR YEAR IN HIGH school, my class went on a field trip to a museum in Indianapolis, sixty miles north of our town. We stopped at a mall for lunch, and when I noticed a kiosk displaying hundreds of six-inch standing flags from all over the world, I approached and shyly asked the salesperson if he sold the Vietnamese flag (I had no idea what the flag looked like, so I couldn't find it myself). He handed me a red flag with a yellow star in the middle.

When I returned home that day, I proudly set the flag on the kitchen counter next to the telephone, believing that my father would be grateful.

Instead, he scolded me.

"Why did you do this?" he asked in a harsh tone I'd rarely heard from him. "This isn't the *right* flag."

He took the flag away immediately.

I wasn't sure what he had done with it—whether he'd hidden it or thrown it in the trash—but within a few days, a different flag sat on our kitchen countertop: a bright yellow flag with three red horizontal stripes.

"This is the *true* Vietnamese flag—the one of my homeland," my father informed me.

Much later in my life, I reached the conclusion that our relationship had always been beset, and perhaps even defined, by the disappointments that remained unspoken. My purchase of the wrong Vietnamese flag. My father's inability to speak to my high school history class about the Việt Nam War. My decision to venture to Hà Nội and not Sài Gòn.

NGHĨA

Connecticut | 1975

BEING AN IMMIGRANT IN A NEW country, I quickly learned there
was so much I didn't know—not only in the hospital, where there was
a lot of clinical work to do, but also in my day-to-day life. Because of
this—even though the hospital wasn't accredited, my year in New
London wasn't wasted. I used that period to learn how to express
myself in English and, in particular, to be understood by my patients.
U.S. medical technology was new and in many ways different from
what I had practiced with in Việt Nam. It was an eye-opener that prepared me for what would come ahead—a grueling five-year surgical
training program.

After a few weeks, I realized there was little I could do without
having a car. In many countries, a car would be considered a luxury
item and a status symbol, but in the U.S. it felt like a necessity. When
I needed something urgently, I had to wait until someone was available to drive me to the store. I could not ask for rides all the time, and
I didn't want to, since my friends had their own agendas and responsibilities, so I decided to look for a car on my own.

Given that I had no experience purchasing a car, I solicited Ed's
help. After I saw a Ford Pinto, an attractive car at the time for young
people, parked at the camp, I was immediately drawn to it. When it
was time to purchase the car, Ed did all the haggling. I never knew if
I got a good deal or not, but I was happy to have a car.

My brother, Tuấn, and sister-in-law were living with me at that
time. Tuấn started out working at a local store, making just enough to

get by. But this arrangement didn't last very long. He'd been accustomed to making large sums of money in Việt Nam and knew that the job as store clerk would not lead him anywhere, so he decided to further his education. With the help of a sponsor, he began looking into the college entrance requirements and making plans to obtain an equivalency degree in pharmacy. He and his wife decided to move to Columbus, Ohio—close to her parents—so he could begin taking the courses he needed to apply for pharmacy school.

It was late October by then, and the changing color of the leaves was so spectacular—something that I would not fully appreciate until later, and something I had never witnessed while living in Việt Nam. I did notice the change in foliage from green to yellow, brown, and red, but I was initially too absorbed in my daily work and helping my brother move to pay close attention to it. Slowly, though, I started to observe the shifting seasons. The leaves gently fell to the ground, forming big piles at every street corner; a few weeks later, all the branches had lost their foliage. This was a completely new experience for me.

That first year, I was also unaware of daylight savings time, so when I showed up at work one day and nobody was there, I asked the clerk if it was a holiday.

"No," he said. "You're just here an hour earlier than usual. It's daylight savings; you're supposed to turn your clock one hour backward."

From then on, I understood the importance of paying attention to the local news so that I could stay apprised about what was happening locally.

Weeks later, we drove to Ohio through the Amish country in Pennsylvania and then through Pittsburgh. The thermometer was dropping, and a cold front moved through the Midwest. Through a new immigrant's eyes, the spectacle of the white flakes flying down slowly and sticking to the windshield before gradually melting away was simply beautiful, and I recognized that there was so much newness in my life in this new country. The seasons and the beauty of nature that I had not experienced in my homeland was quite awe-inspiring.

Later, when my two daughters were born, I would give them Vietnamese names that would honor the seasons: Thu, or "fall," and Tuyết, meaning "snow." Only in adulthood would they learn what their names signified to me: the freshness of starting anew, and the inspiration of the natural beauty around us.

CHRISTINA
Indiana | 2002

BEFORE LEAVING FOR VIỆT NAM, I spent a few days with my father and Alice, my stepmother who was also Vietnamese, in Indiana. They'd been together for five years and married for only two years. Alice and I shared the same middle name, Tuyết, a fact that irked me for some reason. Over the years, I'd heard different versions of how my father and Alice met. A family member told me that they were introduced to each other by my uncle in New Orleans. Another story that I heard from my mother's best friend, Teri, was that they had already met at an event before my mother passed away. She suspected that Alice was after my father from that initial meeting.

For Christmas the first year without my mother, we drove to New Orleans to celebrate with my uncle and his family. By that time, eight months after my mother's death, we still didn't know the name of the woman my father spoke to on the phone, but my sister and I had figured out she lived in New Orleans.

We drove past the exit to my uncle's house, and I knew without my father saying anything to us that we were going to Alice's house first. Although I didn't know the woman we were about to meet, I still wanted my father to impress her and urged him to stop at the grocery store to buy her flowers.

When she opened the door, her mother standing behind her, I couldn't help but think about how different she looked than my mother. She was tall, even taller than my father, and slender, with long, shiny black hair that fell to the middle of her back. In the photos

I'd seen of my mother when she was younger, I'd thought she was beautiful, but she'd gained weight over the years and then become bone-thin when she had cancer.

Alice gave us a tour around her house. She made a lot of art, showing us some of her pieces scattered throughout the home. I was impressed, and I felt she had accomplished so much more than my mother, who I viewed as having been "just" a housewife. At that time, I didn't see how much creative energy my mother had put into raising me and my sister—into nourishing our family.

We went to eat phở at a Vietnamese restaurant down the street, where Alice awkwardly asked us questions about our lives. My sister barely said anything. I tried to be polite, but in the back of my mind, I was thinking of my mother and the last time I'd had phở with her.

Two months before she passed away, she pleaded with my father to take her to the MD Anderson Cancer Center in Houston to see if there was a novel treatment that could save her life. The appointment lasted five minutes. There was nothing they could do. Afterward, we went directly to a phở restaurant, and I stared at my mother with her chopsticks mid-air, gazing blankly into space, reconciling the fact that her life was ending.

Alice brought forth something in my father that I had never seen before—a certain life and vitality. I remember reading love poems he'd written shortly after they met. Later, I understood that she helped my father rekindle and remember his love for Việt Nam. It was during those early years with her that he wrote The Pink Lotus and began working on other books related to Vietnamese history. The love, passion, and healing he found with her also, I believe, helped him chip away at the trauma of leaving his beloved homeland. Even as a teenager who had not yet experienced falling in love, I understood that Alice sparked something within him that had been extinguished—perhaps because his life with my mother was so focused on raising us.

Alice and my father dated long-distance for their entire relationship. In her early forties, as a second career, she finished medical school—her determination likely another characteristic that my father admired about her. She studied full time and sold Mary Kay cosmetics on the side, saving enough money to put herself through medical school. While I was in high school and the first two years of college, Alice was a resident at a hospital in Indianapolis. She drove down almost every weekend to see my father. In the last two years of college, she was admitted to a fellowship at Duke University in Durham, North Carolina—only a fifteen-minute drive from where I lived—and I sometimes visited her there.

I will never forget one of the paintings that she hung above her dining room table in her Durham apartment. It was of her and my father—both wearing áo dàis, traditional Vietnamese attire, and sitting happily in a cyclo, big grins on their faces as they rode through a rice field in Việt Nam. Only later did I think about how much my father must have loved that painting.

After years of long-distance relations, they finally got married when I was a junior in college. For their wedding, they hosted a party in a small ballroom at a hotel in Bloomington, Indiana, about thirty miles north of my father's home. For entertainment, they invited Elvis Phương, a Vietnamese singer known for his appearances on *Paris by Night*—a popular Vietnamese entertainment program. He also, I later learned, happened to be a childhood friend of my father.

I felt a small amount of jealousy—even resentment—toward Alice. I often asked myself why. Was it because I felt that she had replaced my mother? Did I believe she took my father's attention away from me?

Years later, the reason crystallized for me. It was more complicated than that. It was a jealousy that stemmed from the fact that Alice connected with my father in a way I felt I was not able to, around his true love: Việt Nam.

A FEW DAYS BEFORE MY DEPARTURE to Hà Nội, Alice and my dad brought me to a Chinese restaurant where Alice's tennis friends, a group of Vietnamese women, met every Sunday for lunch after playing together at a local club.

The restaurant featured an Asian buffet and was reasonably priced at $7.95 for a Sunday buffet. Porcelain white teacups were neatly placed in the center of each table.

Alice led us to a table where two Vietnamese women were already seated—both in cute tennis outfits—short skirts with matching shirts—and with their makeup perfectly intact. She introduced them as Thủy and Hiền.

Seeing these women, I didn't think Alice meshed well with this group: she was not the type of woman who would so meticulously consider her appearance after playing tennis. When she did dress up, she always looked uncomfortable and awkward. For her wedding party, she had hand-sewn white, tutu-like dress. One time, I remember her wearing a sparkling gold shirt paired with light pink leggings. She was also not the type of woman who could effortlessly participate in chit-chat—a characteristic I appreciated in her.

"Christina is going to live in Việt Nam," she informed the women abruptly. "She's leaving in a few days to go to Hà Nội."

This tendency of Alice's to interject statements at uncomfortable moments was a trait I had noticed about her and echoed the awkward manner in which she'd tried to become part of our family over the years.

Still, in this moment, I could sense what was underneath her statement to these two ladies: she was proud of me.

I sat there quietly, as did my father. I looked down at the placemat—emblazoned with the Chinese zodiac—and although I knew the characteristics of my sign, the goat, I read the description carefully: *Goats are able to persevere through any difficulty. This is their most notable trait. They are strong and resilient, though their gentleness might be misleading.*

When I looked up, I could see the women assessing me, then glancing coyly at each other.

I expected at least to receive some half-hearted encouragement from these women—words of affirmation, compliments on my bravery in setting off to explore the unknown. Similar to what I had wished for, hoped for, from my father.

"Oh, she's going to hate it in Việt Nam," Thủy said. "What is she going to do there?"

But she addressed this to Alice. She and her friend didn't look at me now, and I didn't engage with them either. I was still timid around older Vietnamese people, not knowing what to say or how to address them politely.

I wanted to tell them that going to Việt Nam would be magical. I wanted to tell them about how Lara would be waiting for me when I arrived, and how Thi had introduced me to two of her closest friends from Hà Nội, Anh and Nguyệt, two local Vietnamese women who had been like sisters to her when she was there. I wanted to share how I already felt deep bonds were forming with those women.

"Is she single?" Hiền added. "And how old is she?"

"She's twenty-two years old—and she's going alone to Việt Nam," Alice said proudly in my defense.

"She's too American, she's only twenty-two years old, and she's single," Thủy said dismissively.

"And it's so dirty there," Hiền said, shaking her head. "She'll return to the States quickly. I don't think she'll stay there."

"I don't even think they have real bathrooms there," Thủy said with a chuckle.

"She'll be fine," Alice quickly responded.

I remained silent, not realizing that this disapproving tone and interrogation style was somewhat typical in Vietnamese culture—I hadn't spent enough time with Vietnamese people outside of my nuclear family to have been exposed to it before. I didn't know then that soon enough I would be under the scrutiny of a number of Vietnamese people—strangers who would bombard me with questions about my age, marital status, and salary, among other things.

It dawned on me that for these women going to Việt Nam was not a great adventure as it was for me. It was the country they'd left behind to create an opportunity for a better life. Although I wanted to argue with them and convince them to be equally excited for me as Alice was, I was too timid to voice my opinion. They couldn't understand that going to Việt Nam was a big step forward in my life—a journey into the unknown.

In his typical fashion, my father said nothing to these women who chatted about everything that was wrong with my plans. I desperately needed something from him at that moment; I wanted to plead with him: *Say something. Anything. You're proud of me. It's a big adventure. Don't be scared.*

Instead, silence.

Alice, on the other hand, stepped in with some positivity: "Life is visible there," she declared. "It is lived on the streets and in every store—you can see so much life. Sometimes people have a storefront where they sell things, like a convenience store or a shop that fixes motorbikes. Then, upstairs, they have their living quarters. It's a lot different from here."

What she said fascinated me, but at that moment I couldn't understand what "visible life" really meant.

THE EVENING BEFORE MY DEPARTURE, WE went to a bookstore. My father picked up a memoir about Việt Nam—*The House on Dream Street*, by Dana Sachs, an American journalist who wrote about her experience living in Hà Nội in the late nineties.

He handed me the book. "This looks interesting for you."

I wondered if that book and her specific journey would be something my father was curious about too. Perhaps he meant it as a genuine gift, but it seemed to me that my father viewed my journey to Việt Nam as what it had been for Sachs—a naive American's adventure in Hà Nội. Regardless of intent, by purchasing the book and giving it to me before my departure, that's the message he seemed to be sending.

THE JOURNEY

NGHĨA

Việt Nam | 1974

My journey to the United States, that peaceful and unfamiliar land, began in January 1974 when I was drafted into the South Vietnamese army. I was twenty-seven years old. Almost two decades had passed since Việt Nam had been partitioned into two countries. During that time, I'd lived, grown up, studied, and worked in a war-ravaged country. All I knew was war. Signs of it were everywhere: on the walls, in the newspapers, in movie dialogue, in the lyrics of songs, and especially on the faces you passed in the street. There was a feeling of sadness, despair, and fatigue hidden behind this Asian mask of serene acceptance. One could sense pain, disappointment, suffering, and now the agony of defeat. It was difficult for the Vietnamese people to avoid the welling up in their eyes, tears slowly running down their bony cheeks.

All students at this time received their military training while in college. When my classmates and I graduated in December 1973, we chose our units. By January 1974, we were ready for duty.

Unlike U.S. servicemen, we would remain in the army for the duration of the war, not for just one year. Our service could last five or ten years, or until we were disabled or died, or until the war ended. Although it had been going on for almost two decades, the war, like tropical monsoons, never seemed to end.

As a physician, I reported to the medical support team in the city of Cần Thơ in the fourth Military Region (MRIV) in the Mekong Delta. Compared to the northern front, which was close to the demilitarized zone, the area was relatively peaceful. People attended to their private business without any disruption, and there were no night curfews. My colleagues, however, were scattered all over the country: in the northern region and the southern part of South Việt Nam, attached to combat units or at military hospitals or dispensaries.

Although I had never been to the Mekong Delta before this, I knew the region was South Việt Nam's rice basket. Cần Thơ, a provincial city on the Mekong River, was quiet and bucolic with its laid-back people, its golden rice fields, its multiple arroyos, and its brackish rivers upon which sampans filled with fruits, flowers, and local products glided gracefully on their way to the floating markets. The sampans were powered either by motorized engines or by the strong arms of teenagers, usually girls (boys were drafted by both insurgent and national armies) who worked rhythmically with a pair of wooden oars. I remember hearing the six-sentence songs characteristic of the delta region, which frequently dealt with love and separation. Romance, music, simplicity, and rusticity characterized the delta people.

The waters of the Mekong River, mostly limpid at its source, were of an indescribable dark color by the time they reached the city after crossing five other Southeast Asian states. They served as a dumping ground for all the people living and all the agricultural industries settled on its edges. These same waters, however, carried with them the rich silt that gave the delta its unique fertility. Fish and shrimp somehow managed to survive and even thrive in that milieu, to the delight of delta inhabitants. Large catfish—some up to three hundred pounds—had been fished out of the same waters forty miles upstream.

Regardless of what would transpire in the years to come, this is the image of South Việt Nam that would remain in my mind: a peace-loving people, poor but happy until war came to them and destroyed their livelihood. They had enough to eat—rice, catfish, and plenty of tropical fruit—and they were satisfied despite not being materially rich.

UPON ARRIVAL AT OUR UNIT, MY friend and I were assigned to sign the death certificate of a first lieutenant who had passed away the night before. The macabre assignment was not what we expected on our first day of duty.

We'd heard that he was the commanding officer of a fortified camp sixty miles south of town and was checking the perimeters of the camp when he accidentally stepped on a landmine that blew him apart.

When I saw the body, I stood silent, not knowing what to do. The cause of death was obvious: a shattered right foot and leg, along with hundreds of mine fragments scattered all over his body. A young officer whose baby face and healthy body seemed to have been untouched by the war tribulations until that moment.

I signed the death certificate and we left.

I couldn't avoid thinking that a lot of tears would be shed over this man that evening. He was so young—probably only a few years out of military academy—yet already a war victim. His wife and parents would undoubtedly be devastated. There was nothing they could do except weep until their eyes became swollen shut or they ran out of tears. I imagined the widow would ask herself, *Why would this tragedy happen to me? Why me? Why me? Who will take care of our young children? How will we survive?* She might start blaming herself for not taking diligent care of him, or for not having spent more time with him. And the parents would ask themselves the same questions: *Out of the millions of parents in this world, why did this tragedy happen to us?* For this family, he was a son and a husband, full of energy and promises and destined for a bright future. But in this sad moment, he was just a cold and disfigured body wrapped in a yellow flag adorned with three horizontal red stripes—a bright future cut short by the meanness of the war.

I thought to myself, *War is brutal, senseless, and unforgiving.*

The vision of this mutilated body followed me for some time. It wasn't that I hadn't seen dead bodies before. There were many of them in the hospitals where I received my training. It was the degree of senseless mutilation that this man had suffered, and the fact that he was so young and already dead, that impacted me.

For many nights, I couldn't sleep; I was haunted by the vision of his body. It reminded me of the smell of decaying organs that persistently stuck to surgeons's hands for days despite repeated handwashing. As for the officer, I knew he was at peace and no longer suffering. It was his family's turn to go through the agonizing pain of grieving.

This tragedy, of course, was not unique. At that time, thousands and thousands of soldiers suffered from the same fate each month all over South Việt Nam. Each war victory was built on a mountain of dead soldiers. The only victor was death itself.

I thought to myself that it could just as easily have been me or my friend. Life and death were just a matter of luck or fate for all of us during that period. This notion was reinforced by the escalating daily casualties, which rendered many of us somewhat cynical. These violent killings, and the senseless murder of untold numbers of innocent people, scarred our young hearts to the point that we were no longer able to handle the suffering and pain. It was not that tears would no longer flow down our bony cheeks. They just flowed slowly and in lesser amounts than the torrents of years past.

The tragic end of this officer's life reminded me of one of my classmates, a sweet and good-hearted student who'd died in 1967 when a missile—shot into Sài Gòn by the Việt Cộng communist insurgents—hit his home one night, killing him and his whole family. I only realized that we had lost that young, innocent classmate when the bad news spread all over the campus a few days later. Missiles landed in various parts of the city a few times each month, forcing us all to lay sandbags inside our homes and take cover when we heard the hissing sounds of flying rockets or siren sounds announcing incoming missiles.

In the 1960s and 1970s, Sài Gòn seemed to be untouched by the war according to local and foreign correspondents. But in reality, the Saigonese lived day by day, not knowing what would come next. A person could be there one day and gone the following because of attacks by the Việt Cộng, who threw grenades on people going to markets or movie theaters, blew up buildings Americans frequented, and shot missiles into the city. This was the reality of life in a war-torn country.

Life in the countryside was less hectic and much safer than in populous Sài Gòn. The insurgent Việt Cộng could make a name for themselves in the news if they struck large cities; small towns or the countryside, not so much. But, everywhere, including in the Mekong Delta, war and its debris were palpable.

Somehow, life at that time reminded me of the sacred lotus flower, which is planted in mud and which must rise through muddy waters before opening its petals. It is no surprise to me that the lotus is known as a beautiful survivor.

Like the lotus, I felt a kinship with my fellow colleagues in the Delta. We had to persevere through these times and, hopefully, find a way to the sunlight.

CHRISTINA
Virginia | 1998

THE FIRST TIME I HEARD MY father give more than a one- or two-line response to anything was at my mother's funeral. The second time, about a year-and-a-half later, I listened to him speak at a reunion in front of his Sài Gòn Medical School class in Tysons Corner, Virginia. I was a freshman in college and drove from North Carolina to meet my father and Alice, who flew in from Indiana. My father's classmate, whom he had seen in New Orleans while visiting my uncle a few years prior, called him one day unexpectedly and told him about the reunion. He said it would take place at a classmate's house—coined the "White House," because it was a replica of the official home and workplace of the President of the United States—and encouraged my dad to attend. He agreed—interested, I imagine, to see other faces from his past for the first time in a long time.

I merely thought I would be accompanying him and Alice to the reunion, but I wasn't expecting to hear him give a speech. For most of my life, I thought of him as the man who didn't speak, and I lived in fear of even trying to communicate with my father, because he usually responded with no more than a nod, a "yes," or a "no." It was difficult to connect with him. Whenever my friends came over to my house, my father simply stayed in his room and would try not to run into them or have to communicate with them. This created a sense of fear within them as well—all my life I'd felt that I was tiptoeing around him.

Because we always lived in small towns, some of my classmates's parents knew my father on a professional level. As a doctor, he seemed to be so different from who he was as a parent. Years later, they would comment about how kind, attentive, thoughtful, and composed he was with his patients, and how he would carefully explain to each one the details of their medical condition. It was hard for me to believe that this man I was hearing about was my father; that there was a part of him who was communicative.

While we were in Northern Virginia, we toured the Việt Nam War Museum and saw the famous wall where the names of the more than 58,000 soldiers who died during the Việt Nam War are inscribed. We also visited Falls Church, Virginia, home to the Eden Center—an economic hub for the Vietnamese community, filled with all kinds of shops.

In the middle of the Eden Center parking lot, a South Vietnamese flag—three red stripes on a yellow background—was flying high in the strong winds. This flag was banned in these immigrants's homeland, South Việt Nam. As my father had reminded me when I was in high school when I purchased the current Vietnamese flag, the yellow flag was the correct one. I wondered, but never asked, why my father never lived closer to a Vietnamese community and why we'd always stayed so isolated, moving to small towns where the Asian population made up less than one percent of the total. Even as a college student, I knew that having a broader community of Vietnamese friends, beyond our family unit, could have helped my sister and me feel less alone, particularly after my mother passed away. Then again, I was also never drawn to these communities myself. I couldn't imagine living in Little Saigon, or outside of New Orleans, embedded so deeply within a Vietnamese community. Similar to my job in corporate America, that world felt suffocating to me.

WHEN WE ARRIVED AT THE "WHITE House," I was surprised by the size and the glitz of it. The floor seemed to sparkle. Through the lobby, I could see the elegant living room, which boasted a luxurious white sofa. I thought of our own house in Indiana, which seemed so simple and small in comparison.

The hostess brought us onto an elevator and down to the basement, which had been converted into a party room for the evening: at least ten round tables and an expansive buffet of food were set up.

As the food was served, each of the guests was given an opportunity to speak. There was a lot of bustle and activity, and as someone who didn't understand or speak Vietnamese, I felt entirely out of place. As people spoke, I simply observed and soaked in the environment. Suddenly, I was relieved that Alice was there because I couldn't imagine navigating that event alone with my father.

Later, I would learn through my father's writing about some of the classmates he'd reconnected with there. They shared with him how their lives and paths had taken shape since leaving Việt Nam: many were running private practices in the U.S. or Canada. Some had specialized in gynecology, pediatrics, anesthesiology and surgery. One had never managed to pass the equivalency test, despite several attempts, and ended up working in a factory. Another had passed the exam but couldn't find a spot in a residency program. Some had escaped in 1975, at the end of the war, but the majority had been stranded and ended up serving time in a reeducation camp.

I was surprised that some of the people who gathered that evening avoided the topics of Việt Nam altogether—the memories, I suppose, were too difficult to surface. Those classmates chose to focus on their experiences, and their relative success, since arriving in the States.

I didn't expect my father to stand up and speak that day. When he did, I felt a nervousness in the pit of my stomach, as if I was the one who was talking to a group of unfamiliar people.

With a paper in front of him, my father began, in English:

Once upon a time, I was born in one of the most beautiful countries on Earth. Unfortunately, this country was divided and slowly devastated by one of the longest wars in history. I was baptized during the war, lived and grew up with the war, and only escaped after the war ended.

I saw my country divided into two, with nearly a million people fleeing the communist North to make a new life in the pacific South. I struggled through school and college amidst the background of war, revolution, uprising, uncertainty, and devastation . . .

Upon graduation, I was drafted into military service to serve my country. Soon the war ended with the collapse of my homeland.

It was then my turn to flee the communist regime. And along with another hundred thousand people, I jumped onto a boat and drifted toward the unknown . . . knowing only that I had lost my homeland, my family, and my way of life. What struck me most in this small boat on the empty and vast sea was not the fact that I had lost my identity, but the fact that, for the first time in my life, I had gained the freedom I had longed for, the inner peace that I had always dreamed of . . .

I landed in a vast, modernized country—the most advanced on Earth. In a country totally different from my former one in thinking, customs, and way of living. Through many grueling and difficult years of retraining, which did take a toll on myself and my family, I settled down in a small town trying to make sense of my life.

The scenario repeated itself a thousand times all over the world for my former countrymen. On this day before Labor Day, thirty of my class-mates gathered here in Virginia to celebrate their first class reunion in a quarter-of-a-century and to share their perspectives.

This letter is dedicated to our families and loved ones who lost their lives in search of freedom; our colleagues and countrymen who could not escape and are still enduring the communist regime in Sài Gòn; and my classmates of the University of Sài Gòn School of Medicine. I share their struggles, their pains, their fears, and their home, but I did not know then that we could have gone this far.

I was struck by my father's words. His deep wisdom moved me, stirred something within my own bones. Perhaps it was this speech that created the longing within me to go to Việt Nam, to unearth and discover the country that my father seemed to love so deeply.

As I looked around the room that day, though, I couldn't help but feel that my father's colleagues, the other doctors, didn't seem to share my father's sentiment and longing. Maybe only a handful could actually relate to his depth. Perhaps for them, Việt Nam was something different. Perhaps many of them, like the couple who owned the "White House," preferred to focus their energy on building the lives they'd created in the States; maybe, unlike my father, they didn't want to put their energy into uncovering the past, but preferred to find satisfaction in the present, in their new homeland.

When I ventured to Việt Nam on my own a few years later, it was because something was stirring within me, calling me to know and understand my father—not the man I knew as my dad, but the one who'd spoken at that reunion. He was deep, he was wise, and although he was a man of few words, I'd come to realize that there were boiling depths beneath his quiet disposition. On some level, I recognized that the father I was searching for would be found in my full immersion in Việt Nam.

NGHĨA
South Việt Nam | 1974–1975

EVERY FOURTH MONTH, I WAS ON rotation at the Chi Lăng military camp, a training center for new military recruits from the MRIV region, in the southwestern corner of South Việt Nam near the Cambodian border and about fifteen miles from the provincial city of Châu Đốc. Located by the Hậu River, a branch of the Mekong River, and the Vĩnh Tế Canal, Châu Đốc was historically a territory of the kingdom of Funan, which ruled over present-day South Việt Nam, Cambodia, and Thailand from the first to the fifth centuries CE. It was a powerful trading state with its capital at Óc Eo, a hundred miles from Châu Đốc.

During my time there, the camp had a clinic and a ten-bed hospital run by a physician and three male nurses. Around this same time, an epidemic of Dengue hemorrhagic fever had swept through the area, affecting the recruits of the crowded training camp. Overwhelmed by the sudden influx of sick patients, the physician stationed there requested help, so every month one of us from the Mekong Delta was sent there to assist him with the care of the patients.

The hamlet surrounding the camp was quiet, on the verge of utter boredom, particularly in the evenings. The general area was arid and rocky with minimal vegetation, creating the look of a lunar land-scape bordered by a mountain rather than a tropical paradise. Despite its lack of entertainment, the hamlet offered a much-needed outlet to the rigors of the camp and survived because of the presence of the recruits. In some areas, the single road was asphalt before becoming a plain dirt road a few miles from the hamlet. Access to the camp was so difficult that the military police didn't even bother patrolling the roads.

On Sunday afternoons, the local cockfights provided the only excitement for the entire week. There was no movie theater or indoor entertainment. The few villagers entertained themselves by sitting in straw-hut coffee shops and smoking and drinking beer or coffee while listening to the melodious voices of Khánh Ly and Lệ Thu, well-known folk singers at the time. Trịnh Công Sơn and Phạm Duy's "anti-heroic" and peace-loving songs also blared out of cassette tapes.

When in rotation at the camp, I was lodged in a compound previously built for American military advisers who had left South Việt Nam a few years earlier. The buildings were deserted, and the lack of maintenance was apparent. The large, empty rooms felt like cavernous hangars rather than comfortable sleeping quarters. The doors needed to be repaired; their wood, which had been warped by inclement weather, had separated from their frames at the corners. In the morning, sun rays—our wake-up signal at the camp—penetrated through the cracks and lit up the windowless rooms. The air-conditioners and fans had been removed a long time ago to outfit the local officers's mess on the other side of the camp. A single light bulb dangled from the ceiling at the end of a foot-long cord. The walls were empty of any paintings or decoration.

In a compound that could accommodate at least eight people, I would be the lone guest. The front entrance housed a pool table that nobody used. The tennis court, which at one time must have been busy, was completely deserted—devoid of the sounds of running feet, bouncing balls, or the impact of the racket as it made contact with the tennis ball. The eerie feeling of the deserted compound, in my opinion, reflected the overall mood of the nation at that time. Lights were off; the Americans were gone. The Vietnamese had to struggle with a bare minimum.

One night, I was assigned to talk to a group of recruits about Dengue hemorrhagic fever; the mosquitoes and viruses that brought on the disease. There had been a few deaths in the camp, and the commander thought it was important to advise recruits about the illness.

Looking into the tired and worried faces of these teenage soldiers who sat on the bare ground listening (or pretending to listen) to what I had to say, I couldn't help but think that I had been in their exact position a few years earlier, during my four weeks of military training at the Thủ Đức military camp north of Sài Gòn.

Soon, these men would be dispatched to their units to continue the fight and become baptized by encounters with the enemy. They would either become grown-up men hardened by conflict and destined to kill, or they would be killed in the long war. I thought the nation owed each of these young men much respect and admiration. They had been plucked out of their families to answer the call to defend the nation and should be given dignified recognition no matter how the war turned out.

Unfortunately, this would not prove to be the case for many Vietnamese who served their country.

One Sunday in July 1974, a group of Vietnamese students who were doing their studies overseas returned home during their summer vacation. They'd been enrolled to talk to military officers in an attempt to bridge the gaps between officers and overseas students.

The event was a surprise to all of us. No one knew how long this program had been in place and what the government was trying to accomplish.

Any attempt to bridge the gap is helpful, I thought, *although it may not always be successful.* Those who traveled overseas to further their studies belonged to an elite group. They were either smart enough to get their own scholarships or their parents were rich enough to enroll them in a university overseas. On top of that, they received deferments that could last a long time, maybe for the duration of the war. They didn't have to worry about the draft or the uncertainty of life in a country ravaged by war.

As for the students who had remained in our country—life in South Việt Nam could be grim. Every day was a constant reminder of war:

the draft, the wounded, the widows, the disabled, and so on. They had to enroll through local universities to receive military deferments until graduation, after which they were required to enroll into military service. Life was different for these two groups of students.

By the end of April 1975, I was still stationed in Cần Thơ after having completed an almost month-long rotation at the Chi Lăng camp. Awaiting the necessary papers to return to Sài Gòn to visit my family, who I had not seen for some time, unexpected news arrived: I was ordered to report to the island of Phú Quốc, an island in the southwestern end of Việt Nam about 100 miles offshore from Rạch Giá, the provincial city of Kiên Giang Province. I was being sent there to take the place of a colleague who had recently gotten married and was going on a honeymoon.

The mission at Phú Quốc was designed to provide medical assistance to the refugees from central Việt Nam who had been recently relocated to the island. While I had never visited Phú Quốc before, I knew it was famous for its nước mắm (fish sauce), which added a salty flavor to food and defined Vietnamese cooking.

I was irritated by this order, to say the least, but there was nothing I could do that would change it. So, I headed back to the southwest.

In retrospect, that last-minute order was a blessing in disguise—but I would only realize that fact weeks later.

CHRISTINA
Hà Nội | 2002

I ARRIVED AT NỘI BÀI INTERNATIONAL Airport, approximately thirty miles outside of Hà Nội, around midnight on a muggy evening in the middle of September. As I walked out of the airport, a thick layer of heat immediately overwhelmed me. I scanned the sea of unknown Vietnamese faces for a familiar one—that of my friend Lara, who was coming to pick me up. With only a handful of contacts in Hà Nội—Lara, Thomas, my future UNDP colleagues, and Anh and Nguyệt—I was determined to create some semblance of a life there.

During my layover at Seoul's Incheon Airport, I noticed a group of foreign exchange students. They were huddled together on the floor, chatting, listening to music, and skimming through Việt Nam guide-books. Watching them, I wished that I was also traveling with a group—that I had others with whom to clumsily make my way through the initial days of newness and uncertainty of living in a foreign land. I wondered how I would survive the transition alone. Lara had offered me a room in her aunt's place in Hà Nội—or, rather, she would share her room with me. She told me the cost would be $300, including meals. I agreed, even though I wasn't sure I wanted my meals prepared for me. Alice had commented that it sounded like too much money for a room in someone's house in Việt Nam, not to mention a shared room. And I didn't know where the house was located. But I didn't have a reference point for the cost of renting space in Hà Nội, or know at that time that the price of almost everything in Việt Nam, from renting a motorbike to buying a bottle of water, was negotiable.

I also didn't care; I was so nervous about all the newness that I would experience in Hà Nội that I didn't want to add finding an apartment to my list of things to do.

Lara had emailed me a list of items, including Ziploc bags and paper towels, that she wanted me to bring for her aunt. *If these are gifts*, I thought, *what other amenities won't be readily available in Hà Nội?* She'd also told me that I should bring enough tampons for my entire trip. *The government is against tampons because it encourages women to stick things in their vagina*, she'd explained in her email.

A woman stepped out of the crowd, waving and smiling. *Lara!*

I sagged with relief. At least this part of the journey had been easy.

I WAS SO TIRED THAT I didn't pay much attention to the long drive to the city center that day. I had no concept of how Hà Nội was mapped out, nor which part of town Lara's aunt's home was located in. I later learned her house was in a district called Tây Hồ (West Lake), named after one of the largest lakes in the northwestern corner of Hà Nội, a fifteen-minute drive from the city center. All around the lake, there were beautiful, two-story, gated villas shaded by large palm trees. These villas were often rented out to foreigners—usually embassy or development workers who were on international contracts and opted for more space, fresh air, and less noise than apartments in the city center.

At that time, the neighborhood, along with much of Hà Nội, had not reached its full development potential. The main street, Xuân Diệu, that led to West Lake had only a spattering of stores—a bamboo furniture store, a lamp store, and a few Vietnamese restaurants. The Sheraton, with its unkempt landscaping and unlit but still recognizable "S" logo, had been abandoned by investors who'd run out of money before completing the hotel's construction.

The ngõ, or small alley, where Lara's aunt's house was situated was part of a maze of tiny, meandering streets that, taken all together, created the feeling of a mini village of clustered homes. Many Vietnamese families capitalized on every square foot of their space, using the first floor of their home as a storefront, selling random packaged goods, or operating as tailors, motorbike mechanics, or hair stylists, and more. I started to believe that all Vietnamese were in some way salespeople—and I finally grasped what Alice had meant by "visible life."

After spending a few days in cô Hoa's house, I learned more about the way in which Vietnamese people lived. I also learned that "cô" was the correct way to address an older woman who was younger than your mother. Chị (older sister), anh (older brother), and em (younger sibling) were used for people of the same generation; bác was used to address a person older than one's parents; and so forth. It was confusing in the beginning, and I always feared guessing someone's age incorrectly and inadvertently offending them.

Lara told me that her aunt's house was a traditional Vietnamese home, built tall and deep rather than wide because of the limited space in overcrowded Hà Nội. Multiple generations sometimes lived in one house. There would be a shared kitchen and common space on the first floor, and then each generation of the family might have their living quarters on another floor. She explained that in some Vietnamese homes an entire family lived in one room—making my own mother's insistence that my sister and I sleep in the same bedroom as her when we were children make a little more sense. I'd previously found it strange that my mother never allowed us to have our own rooms as children; now I understood that it must have been comforting to her.

Lara and I shared one of the bedrooms on the second floor. Painted in a dingy light green color—the same color that covered the kitchen walls—it had fluorescent lights, which I found depressing, and two foldable mattresses, purchased on one of the streets in the Old Quarter where bedding and mattresses were sold, pushed together on the floor.

I started to question the cost when I first saw this setup. *For this, $300 feels a little steep*, I thought, disappointed.

The whole house was unadorned and basic, with the occasional painting or engraving of a seascape hung here and there, reminding me of the understated and minimally decorated homes that I had grown up in. I'd always compared our family's home to those of my American friends; theirs seemed more decorated, cozier, and somehow more put-together. Now I began to understand that this was simply the Vietnamese style.

In cô Hoa's home the sitting room was located on the first floor, directly opposite to the kitchen. It was filled with six tall wooden chairs, engraved with a flowery design, that were placed around a low table. The room, neither beautiful nor comfortable, was used functionally, to entertain visitors—otherwise, it sat empty.

Over the weeks to come, I saw Lara's aunt serving friends and family members in that room, a steady stream of visitors that I had to learn to identify in the Vietnamese way. She kept her tiny teacups and teapot ready on the low table, in anticipation of the next visitor.

I didn't know how Lara's aunt explained who I was to her visitors; they spoke in Vietnamese, so I did not fully understand their conversations. I didn't mind. After having grown up with my parents speaking to each other in Vietnamese and not comprehending a word of it, I was used to it.

I started to notice that the visitors often commented about my appearance, and the word "béo," which means "fat," became familiar to me. When I complained about these comments to Lara, she simply advised me to brush it off.

"That's just how Vietnamese people are," she said with a shrug.

EVERY MORNING FOR THE FIRST FEW weeks, I woke to a host of unfamiliar sounds: the crowing of a rooster in the back courtyard, the banging of pots, the construction from the neighbor's house next door, and the indecipherable words blaring through the loudspeakers hung on telephone poles near the house. The Vietnamese loved the mornings; this I learned almost immediately.

Locals arrived at Hoàn Kiếm Lake, the lake in the center of Hà Nội, before sunrise each day. Men lugged their weights and set up on the sidewalk, sometimes in the middle of the street. Old people did tai chi, women in clusters took aerobics classes. Music blaring, the instructors called out, "*Một, hai, ba...*" as they led the exercises. Other groups convened to play badminton.

I dreaded the breakfast that cô Hoa made for us. I was never sure what she would prepare. Unfamiliar food items were covered with a plastic, cage-like object to protect them from the swarming flies. Sometimes she gave us leftovers from the night before—once it was thịt kho, a caramelized pork dish; another time it was French bread with chả lụa, something that my father had often eaten for breakfast. The meals were always followed by fruit—mangosteen and rambutan or miniature bananas, which did not taste differently from normal bananas but which I for some reason loathed.

It wasn't that the meals were bad; it was just that sometimes I didn't feel like eating, particularly a heavy meal, first thing in the morning. And we were expected to finish everything that was prepared.

As my stomach filled, a nauseous feeling sometimes overtook me.

Meanwhile, cô Hoa would be standing near the kitchen table, saying "ăn đi"—basically, encouraging me to keep eating.

Now that I was surrounded by dainty and petite Vietnamese women, most of whom were around my height but weighed twenty or thirty pounds less, I felt even more self-conscious about my appearance than I had before my journey there. While I had never been thin—I had broad shoulders and a stout build—when I arrived in Hà Nội, I probably weighed more than I ever had in my life. So cô Hoa's urgings to eat more didn't make sense to me; I thought she should want me to eat less for breakfast, since everyone seemed to be commenting that I was overweight.

Cô Hoa and I could barely communicate with each other. Her English was basic, at the same level of my non-existent Vietnamese. Lara ended up translating the handful of words, mostly simple questions, we shuffled between us when we made conversation. Cô Hoa's piercing gaze made me feel that I would simultaneously offend and disappoint her if I didn't finish what she prepared for us, reminding me of when I was a child in my mother's kitchen and being told to finish everything on our plate, despite my pleas that I was full.

One morning Lara explained to me that I had to "mời" cô Hoa (invite) her to eat breakfast, since she was the eldest person at the table.

I was afraid of fully embracing the Vietnamese language. I had started to take classes, but for whatever reason, I was embarrassed that I didn't commit myself to learning to speak. I depended on Lara, or someone else around who spoke Vietnamese and English, to help me translate, and did everything possible to avoid formally addressing anyone I encountered there. Speaking Vietnamese was something that I had wished my father had pushed me to do, but since there was a difference between northern and southern Vietnamese, I wondered if he didn't care—if learning northern Vietnamese was worse in his eyes than not speaking Vietnamese at all.

I could understand how Lara bore a certain responsibility to abide by her family's rules. She was, after all, a representative, an emissary, of her American family. Almost every family, I began to understand, was split in these ways—those who had left Việt Nam to move to countries all over the world, and those who had stayed back in Việt Nam. For both sides of the family, the feelings were complicated. There were impressions to uphold and secrets to be kept; before her arrival, I am certain Lara received detailed information on what should and shouldn't be said to her family members.

Because I didn't have any family in Hà Nội, or anywhere in Việt Nam (not that I knew of at the time, anyway), I wanted to be completely free from the responsibility of family. I hadn't ventured to Việt Nam only to abide by rules imposed by a friend's aunt.

One such rule was our 10 p.m. curfew. Cô Hoa didn't want to be woken up to unlock the front gate, and we weren't allowed to have a key. Lara didn't seem to mind this schedule, as she diligently worked on her research project in the evenings and then went to sleep early; for me, though, I felt that I was missing out on fully experiencing Hà Nội. The initial gratitude I felt for staying in a Vietnamese home quickly dissipated. I wanted to explore Hà Nội, get to know the city, cultivate a broad circle of friends—I wanted to be free, not confined to rules imposed by someone else's family. And, yet, ironically on some level, I went to Việt Nam to find and understand the meaning of family. I was still too steeped in this notion of American individualism to fully embrace the Vietnamese family.

NGHĨA
Phú Quốc | 1975

FROM CẦN THƠ I TOOK THE bus to Rạch Giá—located on the Gulf of
Thailand, about fifty miles from Châu Đốc and a few miles from Oc Eo,
the famed capital of the kingdom of Funan. Rạch Giá was the last
frontier of South Việt Nam on my way to Phú Quốc. There, I was told
that the next and last boat to the island would depart at 5 p.m. local
time. I sat in a cafe on the bank of the river, sipping lemonade and
watching workers loading a ninety-foot-long, two-decker commercial
boat in preparation for departure.

When I finally boarded the vessel, I stayed on the top deck to savor
the breathtaking sunset and the calm waters of the gulf. Most of the
people decided to stay in the hull, where they felt protected from the
sun, winds, and weather, and where commodities were available. A
few people even managed to string up hammocks in preparation for
the long night.

I remembered that Nguyễn Ánh, who in 1802 became King Gia
Long, had made this same trip many times between 1784 and 1788
when he was harassed and hunted by the Tây Sơn rebels. Each time
he lost a battle to the insurgents, he jumped aboard a boat and sailed
to safety either to Phú Quốc and nearby islands or to Siam (Thailand).
And each time, after regrouping, he came back to put up a new fight.
It took him twenty-five years of hard battles and persistent will to
recover his throne.

Thinking of this story, it dawned on me that in its long history—
from 937 CE until the present day—Việt Nam had frequently been

convulsed by wars. Many of those wars were against invaders (China, France, Thailand, Japan, etc.), but a number had also taken place among the different people who lived on the land called Việt Nam.

Tired, I laid down on the deck and slept without bedding or cover. This was military life in its unsophisticated form. I didn't realize then, and I couldn't have predicted, that there would be many more nights in my future when I would have to sleep aboard a ship.

THE FOLLOWING MORNING A COOL BREEZE woke me up at 5 a.m. A new day had begun; the air was calm, the skies clear. The sunrise was as beautiful and serene as the sunset. The cloudless sky offered its most vivid and brightest colors.

The boat anchored a few miles from shore, awaiting permission to dock. When we tied up at the local pier, it was breakfast time.

I quickly ate breakfast at a nearby cafe—one of various straw huts with worn-out wooden tables and chairs on an earthen floor. Then I inquired about the directions to the camp.

I was told it was about two miles north. I decided to walk there, following the lead of the locals, on the dirt road, which was riddled with huge potholes carved out by the monsoon rains.

At my destination, I found a mini-city—nearly 40,000 people living in tents or wooden buildings with bare minimum conditions. Members of my team had arrived earlier with their equipment and vehicles and were waiting for my arrival.

My bed—a wooden divan without a mattress, covered with a mosquito net—was in a corner of a cavernous hangar. The doors were kept open all the time. The storage area had recently been converted into a housing unit. I couldn't complain, since I had at least a corrugated roof over my head.

On average, I saw forty patients a day at the clinic—the majority of them suffering from common cold, flu, rashes, bruises, or cuts. Two other physicians from another unit also worked at the clinic, and together, the three of us covered the medical needs of all 40,000 refugees.

As for entertainment, there was neither a newspaper nor a television to be found at this remote camp. However, the beautiful white-sand beaches and turquoise blue waters, still pristine and unspoiled by civilization, provided a magnificent alternative to the lack of amenities. The water temperature was warm and the ideal place for swimming and sunbathing. I wondered why the local government had not thought about opening a resort in this area, as I believed it could certainly become a vacation destination for the Vietnamese. There was a village, complete with a market, restaurants, and fisheries, and, of course, the fish sauce industry the island was famous for.

But my mood and mind were not on sightseeing or visiting local industries. It was the war that had sent me, and all these thousands of refugees, to this beautiful and isolated island. We were all victims of that monstrous war, initiated by the belligerent communists who only wanted to take away our land.

I WAS ONLY ON THE ISLAND for seven days.

During that time, we were all oblivious to what was happening in Sài Gòn. Since not a single member of my team carried a radio, we hunted for news—which was getting worse by the day—by finding people who had access to it, or who had arrived on the island more recently than we had. I requested permission to visit my family in Sài Gòn, but I didn't receive an answer.

We learned that President Nguyễn Văn Thiệu had resigned and been replaced by General Dương Văn Minh.

People's faces stayed calm, but underneath, the locals were grave, reserved, and resigned. Something ominous was about to happen.

We were already shocked by the news over the loss of Central Việt Nam. Battles were being fought everywhere around Sài Gòn, and the shelling of the city by the communists continued.

Around noon local time on April 30, General Dương Văn Minh, the last President of South Việt Nam, went on the radio to announce the unconditional surrender of the government of South Việt Nam.

The mood suddenly turned somber and grave. The moment of silence was short, probably just a few minutes, but seemed to last an eternity. No one raised their voice. The shock of the loss was so brutal and immediate that it blocked our vocal cords and left us speechless.

Reactions among the islanders ranged from utter disbelief to calm resignation to pain and of course, anger. Tears were seen rolling down everyone's cheeks. The news, although somewhat expected, was stunning. No one had dared to predict that such an unconditional and immediate surrender would occur.

The Republic of South Việt Nam had been wiped off the map. The land that our forefathers had lived on since 1600 had been taken away from us. What we had fought for so long and so hard during these twenty-one years had been forever lost. The more than 400,000 brave men and women who had dedicated their lives to this cause, along with the untold numbers of civilians who had also died during this conflict, had thus died in vain. Torrents of tears had been shed during that war; countless families had been uprooted and displaced; hundreds of towns and villages had been torn down, shelled, or bombed. And it had all been a waste. The sacrifice of so many people had ended in smoke.

The long, bloody, and arduous fight had been for nothing.

We fought for twenty-one years only to lose everything—the war, our homes, and our country—in the end, I thought. We had put up a good fight. We could have done it better but had not. The U.S. had tried to help us, but its efforts had not changed the equation—and any military or economic help from outside always has its limits, to say the least.

Each of us was devastated by the news—some more, some less. For me, the horror of the loss was staggering. There was nothing to do now but leave—run far away from these communist monsters and look for freedom somewhere else.

THERE WAS ONLY ONE THOUGHT ON my mind: escape.

I saw the two other physicians packing their belongings in a Jeep. I'd had little contact with them since arriving on the island; I didn't know where they were going.

I gathered my troop of five men, military nurses who had helped me during the last seven days, and told them, "You have all heard the news that Sài Gòn has surrendered. You are free men now. You can do whatever you want. Those of you who want to remain in Việt Nam can stay here. Those who would like to escape from the communists can follow me."

All five men had families in the Mekong Delta and decided to remain behind. I thanked them and said good-bye. Then I followed the two other physicians and their families to the port where I had arrived only one week earlier.

I went straight to the dock and saw many PT boats with their engines running. One boat took off right as I reached the pier. I found another one that was ready to leave and got permission to board. The boat rapidly took off to the sea. There were twelve of us: the captain, his wife and daughter, three crew members, two other physicians and their families, and me.

Back at the pier, I could see stranded families yelling and screaming, begging the captain to take them aboard. He didn't slow down. He simply pointed toward the remaining anchored boats offshore.

I didn't know what the future had in store for me. I didn't even know where the tiny boat I'd boarded was going. All I knew was that I wanted to get out of Việt Nam, out of this unending fratricidal war, and especially out of the reach of the communists. I had been attached to my country as long as it was free from communism. Now that the land I'd called home for almost three decades had been taken away from me, I had no more sacred land to fight for.

For the first time in my life, I had no country to call my own. As that realization hit me, a strange, indescribable feeling came over me.

An hour earlier, everyone on the boat had been connected to a land called South Việt Nam. Then suddenly, there was no more South Việt Nam. What we had called motherland or fatherland no longer existed. What we had cherished most was lost. We were all orphans. I never thought that I could be without a country. The suddenness of the disconnection stunned me.

In that moment, I understood what Phan Bội Châu, one of our country's greatest non-communist revolutionaries, meant when, in 1908, he wrote that there was "no greater loss than that of losing one's country."

CHRISTINA
Hà Nội | 2002

MY ARRIVAL IN HÀ NỘI COINCIDED with Tết Trung Thu, or Mid-Autumn Festival, which historically marked the end of the summer harvest, but had over time become a celebration almost entirely for children. Festive lanterns adorned the streets of the Old Quarter. Neatly packed mooncakes, in a variety of flavors like mung bean, coconut, and durian, were piled high in a triangular shape in front of stores, providing yet another opportunity for the enterprising Vietnamese to set up shop. The festive atmosphere, which enveloped me much more than any holiday celebration in the U.S. ever had, permeated the city. It felt like a season of new beginnings—a time when children returned to school and when flocks of expats like me descended onto Hà Nội to begin their lives anew.

It didn't take me long to realize that Hà Nội was more like a provincial village than a bustling metropolis of 7 million people. I started to notice familiar faces around town. I spotted the foreign exchange students I'd initially encountered at Incheon Airport at various places throughout town on a regular basis. Initially, I thought these chance encounters meant these people were supposed to be part of my Hà Nội life, but as the city became more familiar to me, I realized that most foreigners centered their lives on District 1, which covered only a small section of the town.

There were only a handful of bars, restaurants, and coffee shops that were targeted toward expats. The run-down street stalls in obscure locations known for one specialty dish—like chả cá, mì xào, or bánh cuốn—were novel to me, but during those initial weeks, I yearned for the familiar comfort of home. I wanted to find cafes that served cappuccinos instead of the strong, bitter cà phê sữa đá (iced Vietnamese coffee) that I had only tasted a few times in the past. The venues in District 1 that catered to foreigners served as my touchstones as I navigated Hà Nội's unfamiliar environment. I wanted to nestle myself in a cozy spot where I could sit for hours and read, rather than perch on a one-foot-tall stool on a sidewalk feeling overwhelmed by the honking sounds of the motorbikes and the endless parade of vendors selling everything from fresh tropical fruit to ceramics.

One of the popular cafes I frequented, Puku, was located on Hàng Trống Street, close to the Old Quarter—a neighborhood of thirty-six meandering streets, each named after the items that were historically sold on that street. Hàng Bạc, the silver street. Hàng Đường, the sugar street. Hàng Muối, the salt street. Hàng Gà, the chicken street, and so forth. Puku was founded by three entrepreneurial New Zealanders and a fourth Vietnamese business partner who'd seen a need for Western-style cafes in Hà Nội. The simple establishment had walls painted in navy blue and emerald green, dark wood tables handcrafted in Việt Nam, and colorful hanging lamps that provided a warm ambiance. Piles of magazines and books left behind by tourists filled a wooden bookshelf along the wall. The close-set tables, only a few inches apart, made it easy to strike up conversations with others who also enjoyed the "Kiwi" breakfast and menu with the kinds of sandwiches and basic salads with which Westerners were familiar.

At Puku, I began to meet other expats—people who at first were strangers but quickly became friends as we ran into each other repeatedly at the quaint venue. The varied reasons people chose to journey to Việt Nam, and in particular Hà Nội, intrigued me. I met English teachers who taught Vietnamese children in schools called Language Link (their marketing tagline: *Your international link to success*). Teaching was not their chosen profession, but rather a way to earn a decent salary while leading a temporary, and relatively stress-free, existence abroad. Many of my new UNDP colleagues—the ones venturing from France, Ireland, and Sweden—landed in Hà Nội because it was their next international post. Then, of course, there were a handful of people who didn't have a real plan to live in Hà Nội, they simply arrived there after traveling through Southeast Asia and decided to stay. An American woman in her early thirties told me about deciding to leave her California life behind and spontaneously rebuild another one in Việt Nam after a recent divorce.

In addition to these expats, I had started to meet other young Vietnamese Americans, also recent college graduates, who were on exchange programs or had come on Fulbright scholarships. Two people in this group—Mai and Minh—became my closest friends in Hà Nội.

There were different levels of expat living: those who had come without a plan; some with well-paying jobs at international organizations that offered benefits and assistance with working through the details of the transition to life in Việt Nam; and some, like me, who'd taken a gamble and accepted an unpaid internship or something similar Việt Nam, believing that the time there would be more valuable than financial compensation.

THOMAS, WHO WORKED AT THE ASIA Foundation, was one of the expats I knew in Hà Nội who earned a solid salary and benefits. I'd only communicated with him sporadically before my arrival in Việt Nam, yet among the whole host of new people in my life, comparatively he felt like an old friend. Perhaps my affection for Thomas was premature, but his friendship comforted me. Maybe we'd met in another life, or perhaps it was knowing that he was from North Carolina, the last place I'd called home, and graduated from the same university. Immediately after my arrival, we met for dinner at Au Lac café, a courtyard restaurant across from the historic Sofitel Metropole, and I discovered in conversation that he'd graduated from Carolina the year I started. I also learned that Thomas was gay, and his partner lived in Singapore, which immediately deflated the dream that we could potentially be romantically involved. Nevertheless, I was happy to have Thomas as a new friend.

A week or so later, he invited me over for dinner at his place.

Thomas lived on a street lined with cafes and food stalls that circled Trúc Bạch Lake, another popular lake in Hà Nội. Trúc Bạch was separated from Tây Hồ, the area where cô Hoa lived, by Thanh Niên Road, coined "Lover's Lane" because young Vietnamese lovers gathered along it on the backs of their motorbikes, embracing each other tightly, pleased to have escaped their parents' watchful eyes.

Admittedly, the view was impressive and romantic—the sun setting over Tây Hồ in the distance, the sprinkling of swan-shaped paddle boats gracefully moving over the water's surface. Both Trúc Bạch and Tây Hồ were popular places to live for expats who wanted to escape the polluted city center.

Like cô Hoa's house, Thomas's place was situated in a ngõ that was part of yet another maze of tiny, winding streets. His house, however, had been reconfigured for a foreigner. Savvy Vietnamese people could make additional money through real estate by renovating their house to meet an expat's standards and choosing to live in a smaller place or move in with their families. The most lucrative rentals for Vietnamese were to international organizations or businesses that paid the landlord directly for rent, sometimes even fronting the renovation costs.

I noticed his Honda Wave motorbike parked inside the front area of the kitchen.

"Do you drive that?" I asked him.

"Only around town," he said. "Sometimes to work. I don't drive very far with it."

Having experienced the streets of Hà Nội, with their constant barrage of sounds and the sheer number of people, I appreciated Thomas's need for a comfortable space to retreat to, to escape the chaos of daily life in Hà Nội. He'd created a home in which his belongings were organized neatly and there were photos to remind him of friends and family back home all around. Fluorescent lights had been replaced with a colorful array of lanterns and charming lamps that created a dim, welcoming light in the common areas. The brown couch was sprinkled with a vibrant assortment of silk and velvet pillows that he'd purchased from Dome, a popular housewares store started by an Australian woman.

Thomas told me the first time he moved to Việt Nam was to study Vietnamese for a semester during college. The second time, after graduating from college, he returned to lead the American Chamber of Commerce in Hà Nội. Now, he was working as a program manager for the Asia Foundation.

"I can't imagine coming back to Hà Nội so many times," I said to him.

"It's a city you'll probably keep returning to," he told me. "I don't know why. There's just something about it. You'll see."

We looked through some of his old photos. He showed me a picture of him with an elegant, beautiful Asian woman, taken at a launch party for the first Louis Vuitton store that opened in Hà Nội.

"She's from Hong Kong," he told me. "She moved to Hà Nội with her husband, but because she didn't have a work permit, she couldn't be employed in Việt Nam. Yet, with her entrepreneurial spirit, she saw the potential of the hand embroidery that Việt Nam had been known for, as well as the availability of raw materials." He went on to explain that she'd begun working with a seamstress and started making handbags at a small studio, and eventually, she'd earned renown for her signature style: bold, bright handbags adorned with sequins and embroidery.

I was pleasantly surprised to learn about these people—the ones who not only decided to live in Việt Nam but also to build a business and stimulate the economy by employing local Vietnamese. It left a significant impression on me.

He pulled out a picture of another villa in Hà Nội that was indistinguishable to me from the one we sat in now. "That's where I used to live—on Hàng Trống Street, across from Puku," he said. "It'll always be one of my favorites." Thomas spoke with a lingering sense of nostalgia for a place where he currently lived. Each round of his Hà Nội life had been defined by a different experience, another phase in his life—first experiencing another country for the first time, then gaining work experience, and finally, returning at another point in his career.

Even if he was finding happiness in this latest stint in Hà Nội, it seemed clear that he had a longing for a previous time. I wondered if I, too, would have a long-lasting relationship with Hà Nội—if I'd return again and again.

"I can't wait to start my life here," I said. I thought about all those expats I'd met at Puku, who seemed so comfortable in their lives. I longed for that.

"You should just dive in. You won't regret it," Thomas said.

AFTER VISITING THOMAS'S PLACE AND GLIMPSING the wide range of expats in Hà Nội, I knew I wanted to move out of cô Hoa's house and experience Hà Nội on my own. I wanted to be free and not confined to the rules of a Vietnamese family.

I asked one of my UNDP colleagues to put me in touch with a housing agent who could help me look for an apartment. I told him my budget and that I wanted to be in the city center—close to all the action, not in Tây Hồ or even Trúc Bạch Lake. He found me a small one-bedroom apartment, only a ten-minute walk to the UNDP office, in a building located on Nguyễn Du Street. It had three units—one for the landlord; one rented by Claire, an Australian woman; and the one I was offered.

The apartment itself was tiny and awkward and required walking outside on a small balcony to go between the living space, with its small kitchenette, and the bedroom. When I saw it, however, I immediately took it. It was only $50 more than what I'd been paying for the shared room with Lara, and it was in the center of town—not fifteen minutes away by motorbike.

Lara and her aunt dropped me off at my apartment with my two bags, one silk blanket, and a couple pillows that I'd recently bought.

In the taxi ride over, Lara said in a sweet, sisterly way, "We're worried that it's too early for you to live on your own."

Truthfully, I was worried too. But I also felt that I was getting ripped off by living with cô Hoa—and this was the first time in my life that I'd had the chance to live alone. I'd always lived with housemates in college, and after graduating and getting a job, I'd still lived with other people.

It was time to spread my wings.

BEING IN MY NEW SPACE ALONE didn't start well. For weeks after moving into my new place, I felt a sense of emptiness and discomfort.

Every evening when I returned home from the UNDP offices, I would rush up to Claire's apartment to see if she was home; if she wasn't, I would head out to Puku to escape the silence of my own apartment. I started to have an inkling of desire to decorate, but I was reluctant to make this place a home.

One morning, I woke up to the sounds of a person scuffling around in our courtyard. When I looked outside, I discovered that someone had stolen the bikes that Claire and I had chained up outside. That someone could so easily jump the fence or unlock the front gate and access our courtyard only added to my fear of being there alone, and seemed like further evidence that my decision to live on my own had been premature.

A few days later, I met an American girl, Monique, also a recent college graduate, at an internet cafe. She told me that she was looking for a house with two other Americans—one of whom was working with her at the Việt Nam News and the other of whom was teaching English. They'd already started looking at different neighborhoods around town, and the one that they were most interested in was in the south part, about a ten-minute motorbike ride from where I was currently living.

She sent me a message once they signed the lease.

While the villa had a lot of space and a cozy courtyard, it was not in the most beautiful part of town. Getting there required driving on one of the most traffic-laden streets. It was a downgrade from my current apartment, which was centrally located and in a charming neighborhood. Still, I decided to move in with them. I needed comfort and companionship.

I counted the days I made it in my own apartment. Only nine.

NGHĨA

The Vast Ocean | 1975

THE TINY BOAT KEPT POWERING AHEAD, but the roaring engine didn't distract me from my thoughts. No one was talking. There was total silence besides the engine noise and the sound of waves crashing into the sides of the boat.

Phú Quốc Island soon became a dot on the horizon. The captain proceeded to disarm us—to prevent a potential mutiny and to preserve safety on the boat, he said, before informing us that we were heading to either Malaysia or Thailand. I didn't care where we landed. I, like most everyone else on the boat, had never set foot outside Việt Nam before, and in my eyes they were essentially the same: a foreign land.

On the boat, I realized how vast and unlimited nature could be. I could look so far to the horizon and see only waves and the deep blue ocean. Somehow, that made me feel secure and free. It was a strange feeling—one that I had never felt before. The war was finally over. Twenty-one years had passed since Việt Nam had been partitioned into two countries. All I knew was war. Now, I was free but without a country, without a job, without a home, and without a future. An eerie calm set in.

I started to think about how I did not have to wear a military uniform anymore or keep my clothes straight and wrinkle-free. I didn't have to salute anybody or have my every move restricted by military rules and regulations. I didn't have to present my identification card at every street corner to the military police. Nor did I have to hold on to and care for a gun, bringing it everywhere I went. There would be no more shooting, shelling, bombing, or pounding of artillery. Most importantly, there would be no more killing.

I was free.

We had been on the water for maybe half an hour or an hour when I suddenly saw out ahead of us a ten-story transatlantic ship with three or four dozen local boats of all sizes and shapes swarming around it.

I would find out much later that with the imminent collapse of South Việt Nam, the U.S. government had ordered all available ocean liners, including the U.S. Seventh Fleet, to anchor outside the country's territorial waters in order to pick up potential refugees. That was why the *Pioneer Contender* had been anchored in the middle of the ocean since March 1975. It had brought refugees from central Việt Nam to Vũng Tàu on various occasions and carried other refugees to Phú Quốc Island. Now, it was her turn again—this time to pick up many of her previous passengers aboard and transport them abroad.

We were fortunate to bump into the *Pioneer Contender*; had we not, we would have been forced to head to Malaysia or Thailand on the tiny patrol boat with its unforeseen problems—a trip we weren't prepared for, since in our rush to leave the island we had failed to bring either food or water with us.

The patrol boat headed toward the ship and docked against rows of boats. We walked across the other boats to get to the stairs, then waited for our turn to climb aboard the big ship.

Elderly people and children were allowed to get up first. They slowly moved up the steep and swinging stairs. Scared women had to be led or even carried on board. The transfer of people from native boats to the ship proceeded at a slow pace. Refugees then spread out on the deck itself or down the cargo hold. At the end of the day, we were offered sandwiches.

I fell asleep quickly that night, even though I was stressed and depressed by that day's turn of events. The night before, I had slept in a warm bed in my homeland. That night, I was for the first time "homeless" and sleeping on a hard, cold deck somewhere on the vast ocean. The only thing I could claim as a roof was the sky, whose scintillating stars contrasted with my deep sorrow and anguish.

In spite of the agonizing situation, I slept well that first night.

I AWOKE THE FOLLOWING MORNING WONDERING about our location. We were advised that the ship had hugged the Vietnamese coastline all night long and headed north. At one time, we passed close to Côn Sơn Island, where political prisoners and captured Việt Cộng were held. We could not understand why the ship had headed north instead of east or south; a northward direction meant Sài Gòn, while an eastward course signified the Philippines and therefore freedom. The only thing I was worried about was being returned to the new Sài Gòn government against our will. That would mean imprisonment for sure.

By the end of the second day, we were anchored in front of Vũng Tàu, at the mouth of the Sài Gòn River, close to half-a-dozen large ships and a myriad of smaller native ones. Known as Cape Saint Jacques under the French, the spot had been renamed Vũng Tàu—literally, a "mooring place for ships"—after the French were expelled. In the fourteenth to fifteenth centuries, trading ships had moored in front of the cape before entering the Sài Gòn River and trading with the locals either in Vũng Tàu or Sài Gòn. Sài Gòn had soon taken over the trading business, while Vũng Tàu became a seaside resort. Now, it had been made into the meeting place of all the rescue ships of the U.S. Seventh Fleet before they headed toward their final destination.

The rescue operation continued for another day or two while flotillas of refugee boats from Vũng Tàu and Sài Gòn converged on the anchored ships. Boats of all sizes and shapes—some civilian, others military, all filled with refugees young and old—headed toward the big ships. They were fishing boats, trawlers, ferries, tugboats, and military vessels; anything that could float had been rapidly resuscitated and used. The native boats docked on the sides of the ships, and people were transferred to the big ships. Once empty of passengers, the small boats were set on fire and pushed away. At night, it made for an eerie picture: small boats on fire floating on the ocean.

And then, the last spectacle of the war: people jumping off the ship to kill themselves. A soldier turning a gun on himself. These people who took their lives must have looked at the ongoing debacle before them—the people rushing to the ships, the coastline of Việt Nam—and felt they could stand no more. The thought of losing their country and their families, of perhaps not being able to return to Việt Nam ever again, must have been too much for them.

AFTER PICKING UP MORE PASSENGERS, THE *Pioneer Contender* sailed again, heading east this time, with thousands of passengers on board.

A heavy weight lifted from my chest, as an eastward course meant freedom.

I had never seen that many people crowding on a ship before: anxious women holding on to their children, elderly people walking slowly, sad-looking soldiers still in uniforms, and people clutching their meager belongings in their arms. They huddled in groups or laid on the deck, submerged in their thoughts, barely talking to each other, their minds a hundred miles away from that place. We were all focused on the past, the future, our families, and our survival. This was an image of extreme despair and anguish: a group of defeated people who had lost everything—jobs, houses, belongings, and country—trying to assess the damage and figure out the future.

Who could ever imagine leaving everything behind for a bleak and uncertain future? The 1620 pilgrims were better prepared than we were, for at least they knew where they were going, planned ahead, and brought provisions with them. We 1975 Vietnamese refugees just ran away with nothing more than the clothes on our backs.

Still, that night I slept well once again—maybe even better than I had the first night—because I was assured that we were not going back to Việt Nam.

THE FOLLOWING DAY, THE SHIP SAILED between a series of islands that I was told were the Philippines. The view was certainly beautiful, with tropical islands on both sides of the ship. I saw a few fishing boats close to the islands, and dolphins frolicking in the sparkling blue water. Here and there another ocean liner passed us by.

We soon settled into a boring routine broken only by mealtimes. In front of and around us was the immense sea, all the way to the horizon. Days were hot; the bright and shining tropical sun cooked us like bread in an oven. Luckily, the ocean breeze somewhat softened the heat effect. Those who could not stand being in the sun hid in the cargo bay—but it was packed down there during lunch time, and I found the heat just as intense.

Most people migrated back to the deck as the temperature cooled down in the evening. Nights were tolerable and even beautiful under the starry sky. The weather was gorgeous during the whole trip: the absence of storms prevented many of us from falling sick from the combined effect of heat and dampness—although an epidemic of conjunctivitis did spread among the refugees toward the end of the trip, due to the closeness of the quarters. Many woke up with swollen, teary, red eyes in their last days on the ship.

Those were the beginning days of my free life—filled with uncertainty about my future, the starry sky my only guide.

CHRISTINA
Hà Nội | 2002

THE UNDP OFFICES WERE LOCATED IN a gated French colonial building on Lý Thường Kiệt. The faded yellow exterior and green shutters gave the building an air of importance. It appeared that it had once been a beautiful building, but now it was run down. The UNICEF sign hung on the front, even though their offices had been moved to the other side of town a few years prior. The inside, meanwhile, was as worn down as the exterior. The staff often complained about the building's infrastructure: in the summer months, the building was too warm, and the floors throughout the building were slanted.

I had initially been assigned to sit in the basement and share a small space with a Swiss intern—but when chị Thanh, the coordinator of our department, learned that I was sitting downstairs, she'd advocated for me to come up and sit next to her.

Thanh was a serious and plain-looking Vietnamese woman with a short-bobbed haircut, glasses, and bangs cut straight across her youthful face that made her look much younger than her actual age, which I assumed was late twenties or early thirties.

I hadn't put much energy into my internship. I was too focused on the newness of Hà Nội and my ever-widening social network. My colleagues, from the Vietnamese staff to the foreigners, many who were part of UNDP's young professional program, were impressive—intimidating, even. My supervisor, Đức, a Vietnamese man in his early forties who was head of the social and economic development unit, spoke quickly and fluidly about the development of Việt Nam. One of the staff members who worked in the Resident Coordinator's office said that he was one of the smartest men in Việt Nam, and I believed it. He'd earned a PhD in the States, and then, when faced with the decision to stay or go back to Việt Nam, he'd returned. He spoke so rapidly about projects, ideas, and people that it was challenging for me to keep up with him. I couldn't really figure out how I could contribute to the department, or to these conversations, since I had not studied international development and this was the first time I'd worked in a developing country.

Since Đức was so busy running the department, I didn't meet with him much. Instead, I spent most of my working day with chị Thanh, who, as coordinator, had a hand in overseeing all of the team's projects—including the one I was assigned to, which involved the organization of the first HIV/AIDS Policy Forum led by UNDP and a government counterpart. Prior to that, the Vietnamese government had not officially wanted to address HIV/AIDS as an issue in Việt Nam, claiming instead that it was a disease linked to "social evils" like drugs and prostitution.

From the moment we started working together, chị Thanh felt like an older sister to me, a pattern that seemed to repeat itself on this Vietnam adventure. Until I moved to Hà Nội, nobody, not even my parents, had ever called me by my Vietnamese middle name, Tuyết, which translated to "snow." I'd never even told anyone my full middle name—Thị Ánh-Tuyết—because it looked long and awkward to me. When I was a child, I thought the three names looked so strange, so if it appeared on my paperwork, I would simply remove the "Thị Ánh," hoping it would be more acceptable. And when anyone in the U.S. tried to pronounce Tuyết, it usually sounded like they were saying, "Twit." But in Việt Nam, my middle name gave me an entirely new identity; it sounded melodic. Every morning, when Thanh addressed me as em Tuyết (since I was younger than her), a feeling of tenderness washed through me. I was beginning to understand how beautiful the way Vietnamese people addressed each other was. And Thanh even commented on the beauty of my full Vietnamese name, Thị

Ánh-Tuyết: "They named you well," she told me. "It is a name, you know, that is often associated with creative people. There's even a famous singer named Ánh-Tuyết."

Chị Thanh intrigued me because she was forceful about her opinions, which at that time felt strange to me, not only for a Vietnamese woman but for any woman. At almost twenty-three years, I still felt young and naïve—I was just learning to find my voice.

Thanh told me what she didn't like about the job, about the bureaucracy that we worked in. When I heard her in meetings, she spoke with grace, passion, and conviction about standing up for people, about helping those who didn't have a voice. She didn't see the broader policy implications; she focused on the individuals, wanting to fight for those people. Over time, I realized that she loathed working for an organization that she considered bureaucratic. Most young Vietnamese women, it seemed to me, would have been proud to work at the United Nations, particularly because the salary there was significantly higher than it was at most organizations in the country. There was a part of Thanh that, very much like me, yearned for something more. She reminded me of a woman warrior: her fight was for the vulnerable population. I began to think about where, as a professional, I would find the same fire as chị Thanh.

Thanh was not the traditional Vietnamese woman that I had expected to encounter in Việt Nam. By Vietnamese standards, she was already considered too old to have a family, yet she still maintained her commitment to family by living at home.

Prior to my arrival, I'd thought that most Vietnamese women would be more family oriented and less daring than the women I was fortunate enough to befriend while I was there. One colleague told me that she had a baby at home and would return home during her lunch to breastfeed the child. She also said, casually, "I go to the market to get fresh food to prepare for the family around 6 a.m. before going to work." I couldn't imagine how these women managed all facets of their lives so efficiently, seemingly without any resentment for not being able to live their independent lives.

There was a level of duty and responsibility toward family I was not accustomed to, and wasn't sure I ever could be. I thought about my father and wondered if that was another way that I'd disappointed him.

ONE COLD, FALL MORNING IN HÀ NỘI, when the weather was crisp and overcast, Thanh invited me to go eat at the stall across the street with her.

By this time, I understood why Vietnamese people wanted to eat phở in the morning. This had baffled me for years—until I moved to Hà Nội. There was something about the chill morning air that made it feel normal to eat a hot bowl of soup first thing in the morning. The warmth of the broth comforted me.

I knew that it didn't get as cold in the South, so I was curious if morning phở had the same impact there. I'd learned that there was a difference between northern and southern phở. Northern phở tended to have wider noodles, with a simple and clear broth, and northerners preferred to eat phở with chicken meat or simple minced rare beef. Southern phở, on the other hand, had thinner noodles, the broth was sweeter and bolder, and the meat dominated the flavors, with many parts of beef, such as sliced rare beef, bone marrow, tendon, fatty flank, brisket, and meatballs.

"The place where we're going is one of the best places to get phở, one of the most famous in Hà Nội," Thanh said to me as she grabbed her wallet and coat, eager to step outside.

Like most of the delicious places in town, it was a run-down street food stall, with the ubiquitous blue stools and the plastic container holding chopsticks, napkins, and hot sauce in the center of the table. Most vendors were known for one thing, and oftentimes exclusively served that dish. As I'd become more familiar with Hà Nội, I'd started to figure out where to eat the best dishes in town, but I was still learning.

After we sat down, chị Thanh picked up a pair of chopsticks, wiped them down with a paper towel, and handed them to me before cleaning a set off for herself.

We spoke about work and our impressions about the meeting we'd attended the day before as we waited for the woman running the stall to serve us our piping hot phở.

I also had some news I couldn't wait to talk with Thanh about: "I stopped by Bobby Chinn's restaurant, and I actually met him," I blurted out.

Bobby was an attractive half-Egyptian, half-Chinese man who had been running restaurants in Việt Nam since the early nineties. His namesake restaurant was located in a prime location at the south-west corner of Hoàn Kiếm Lake. Red silk and dried rose petals hung like garlands from the ceiling, and in the back of the restaurant the most glamorous Vietnamese and expats smoked hookahs and nibbled on grapes stuffed with goat cheese on low-slung sofas.

"He told me that I should work at my internship during the day and help him do the marketing for the restaurant in the evening," I continued.

I was so excited about all the possibilities around me that the idea of development work now seemed boring to me. In my spare time, I'd been scoping out houseware stores, and I now dreamed of opening a small business one day, importing homewares from Việt Nam.

"Tuyết, I think you should focus on the internship and on learning Vietnamese," Thanh cautioned me. "Take things slowly, and step by step."

I knew that she was right, but everything else seemed so much more exciting. I wasn't focused enough to study Vietnamese (I would regret this later), and even though I had a great internship at a prestigious organization, I found the work boring. I wanted instant gratification; I desired an exciting life. In all areas of my life, I was jumping—from country to country, job to job, home to home. The search, the discovery, was the most important thing for me at the moment.

I couldn't help but broach the topic of family and marriage with Thanh. I'd had enough initial interactions with Vietnamese people over the course of the month that I'd been there that I knew the important reference points: your age, your marital status, and your salary. After someone found out that I was single, the next comment would generally be "Why are you alone?"—as if no one would ever choose to live a solitary life.

I'd started to meet other women who were defying my ideas of traditional Vietnamese women, including Anh and Nguyệt, two of the women Thi had introduced me to. When Thi had written to me about Nguyệt, she'd described her as a Vietnamese woman who was the perfect balance between a modern woman who was claiming her independence, and a traditional woman who maintained her Vietnamese values and close ties to her family. When I met Nguyệt, she was exactly how Thi had described her. There was an independence, a fierceness, and a gentleness at once. She was concerned about where I was living and if I was comfortable living there. I knew she was in her late twenties, but she spoke nothing of a desire to be coupled off, or an interest in being bound by duty and tradition. It surprised me to meet Vietnamese women like this. In many ways, I admired them for balancing both family and their individual desires. In that sense, I felt fully American, driven by a rugged individualism and lacking the emotional wherewithal to focus simultaneously on my own journey and that of others.

As we finished our phở, sipping the last drops of the soup, I asked Thanh if she wanted to have a family.

"Yes, I do want to have a family," she said. "But I also want to study human rights in Hong Kong. I want to learn about the world. I want to have the opportunity to get out of Việt Nam."

When it was time to pay for our phở, Thanh insisted that I let her pay. I noticed that had happened a lot when I went out with Vietnamese friends.

When Thanh looked at me and said, "Be quiet, Tuyết; she'll charge a different price because you are Việt Kiều." I was just beginning to understand what it meant to be Việt Kiều.

NGHĨA

Guam & Fort Indiantown Gap, Pennsylvania | 1975

AROUND MIDNIGHT ON THE SEVENTH DAY of the sea trip out of Phú Quốc, while the skies were still dark, part of the horizon suddenly lit up. A few people woke up, surprised by the brightness of the sky. Their excitement in turn stirred other people.

A feeling of joy lifted my heart. I knew land was there on the horizon, although I couldn't put a name or a location on that place; only a large population could make an area that bright in the middle of the night. Our seven-day-long, monotonous trip was coming to an end.

Although it was past midnight, no one could go back to sleep, so we all remained there—our chests against the ship's rails, our eyes glued to the bright lights that came closer with every single minute.

The ship slowly approached the land mass. The magical place turned out to be the island of Guam—thirty-two miles long by four-to-twelve miles wide and home to 80,000 people—somewhere in the middle of the Pacific Ocean. It seemed unbelievable that 80,000 people could light up all the sky in the middle of the night.

Exhausted from the journey, I did not pay attention to the size of the island, the neatness of the place, or the employees who were still awake to meet and screen us. I dragged my feet down the stairs. The identification process was long due to the sheer number of refugees.

"Do you have family in the United States?" the interviewer asked me.

"No," I responded.

"Would you like to go to California, Pennsylvania, or Florida?" he asked.

Having never been to any of these places, I didn't know how to decide or to give an appropriate answer. I thought to myself, *What will these places look like? How will one differ from the other?*

Someone elbowed me in the back and whispered, "*California.*"

"California," I responded.

"Okay, then please sign here," the interviewer said.

AFTER A LONG IDENTIFICATION PROCESS, WE were transported to a nearby campsite on the island. It must have been 4 or 5 a.m. when we arrived at our destination. We were each assigned to a military cot, four to five under a large tent. This was the first time in a week that we'd been able to rest in something private resembling a bed.

What astonished me most was that I didn't see any mosquito nets anywhere. To protect ourselves from mosquitoes, which were prevalent in tropical areas, Vietnamese people were used to sleeping under mosquito nets. We'd done so our entire lives, so sleeping without one felt like being naked, unprotected from the environment. But it was so late, and I was so worn out, that I didn't worry about the mosquito net and simply fell asleep quickly.

In the morning, I was awakened by noise outside of my tent: people running and talking, and children crying. The sun was high and bright, and the heat felt palpable.

I peeked out and saw a long line of refugees snaking around a huge tent.

"Wake up," I heard someone say. "Get your lunch, otherwise there won't be anything left to eat."

"Where and how do you get your food?" I heard someone ask.

"Go over there, stay in line, and move accordingly. Your turn will come soon."

After taking a quick wash, I scrambled to get in line. I was surprised to see all the refugees standing neatly one behind the other—a move that was rarely observed in the Vietnamese community.

I learned that food was only provided at mealtimes. There were no grocery stores or vending machines in the camp. Even if we had money, we wouldn't be able to buy food anywhere.

After lunch, we went back to our tents for a quick nap to recover from the ordeal of the night before. Then it was again time to line up for supper.

CONSTRUCTION WAS GOING FULL SPEED IN the camp. Bulldozers were parked close by and uprooted trees still lay on the side of the roads. The ground was uneven, the earth newly broken. Construction materials and machinery were scattered throughout. On the far end of the camp, new tents were erected every day. Eventually, the camp, which was located on the abandoned WWII Japanese airstrip on the Orote peninsula, was filled with almost 3,000 tents housing tens of thousands of refugees. It was first named Camp "Fortuitous," but that was somewhat difficult for the refugees to pronounce, so it quickly became known as the Orote "Tent City."

I found the food they served there hot and delicious, much better than what had been provided on the ship. There in Guam, we ate hamburgers, chicken, mashed potatoes, and green beans—the staples of American food—for the first time in our lives. This was also our official introduction to American society and way of life. Fruit cocktail, uncommonly seen in Việt Nam, was abundant in the camp. Apples and yellow-skinned oranges were served later. In our tropical Việt Nam, oranges tended to come with green skins; these small differences piqued our curiosity and reminded us we were in a different country.

I spent another five or six days there doing nothing except watching a large number of people moving in and out of the area. Each time one group departed, another group came in.

The idleness on the island provided me a lot of time to think about our lives, families, and country. No information came out of the hermetically closed communist Việt Nam; all news was blacked out. I did not know what had happened to my family, still trapped there. On this bright and sunny tropical island, we remained in total communication darkness.

So many questions ran through my mind: What were we doing on this island? How could we have lost the whole country? This must be a bad dream. How could a country of 17 million people surrender to the enemy and collapse overnight? Why had the U.S. not helped us in this tragic moment? Were our leaders inept to the point of losing the war? Have we done our share in this fight? Should we have done more?

Days and nights went by without any answers. After spending sleepless nights tossing, turning, and torturing myself with these unsolvable questions, I just gave up. This maddening intellectual exercise led to nowhere except more self-recriminations, anguish, and pain.

By the end of that first week in the camp, I had lost track of time and dates. We had also temporarily lost our freedom. Our schedule revolved around mealtimes, without which we would go hungry; the times for lunch and supper were dictated by the mess, and deviation from the rules meant a hungry stomach later. We lived together in confinement, separated from our benefactors by camp walls and the language barrier.

I realized we did not even speak the language of our new country. I also considered the fact that were we thrown out among the islanders, we would not be able to survive and be self-sufficient economically. Grasping all this for the first time, the future felt daunting.

For some of the refugees, irritation turned into anger, desperation, and then violence. A few requested permission to return home to look for their families. They felt guilty for having abandoned them. Negotiations with the new government in Việt Nam were slow, as the communists were now in control—governing the whole country, and putting one million southern males into concentration camps. Some refugees rioted, fasted, shaved their heads, and even burned down a couple of buildings before the camp administrators gave in to their demands.

A few months later, armed with an agreement from the new government in Sài Gòn and Hà Nội, a group of refugees were given the opportunity to refurbish the *Thương Tín I*—the same boat that had taken many to Guam—and to make some dry runs with the ship around the island.

Finally, on October 16, 1975, they were given the clearance to return to Việt Nam.

A total of 1,546 Vietnamese made the journey back. It wasn't until ten years later that Captain Trần Đình Trụ, who guided the ship back to Việt Nam, reappeared and told us about the ship's odyssey.

On arrival in Việt Nam, authorities ordered the ship to head to a port in central Việt Nam. All the returnees were imprisoned and Trụ was tried as U.S. spy. He was jailed in a communist reeducation camp for almost a decade before finally being released back to his family.

After his release, he applied for immigration to the U.S. He first landed in San Francisco, and later settled in Texas.

He admitted to having made a "huge error" deciding to return to Việt Nam from Guam.

APPROXIMATELY TWO WEEKS AFTER OUR ARRIVAL to Guam, we were told to pack up and get ready for departure.

We were driven to another camp, where we stayed for another two weeks in sturdy barracks. Amenities were better there than they had been in Tent City. There was even a beach on site, although no one was in the mood to take a swim.

One early morning, we were taken to the airport and advised to rest and wait in the barracks within the confines of the airport. The area was comfortable, with mattresses on bunk beds and air-conditioning. At the end of the day, we were transported to the airfield and boarded a huge Boeing 747 jet.

Soon, we were airborne.

HOURS LATER, WE LANDED IN HONOLULU, Hawaii. We were allowed to debark and stretch out in the empty gate-reception area.

"There's no lei flower reception," I heard one person joke.

"They probably don't even know we're here," responded another.

The plane took off again and made another stop in Portland, Oregon, before continuing to Harrisburg International Airport in Pennsylvania. We then boarded buses that took us to Fort Indiantown Gap Camp. We were directed to a large hall where other refugees who had arrived earlier had gathered. After a short introduction, we were assigned to different barracks.

By the time we left the meeting, it was late in the night, but there were volunteers from the Salvation Army there to greet us and provide us with food. That was the greatest moment of the day for me. The warm smiles and lovely voices of these middle-aged ladies soothed my dispirited heart and washed away my fatigue and loneliness.

After our meal, I headed back to my assigned bed in the barracks, feeling invigorated.

THE FOLLOWING MORNING, REFRESHED FROM A full night's sleep, I started to explore the camp and its amenities. Only part of the camp was accessible to the refugees. It turned out to be rather big, so much so that buses were available to ride within the camp during working hours. Many refugees utilized the buses, which led to excessive crowding. Eventually, people found it easier to walk around the camp in order to avoid the pushing and shoving matches that came with that overcrowding. Walking also ended up being the best way to meet new and old friends, as well as relatives.

One day, while walking around the camp, I saw my older brother, Tuấn, and his wife, Bích, walking toward me. I was shocked. I hadn't seen them for five or six months, and was elated to realize that they'd escaped Việt Nam as well.

"How are you doing?" I asked my brother.

"I'm all right," he said. "How about you?"

I shrugged. "Have you had any news from the rest of the family?"

"Mom, Dad, and our brothers could not escape," he said sadly. "How did you get out?"

"I left through Phú Quốc, then Guam, and now to this camp," I said

"I took the last boat in Sài Gòn," Tuấn said. "All of the boats were filled with people. We were the last passengers on a boat that sailed to the Philippines, then we left from Subic Air Force Base and arrived here." He gestured to our surroundings. "You know, this is one of four refugee camps: Fort Indiantown Gap in Pennsylvania, Camp Pendleton in California, an air force base in Florida, and one in Arkansas."

"I applied to go to California and somehow ended up here," I said.

"The same thing happened to me," he said. Then he cocked his head, looking at me. "Of all the people I would have thought would have escaped, you wouldn't have been it."

"I know," I said. "I was just lucky. They unexpectedly sent me instead of somebody else to Phú Quốc, and now here I am. I imagine the other person is now stranded in Cần Thơ. This must have been fate."

We told each other how we'd applied for relocation. I'd gone through the Catholic charities; he'd applied through a Methodist organization.

"There were so many to choose from that I didn't even know where to begin," I told him.

We exchanged barrack numbers and said that we would stay in touch. I was relieved to have one family member close by as I navigated these uncertain times.

TWO WORLDS

CHRISTINA
Hà Nội | 2002

"VIỆT KIỀU STAND OUT IN THE crowds," Mai told me one afternoon. "They know we are Vietnamese. They must recognize a part of us that *is* Vietnamese. But they can tell the difference between us and them because of the way we dress, the way we walk, the way in which we speak the language."

Before arriving in Việt Nam, I hadn't even heard of the term "Việt Kiều," which referred to overseas Vietnamese or Vietnamese people who were part of the diaspora—those who had left Việt Nam and now lived abroad. I was adjusting to this word and navigating my understanding of my identity: being Vietnamese, being American, and now discovering I was Việt Kiều.

Mai, who was also Vietnamese American and Việt Kiều, told me that she'd overheard Vietnamese people on the streets commenting about her hair—cut short like a boy's and dyed a reddish tint. They'd say things like, "I wonder if she is a boy or a girl."

Mai felt that if she was Caucasian American, or from another country that was not America, she wouldn't receive such criticism about her hair. Being Việt Kiều Mỹ (American Việt Kiều) meant that we were navigating a space of being neither fully Vietnamese nor fully American.

I met a handful of other American Việt Kiều, many of whom had studied public health as undergraduates and now worked for international development organizations. Minh, another close Việt Kiều friend of mine, was on a Fulbright Scholarship to research chữ nôm, a logographic writing system used to write the Vietnamese language between the fifteenth and nineteenth centuries by the cultured elite. Having these other Việt Kiều around me helped me anchor myself in Việt Nam, partly because I recognized that we were all there for a similar reason: to learn more about our cultural history, and to understand ourselves on a deeper level.

I'd heard of other Việt Kiều who'd traveled from France, Germany, and Australia. Within the Việt Kiều category, there was another level of distinction based on the country one's family had emigrated to: an American Việt Kiều, for example, was Việt Kiều Mỹ; a Việt Kiều from France was Việt Kiều Pháp; and so on. For obvious reasons, I felt the most connected to American Việt Kiềus: we were Việt Kiều *and* American *and* had decided, for our varied reasons, to travel to Việt Nam—whether to connect with our heritage, forge our professional paths, or discover ourselves.

During my time in Hà Nội I heard the term Việt Kiều used quite frequently whenever I met a new Vietnamese person or even an expatriate.

"Look you like Vietnamese," said a Vietnamese woman perched on a tiny red stool, selling bottled La Vie water and items like gum and MobiFone SIM cards on a busy intersection in Hà Nội.

"Yes, I am Vietnamese," I responded to her.

Once I confirmed her assumption, I glimpsed a subtle shift in her eyes. Her sense of trepidation and uncertainty about how to perceive a foreigner—her initial hesitation—was overcome by the recognition of my Vietnamese-ness, as slight as it might have been.

"Mỹ, Đức, Pháp?"—American, German, French?—she asked, trying to identify the country which I called home. "Việt Kiều Mỹ," I confirmed to her.

"Oh, Việt Kiều Mỹ." She nodded in affirmation and shot me a knowing glance.

This reverse migration had already begun many years before. And it seemed the number of Vietnamese who returned increased in direct correlation with the development of Việt Nam. I learned that in the beginning phase of the diaspora the overseas Vietnamese wired money back to their families. Then they began making the journey themselves, returning to Việt Nam with suitcases full of Western goods to satiate the needs of their relatives who coveted foreign brands. I had no clue in these early months of living in Hà Nội that I would witness the next generation of Việt Kiều coming back in hordes to build their lives and their careers in Việt Nam, recognizing that there was something quite beautiful about returning to the motherland.

I'd already heard of a few Việt Kiều who had been extremely successful in Việt Nam, and I wondered if one day I would belong to the same category as them. Chad, a Vietnamese American from Washington, had started a chain of Starbucks-like coffee shops—one in a prime location on the southwest corner of Hoàn Kiếm Lake with tables shaded by umbrellas, perfect for lazy days watching the visible life around the lake.

Chad's first cafe was located at the place where I'd met Thomas for the first time, and failed miserably. When his parents had come to visit him in Việt Nam and seen how much he was struggling, they'd urged him to return home. But he still believed in the potential of the coffee market, and had persisted.

Eventually, Chad and his coffee chain unlocked a key formula for any business to thrive in Việt Nam: creating a product that satisfied both foreigners and middle-class Vietnamese people. For the coffee business, this translated to offering a range of coffee options, from vanilla lattes to iced cà phê sữa đá. He created a recognizable brand in his coffee shops, often securing prime locations and creating a consistent ambiance, including lush, comfortable sofas in deep purple and burgundy and old patterned tiles lining the floors, that invited customers to stay.

I didn't know at that time whether I would stay in Việt Nam long enough to make any sort of impact. I did, however, feel a mixture of sentiments about being Việt Kiều and what that meant in Hà Nội: being looked upon with curiosity, kinship—and sometimes resentment.

Being Việt Kiều placed a person in a special category—not fully foreign, not fully Vietnamese. Vietnamese friends offered to help me make purchases so that I wouldn't get ripped off by greedy vendors. An American woman who had lived in Hà Nội for many years told me that being Việt Kiều would be beneficial for my dating life. "The foreign men are attracted to the Vietnamese women because they perceive them as exotic," she explained. "But, oftentimes they connect better with other expats. The Việt Kiều are a mix of both Vietnamese and foreigners." I felt uncomfortable hearing this. I wasn't that ideal blend of Vietnamese and foreign. I was barely Vietnamese, and I didn't see myself as feminine and beautiful as the local women around me. Not only that, but I also didn't go to Việt Nam searching for a man.

My friendships with other Việt Kiều formed quickly; only later would I realize that they would prove to be the strongest friendships of my life at that time and that they would endure. I attributed the rapid nature of our bonds to the fact that time seemed more elastic in Hà Nội. We were less constrained by strenuous working hours. If I'd chosen to move to New York or San Francisco, I doubt I would have been able to see my friends as much as I did in Hà Nội. We met for lunch, dinner, or drinks daily. The new friends who had spent considerable time in Hà Nội passed down prized information: the best tailor, the hidden courtyard café which served egg yolk coffee, the best food stalls—though Hà Nội was far too small for anything to really be kept secret.

I OFTEN GRAPPLED WITH THE FACT that I felt the least Vietnamese of all my Việt Kiều friends. Most of them had grown up speaking Vietnamese at home and had some awareness of Vietnamese customs and traditions. Some of them went by their Vietnamese first names, which they knew how to pronounce, unlike my fear of even uttering my Vietnamese middle name. My family had always lived in small towns, often with only a few Asian families and sometimes no other Vietnamese families. In my high school class of 434 students, I was the only Asian person. I'd often wondered why my parents never wanted to teach us the customs and rich history of their country of origin.

Now, in Hà Nội I shied away from speaking Vietnamese in front of my friends, embarrassed at the way I sounded when I spoke the language. Before arriving in Hà Nội, I hadn't even known that the Vietnamese language was tonal—that a two-letter word, like "ma," could have several different meanings depending on the tone. I also did not know that there was a difference between regional dialects, particularly between the North and South.

Because of my embarrassment, I deferred to my Việt Kiều friends when it came to ordering food or communicating with Vietnamese staff whenever we went out.

Minh often pushed me to speak the language. "Your Vietnamese isn't so bad," he insisted. "You should try to learn while you are here." In retrospect, I wish I had pushed myself to be immersed in the language.

If I ventured out with other foreigners, suddenly, the role was reversed: I was the one who was sought after for help ordering and choosing the best dishes.

Sometimes I wondered what the Vietnamese thought about the Việt Kiều who returned. Were we respected, loathed, admired? Was our presence valued? Were we contributing to the development of Việt Nam? Did women who were around my age wonder, like I did, what their lives would have been like had our places been reversed—if they were Việt Kiều and not local Vietnamese?

I didn't know then that I had merely started to skim the surface of this new understanding of being Việt Kiều.

MY FATHER AND ALICE CALLED ME once a month while I was in Việt Nam. I knew Alice initiated these calls, and not my father, but I simply appreciated the fact that they called. In those conversations, I spoke excitedly about my daily life in Việt Nam, hoping that this enthusiasm would prompt my father to start talking about what he remembered about Việt Nam. I shared with him what I enjoyed and what I found amusing, like the "visible life" that Alice had mentioned was everywhere in Việt Nam.

"I didn't understand what visible life meant," I said to them during one phone call. "But now I do. There's so much life that I can see from the streets."

People walked around outside in their pajamas in the early morning and evening. They'd attach their dogs with a chain to their motorbikes and drive slowly around the block. Sometimes, I could even see people cooking dinners inside their homes. And while my roommates and I peered into the lives of the Vietnamese people who lived around us, they were also witnessing our lives. Our neighbors, the xe ôm drivers, and others who worked on our street were hyper-aware of our comings and goings. They knew where we worked; they knew that we were a group of Americans living together; they even knew what time we returned home on the weekends.

Some foreigners who had been living there for some time told me that the government was watching all of the foreigners and we each had an assigned agent who tracked our whereabouts, often someone who lived in our local neighborhood. I didn't know if that was true or not, but I was enjoying my life too much to worry about whether someone was following me. After all, my life wasn't that exciting and I had nothing to hide: I mostly just went from my internship to meet friends for dinner after work each day.

I felt, though, as if my life had opened up and that I was living—fully and deeply—for the first time. In comparison to what it had been like at my corporate job, life did indeed feel rich. Even though my internship was unpaid and I was living off the money I had made the previous year, I didn't care. The experience was so much more valuable to me than the salary from working at a pharmaceutical company. The newness of everything kept me excited and energized.

I was simultaneously taken aback and unsurprised that my father never asked questions about my life in Hà Nội. He didn't inquire about my impressions of living in Việt Nam; I had to volunteer them. And, still, he never explicitly stated whether he was disappointed that I had decided to move to Hà Nội instead of Sài Gòn. We were different in that sense: If I loved something, I wanted to share it. He kept his love to himself.

I wanted my father to have an intimate portrait of the strangers who were quickly becoming close friends. I wanted to tell him about my colleague chị Thanh, and the group of Việt Kiều who were now my co-explorers in this new land. I wanted him to know about the slightly plump xe ôm driver, Thanh, who wore military-colored attire every day and worked outside of the UNDP offices for years until he was promoted to being the office's security guard—simply because the staff there grew comfortable with him. I thought he would enjoy the story of my friend Minh's xe ôm driver, Trường, who knew the precise time of Minh's classes at the local university. If Minh was running late or had no intention of going to class, the xe ôm driver would call up to his window and tell him that it was time to go. Those were the sweet encounters and stories that made up our daily lives.

On one of the phone calls, I told Alice and my father about how, when I was feeling lonely one time, I'd called one of my new Vietnamese friends and she'd advised me to go to Hoàn Kiếm Lake, the center of life in downtown Hà Nội, to watch passersbys.

"Watch the people," she instructed me. "The old people sitting on the bench, the young children playing, the couples holding hands. Then, you won't feel lonely anymore."

At five in the morning, the early risers convened at the lake for their morning exercise; groups of women would do their aerobics routine, counting một, hai, ba. In the late evening, families strolled around the lake with their children, eating ice cream cones purchased on Tràng Tiền Street. Hoàn Kiếm Lake was never empty, and it was certainly never quiet.

If I mentioned a miscommunication with a colleague or someone I encountered on the street, my father would simply respond, "Oh it's because they are from Hà Nội."

I could tell that in his mind there was a vast difference between Hanoians and Saigonese. The individuals in Hà Nội represented northern Việt Nam, and northern Việt Nam represented communism. Alice and my father warned me that I would be overcharged for the most basic items in the north. I wondered if they knew that most foreigners felt that Vietnamese in general, not just Hanoians, were prone to overcharging foreigners. I couldn't get it through their heads that Việt Nam was a personal experience for me, and not everything needed to be viewed through a political lens.

MY FATHER HAD NOT RETURNED TO Việt Nam since his departure in 1975. Alice had visited once, for a medical mission, and only spoke about the negative experiences she had on her trip there: she'd claimed that medical supplies were left unused in the back of the hospital, and had been dismayed by the conditions in Việt Nam. I, in contrast, felt a sense of wonder about Việt Nam, particularly the natural beauty of the countryside that I had started to visit on weekend excursions—like the huge rock formations in Hạ Long Bay or the mountainous region of Sa Pa. Unlike my father and Alice, I had no prior impressions of the country, no baseline for comparison between Việt Nam before and after the war, no demarcation between North and South. There was simply Việt Nam.

I wanted my father to experience Hà Nội and Việt Nam with me. The only time I sensed excitement—happiness, even—in his voice during one of these phone conversations was when I told him that I was going on a trip to the South. I planned to visit Sài Gòn, Vũng Tàu, a coastal city in the southern part of Việt Nam, and Phú Quốc Island during the week of Tết, the Lunar New Year celebrations. Since arriving in Việt Nam, my Vietnamese friends had been telling me that I should leave town for Tết, because everything shut down for the holiday and it was boring for foreigners, since, unlike the local Vietnamese, we didn't have family to visit and celebrate with. "It's the best time for a foreigner to go to a beach and just relax," one friend said to me.

My father didn't seem to care that my short vacation would also include visits to Sài Gòn and Phú Quốc—two places that I knew were pivotal to his upbringing and history—but there was something about Vũng Tàu that softened him.

"Vũng Tàu is a beautiful place," he told me. "There's so much to do there. Make sure you go to the front beach and the back beach. You can walk up the mountain and see the statue of Jesus. There's also a statue of Buddha you can go visit."

"Thanks," I said, happy that he was taking interest in my trip.

"And take pictures for me," he added.

I heard enthusiasm and excitement in his voice. I didn't know then that he had spent a significant part of his childhood there, living with his grandmother on a longan orchard. He'd never told me that story.

I was only beginning to understand my father's love of South Việt Nam and the gaping space the country he'd lost had left in his heart. *But how can I ever completely understand his Việt Nam, I wondered, since he's never bothered to share it with me?*

NGHĨA

South Việt Nam | 1940s

I WAS BORN IN SÀI GÒN in 1947. When I remember my childhood in
Việt Nam and the backdrop of the war, I think of the motherland, my
own mother, and the role of women in the war. There's a Vietnamese
song that describes the depth of a mother's love. One line reverber-
ates in my thoughts: "Mother's love is like an ocean."

Throughout the war and after the takeover of South Việt Nam,
women held an important role in the economy and education. With
most men gone to war and later to reeducation camps, women took
on jobs previously held, then vacated, by men—anything from
farming to running stores to educating children. Women stood up to
the challenges and needs of the country, as they had throughout history: in France, there was Joan of Arc; in China, there was Mulan; and
in Việt Nam, there were the Trưng Sisters. In times of war, these
women came from nowhere to lead and reenergize the country, but
not only were there war heroes, there were also everyday women who
supported their families and their countries through turbulent times.
I consider my mother, Bạch Cúc (which translates to Daisy), one of
those everyday heroes.

My mother was born in the early twenties, the eldest of seven children (two died at an early age, leaving her with three sisters and one
brother), in Bà Rịa, a small transit town no one would have ever heard
of had it not been situated in a strategic position between Sài Gòn,
the bustling capital of South Việt Nam, and the seaside resort of Vũng
Tàu. Buses loaded with passengers and merchandise that bulged from

their backsides and rooftop made many daily trips between the two cities. Tilting heavily to one side under their cumbersome loads, the buses sputtered through the crowded streets of downtown Bà Rịa. In the process, they generated a lot of noise—driver's helpers banged on the outside of the bus to signal to the driver to stop—and left behind a trail of black diesel smoke.

These buses made a ten-minute stop at the transportation center close to the market to disgorge people, belongings, and at times live poultry destined for sale at the local market, and then to take on new passengers, before heading toward their final destination. The ten-minute stop could, however, last up to half an hour depending upon the circumstances. In a land where rice and food had always been plentiful and where peace had been present for some time, the South Vietnamese tended to take it easy and to enjoy life. They took their time and dragged their feet because there was no pressure to complete any task. Work, although necessary in life, was never intended to be a goal in itself. Celebrations took precedence over other matters and people competed against each other to throw parties to entertain their guests. And there were plenty of reasons to celebrate: weddings, engagements, births, deaths, promotions, and new acquisitions, not to mention all the holidays. Time in this environment became "elastic"; punctuality was never a South Vietnamese virtue.

The passengers who were left sitting in 100-degree heat without air-conditioning often got angry and demanded an explanation when the ten minutes extended to thirty. The driver's assistant, while apologizing for the delay, would state that he was waiting for a few passengers or a shipment that had not yet arrived and promise the bus would leave "soon." That remark was punctuated by either a big smile or a smirk.

The Vietnamese smile frequently and easily. They smile because they are early or late, happy or sad. The smile does not carry any sarcastic meaning, as it might elsewhere in the world; rather, it is intended to deflect attention away from any embarrassing situation. The Vietnamese smile because, as straightforward people, they cannot not fib very well and are often short on words to explain their complex feelings. They also smile when they are caught in an awkward predicament. Unable to produce an adequate explanation for what they have done right or wrong or to express the deep regret they feel, they just awkwardly smiled. This is known as a "sorry smile," a unique Vietnamese trait that is been misunderstood by Westerners and Vietnamese alike but particularly Westerners, who often perceive the smile as an insult.

If, on the other hand, a Vietnamese person does not smile in such a situation, they can instead become angry or blunt in order to protect the deep emotions they're experiencing. For beneath this smile and bluntness runs a wealth of often complex if not contradictory feelings or emotions.

MY MOTHER'S FAMILY LATER MOVED TO Vũng Tàu, where my grandparents had purchased a two-acre orchard planted with longan trees, as well as a condo located about a mile from the orchard. This deal turned out to be a good investment for the future and stability of the family. My grandmother, like many women in Vietnamese society at that time, was a housewife, with at most an elementary school education. In the 1920s and 1930s, women were not allowed to go to school, and without education they could not get a decent job. The orchard, therefore, provided the family with a steady income, although it was not big enough to feed a large family.

Shortly after the purchase of the orchard, my grandfather passed away. Although my mother was still a teenager, she helped my grandmother with chores and with raising her brother and sisters. Suddenly, she was thrust into the limelight, having to play the role of big sister and leader to the family. Her dream was to grow up and finish school like other girls her age, but it seemed fate had chosen another direction for her. Since she was raised under Confucian rules and tradition, she was willing to take up the challenges and this new role.

According to Confucian rules—a relic of past Chinese influence (111 BC–939 CE) that was ingrained in the psyche of Vietnamese of that time—the wife should be obedient to her husband, who provided for her needs. Should the husband die, his wife would raise the children. In the absence or upon the death of the father, the eldest child represented the authority in the family. Family ties in a Confucian world were vital to the stability of the society, and in the era my mother grew up in, no one dared to challenge these two-millennia-old rules unless he (or she) was willing to be ostracized.

The family was a miniature society with its own unwritten rules, regulations, and etiquettes—structures that had been built over many generations. As long as they were alive, grandparents, parents, children, uncles, aunts, and cousins were all part of the family. Everyone knew his/her own place in this "extended family," for respect of the elders was de rigueur in this hierarchical society. The oldest person in the family occupied the best place at the table and was cared for until death. The family concept took precedence over the individual, as evidenced by the fact that Vietnamese and Chinese family names, contrary to Western rules, came first, followed by the middle and then the first names.

AT THE AGE OF TWENTY-TWO, MY mother married my father, Minh Võ, in Vũng Tàu while he was stationed there. Shortly thereafter, they moved to Sài Gòn, where they had their first child a year later. Two years after that, I was born in Sài Gòn, and then, in the subsequent years, three more boys were born, two of them twins.

When I was a child, my mother received a letter from her brother in Vũng Tàu, asking her to help him complete his schooling in Sài Gòn. He'd heard about the big schools in Sài Gòn and their advanced curriculum, and desired to be part of that system. In Vũng Tàu, he would have no chance at all of moving up in society.

My mother was torn between the desire to help her brother and the reality of trying to get her family on steady financial footing. The cost of living in Sài Gòn was higher than it was in the provinces, and she had struggled for years to establish herself and her family there. She worried constantly about the future and saving money for her children, while also needing to devote time to her husband and her growing family.

These were huge decisions for a twenty-something-year-old country woman who was new to Sài Gòn and in many ways lost in the big city. She had no relatives living close by, no friends to rely on, yet because she was the first in her family to move from the countryside to settle in Sài Gòn, she had to make considerations for the rest of her family as well. She wished her father had left her some money to take care of her brother, which would have made things easier for every-body. For some time, she was tormented by her thoughts, unsure what to do—but in the end, she decided to take in her brother, and one of her sisters as well.

Already overburdened with her children and now preparing for her siblings to move in, my mother decided to send me to Vũng Tàu to live with my grandmother. I had no idea why of all my siblings she chose me. But looking back, this decision turned out to be formative for me, because my time in Vũng Tàu allowed me to become acquainted with a countryside lifestyle: slow, gentle, but memorable. My recollection of that time, I would only later understand, would form the foundation of my peaceful thoughts of South Việt Nam—the homeland I would always long for in my mind.

CHRISTINA
South Việt Nam | 2003

WHEN I FIRST VISITED SOUTHERN VIỆT Nam, with Mai and Stephen, one of my housemates, I could see the region's charm and the way it must have lingered in my father's mind. There was an energy in the city that Hà Nội didn't have. It felt dynamic and inspiring. The hot sun beat down on my skin, making me feel like I'd have a sunburn within ten minutes. The smell of exhaust fumes mixed in the air with the odors of pork being cooked on small charcoal grills placed on the sidewalks and the pungent scent of a freshly opened bottle of fish sauce. The stickiness of the humidity seemed more palpable in the tropical environment of the south, with its streets dotted with palm trees.

Sài Gòn, unlike Hà Nội and northern Việt Nam, only had two seasons: hot, and hot and rainy. Hà Nội by contrast, had a brutal winter, which I had already started to experience. The wind pierced through your jacket, chilling your bones, as you rode through the streets on the backs of motorbikes, making the taste of a warm bowl of phở even more delicious. Drivers were barely visible under layers of coats, sweaters, mittens, and masks, which covered their entire faces except for the cut-outs for their eyes and mouth.

In Sài Gòn, when the seasonal rains poured down on the bustling city of around six million people in early 2003, the air remained warm. The enterprising Vietnamese immediately began popping up selling multicolored rain ponchos on the street, and signs for fresh coconut juice and cà phê sữa đá on the sidewalks lured people in to cool down from the melting heat.

The Saigonese on the streets, unlike their Hanoian counterparts, seemed more at ease dealing with foreigners, more friendly and jovial when they encountered one another on the street. Xe ôm drivers, while still generally known for trying to attract foreign customers, called out, "Motorbike you," asking if you wanted a ride somewhere, but if you said "no" they simply shrugged and started chatting with someone else on the street. They preferred to sit on their motorbikes, enjoying the company of their peers, instead of hassling people for a ride—unlike in Hà Nội where a xe ôm driver would relentlessly drive down the street behind you pestering you.

My friends and I noticed immediately that the street vendors didn't gawk at Mai's short hair when we walked down Pasteur Street. Nguyễn Huệ, the main street in downtown Sài Gòn, had been turned into a flower market for Tết, and I wasn't sure if I'd ever seen a market so beautiful, not only because of the explosion of colors but also because of the happiness that people exuded as they strolled to find the perfect Tết tree. Before I left Hà Nội, I'd noticed the vendors selling peach trees blossoming with pink flowers (hoa đào); in the south, however, the Tết tree was an apricot tree with yellow flowers (hoa mai). I found both to be beautiful, and wondered why people couldn't just love the North and the South for their differences and unique beauty—because I, certainly, was falling in love with both of them.

As I explored Sài Gòn, I thought about whether my father had walked down the same path, or if he would even recognize these streets now, given all the changes that must have occurred over the years. There was an airiness, an openness, about Sài Gòn, and perhaps because it had a much larger population than Hà Nội, people there cared less about other people's business. The southern Vietnamese seemed more open to the Việt Kiều, not placing such a clear demarcation between those Vietnamese who were born and raised in the South and those who'd stayed in Việt Nam. There was a greater sense of pride that the Việt Kiều would choose to return, as if Việt Nam had something to offer that our adopted countries did not possess.

Even the food in Sài Gòn seemed richer, more flavorful, than what I'd experienced in Hà Nội. I learned at a restaurant that one of the primary differences between northern and southern cuisine was Sài Gòn's access to the Mekong Delta's fresh fruits and vegetables. Southern dishes like bún thịt nướng, a grilled pork dish over vermicelli noodles, weren't even available in the North, but was on every menu in the South. The phở was served with hoisin sauce, which made the broth more flavorful, and the plate full of bean sprouts and mint leaves seemed more plentiful. Even the cà phê sữa đá seemed richer than the northern version, which was bitter and only had a spoonful of condensed milk and one large ice cube in a small cup. In Sài Gòn, the cà phê sữa đá boasted a certain richness, crushed ice filled to the brim, the darkness of the coffee and any bitterness overwhelmed by the sweetness of the liberally poured condensed milk. It was like starting your morning off with a dessert.

ONE DAY, THE THREE OF US walked around the streets of Sài Gòn looking for the law school where Mai's parents had met in the '70s. As we searched, I was reminded that my parents had met in medical school around that time, though I had no understanding of or context for what their lives had been like there. I knew that my mother had been born and raised in Cambodia, and her family had fled to Việt Nam in the late '60s, because of the conflict between the Khmer and Vietnamese. I also knew that my parents had a son while in Sài Gòn but he'd passed away as a toddler sometime after the war. I never asked them to explain. Because of my mother's death when I was a teenager, she didn't have the opportunity to tell me her story. I wondered if she was still alive whether or not she would've shared her life with me, whether I'd even have the desire to explore their history. As we walked through the streets of Sài Gòn, I could understand why this place had lingered in my father's mind for so long, and even why he'd kept those memories in the treasure chest of his heart.

WE MET A GROUP OF AMERICANS and American Việt Kiều for dinner during our trip. There were so many connections between the two groups it felt uncanny. Mai had been introduced to a guy, David, who lived in Sài Gòn, through a mutual friend in New York. My housemate, Monique, also knew of David because they had attended the same college and had mutual friends. Stephen knew of a girl named Veronica through a D.C. connection, who was also friends with David. Through three or four different avenues, we were connected to this community of young Americans, also recent college graduates like us. Like me, they had journeyed back to the motherland to discover their family's history.

I called this group our "southern counterparts" (a phrase I'd learned from my internship, since all of our projects required a government partner which we referred to as our "government counterparts").

During our trip, I learned more about why everyone had ventured to Sài Gòn and what they were working on. Some of them were beginning their doctoral research, but most of them were teaching English, studying Vietnamese, and just hanging out. This group, just like the South in general, had a laid-back nature that was appealing to me. There was also an openness of energy, a vibrancy, that I loved. Hà Nội in comparison, seemed cold—and not just because winter had recently cast its chill over the city.

It crossed my mind that maybe I should move to Sài Gòn. I had committed to one year at my internship, but suddenly, a year of not getting paid didn't seem so appealing. I felt drawn to the South, and I wondered if that was because of my parents; this was, after all, the city where my father had grown up, and where he'd met my mother. A longing stirred within me; it felt like there were more and more reasons to move to Sài Gòn.

"Maybe I'll move here," I told the group at one of our shared meals. "I really love it." My pull toward Sài Gòn felt just like the urge that had led me to Việt Nam in the first place, and somehow, I knew that I would follow it.

"We might have a room available in our house," David said. "Maybe you could take it?"

The seed of living in Sài Gòn had been planted. Just like the two very different Tết trees in the north and south, maybe I could learn to love both cities.

BEFORE I LEFT FOR MY SOUTHERN adventure, my father had emailed me and mentioned that my paternal grandfather, who was in his mid-seventies and lived in California, would also be in Sài Gòn celebrating the Lunar New Year. He'd given me the address in District 5, or Chợ Lớn, a neighborhood where historically the Chinese community lived in Sài Gòn, and added: he knows you'll go visit him.

This simple statement surprised me. My father wasn't suggesting that I should go visit, or asking if I would. Instead, he was saying that my grandfather knew that I would.

I had only met my paternal grandparents a handful of times in my life and didn't have any clear memories of them. I vaguely remembered visiting them in Little Sài Gòn in Orange County, California, once. My grandfather had taught me to jump rope and then handed me candy behind my back, hiding it from my mother. The only other time I remembered was when they traveled to Indiana for my mother's funeral.

When I met my grandparents as a child, they were already separated. I knew nothing about their story—when they had divorced, or when they arrived in the States. I only knew that my grandmother, Daisy, lived with my uncle Đại, the third son in the family. I wasn't quite sure where my grandfather lived, because I never visited his home.

My grandmother, who had since passed away, was a diminutive old woman, barely four-foot-eleven, and always seemed stern and critical to me. She once told my teenage sister, rather directly, that she'd be more beautiful if she quit smoking. In my memories, my grandfather with his round belly and boisterous laugh, was the opposite of that. I could only describe him as being jovial, and even though I'd had very few interactions with them, I'd always favored him over my intimidating grandmother. My father was the opposite: there was a noticeable distance between him and his father, whereas he carried a deep respect for my grandmother, and had even created a small altar for her in his office, on the highest bookshelf, as if she was watching over him.

I didn't even know my grandfather's name before I met him in Sài Gòn; I had only ever called him grandfather. But after about six months living in Việt Nam, I knew that the proper way of addressing my paternal grandfather was ông—specifically, ông nội, because there was a distinction in how to address grandparents depending on whether they were on the paternal or maternal side.

Following my father's instructions, I found a xe ôm driver and handed him a small sheet of paper with the address scribbled on it. We arrived at the house in short order, and I spotted my grandfather right away, sitting in a folding chair in front of a store that sold propane gas tanks. A large sign that read "Bình Minh Gas" flanked the front of the building.

He smiled at me and waved as I hopped off the motorbike. People often commented that I was the spitting image of my father, so even though I hadn't seen my grandfather in years, I'd known that he would know I was Nghĩa's daughter.

A nervousness ran through me. I didn't know what to say to him. I was also embarrassed that my Vietnamese had not progressed beyond the basics. I recalled that his English was not great either, so I wasn't sure how well we would communicate. My grandfather navigated the empty space, though, with a belly laugh and a reassuring pat on the back. Through his disposition, he more closely resembled my uncle Tuấn, my father's eldest brother, who lived in New Orleans and was always joking and laughing, nothing like my stoic father.

"I told your daddy that you would come visit me," he said.

"I know—you were right," I responded.

"That's me—Bình Minh Gas," he said proudly, pointing at the sign. "But don't tell anyone that I have another business in Việt Nam. They will get me in America for more taxes if they know I have a business here."

"I won't tell anyone," I assured him.

"Here, everyone talks to me," he said joyfully. "But in the States, nobody talks to me. I sit in my apartment and people do not go to visit me. Here, I sit on the street and everybody walks by and waves at me even if I don't know them. Here, I do not feel alone."

I also felt the difference between living in the States and in Việt Nam, but I felt incapable of explaining those complex feelings to him. Life in Việt Nam was more connected, partly from the sheer fact that you saw more people daily. But I knew it was beyond the "visible life." I felt closer to the new friends that I had met because we spent a lot of time together. Even though I knew far fewer people in Việt Nam, I felt more a part of my community than I ever had in the States. So, I understood what my grandfather was saying about Việt Nam.

While my grandfather and I sat next to each other, people scuttled around us, transforming the entire storefront into a makeshift dining room. They set up a table, brought down plates full of food from a kitchen somewhere upstairs, and placed small stools around the table.

I'd heard, although I didn't recall from whom, that my grandfather had had two families when he lived in Việt Nam—one with my grandmother, and another with a Chinese-Vietnamese woman. My grandmother and her children had moved to the States after the war, the other side had remained in Việt Nam.

The front room began filling up with more people, and suddenly I realized that I was the guest of honor—the reason they had made such elaborate preparations for dinner. Out of the corner of my eye, I noticed one man because he bore a striking resemblance to my father, much more so than my uncles. I realized that he must be my father's stepbrother, a son from my grandfather's other family.

He walked up to me and asked me in broken English, a big smile on his face, "How is your father?"

"He's fine," I responded.

"Why doesn't he come visit us here?" he asked.

I shook my head. "I'm not sure."

"We should call your daddy," my grandfather chimed in. "Let's call him. Do you think he will be home?"

They brought down a computer and a phone to hook up to the computer so we could call through the internet.

I heard my father answer with a very distant "hello." My grandfather spoke to him first—asking him how he was doing, and telling him I was there with them visiting and we were going to eat dinner together. Their conversation lasted only a few minutes, and then the man who resembled my father chimed in. My father responded in his typical one-word fashion.

I had wondered whether these two sides of the family had ever met, if they'd known each other growing up, if they had even heard of each other before adulthood. Had there been jealousy between the wives, between the families? Had my grandfather prioritized one family over the other? I didn't even understand if he was now back with his second wife. There were so many questions running through my mind, all of which were too complicated to ask in my rudimentary Vietnamese. I also thought about how different my own life would be if my father's side of the family had stayed in Việt Nam. What if this side of the family had been the one to leave, and we had stayed behind? What if I had grown up in Việt Nam?

I didn't know the answers to these questions, but they bore down on me like the blistering heat of the Sài Gòn sun.

My father's stepbrother spoke with such joy to my father, and when he hung up, he looked me directly in the eyes. "I heard about your dad," he announced. "I know he's handsome, intelligent, and hard-working. The most attractive and the smartest!"

My grandfather made a toast with the small cup of beer someone had just placed in front of him in Vietnamese—"Tất cả là gia đình," which translated to, "We are all family."

The entire family repeated the words, glasses raised: "Tất cả là gia đình."

Silently, I wondered: Were we all family? Would my father consider them his family, too?

NGHĨA
Vũng Tàu | 1950s

VŨNG TÀU ("BAY OF BOATS," ALSO known as Cap Saint Jacques) was a small town sitting on a bay overlooking the South China Sea. With its strategic location, about eighty miles east of Sài Gòn, and its two- to three-mile-long sandy beach, it was a popular weekend destination for Saigonese. Today, I imagine Vũng Tàu must be much more developed, but when I was a child and spent time there with my grandmother, I remember the beautiful French villas and the Grand Hotel that sat along the beach road facing the sea. The beach was bordered by two mountains: a small mountain on the southern end and a big mountain on the northern end.

A scenic road along the coastline and around the big mountain would lead a visitor to an imposing sixty-foot tall statue of Buddha sitting in his usual posture, overlooking the sea with an enigmatic and eternal smile. The statue was erected in the '60s by fishermen with the hope of obtaining the benediction of Buddha: they wanted him to protect them from the rough seas, and to provide them with an abundance of fish, year in and year out. My grandmother was a practicing Buddhist, and we had an evening ritual of reciting Buddhist prayers.

Nearby was the fish market where wholesale seafood could be purchased. Fishermen would drop their daily harvest and sell it to dealers, who would then distribute the seafood statewide. Farther down the road, one would end up in the center of town with its local open market, stores, and bus station. The Catholic church, the local high school, and St. Bethany convent, which I attended, were located a few blocks south of the local market.

South from the beach, along the small mountain road, the post office was on the left-hand side and the fisherman's wharf on the right. Hundreds of fishing boats of all sizes, were anchored in this area. On the hillside of the small mountain were some of the most beautiful white villas in town—each with an impressive view of the bay and the South China Sea, and the most magnificent sunsets and sunrises in the whole area.

Farther south, there was Ô Quắn, or "Windy Beach," also called Roches Noires Beach, which was situated about fifty feet below the windy mountain road. At that spot, the mountain suddenly dropped straight down to the beach. One had to take stairs to get down to the beach itself, which was windier and had a lot more waves than the main beach.

Down the road, there was a giant statue of Jesus with his arms outstretched like the one in Rio de Janeiro. The ninety-foot-tall statue, built in 1974, faced the South China Sea. Past the statue, the road ended up on the back beach, which was much quieter and less crowded than the white sandy beach. Many bars along the beach offered lounge chairs where people could sit for hours, looking at the sea and watching swimmers. Meals and drinks were also served there. I loved the back beach, but it was located so far away that you could not access it without a car or motorbike.

The back road went around the dunes, a few ponds, the main pagoda, the "đình," the longan tree orchard that belonged to my grandmother, and then back to town. On the top of the small mountain sat a lighthouse, built by the French in 1910, that dominated the whole landscape. Driving into town from Sài Gòn, the first structure one saw was the lighthouse. A lighthouse, a statue of Jesus, and Buddha protected this coastal town, and in many ways those three structures represent what I remember of my life there: Catholic schooling, Buddhism at home, and a light of sorts, guiding me back to the peacefulness of my childhood.

Vũng Tàu had a simple, quiet atmosphere and the charm of a small town. The countryside's peacefulness was shattered every weekend by the influx of thousands of Saigonese who doubled or tripled the town's population overnight. Demands for rooms, food, and entertainment skyrocketed and usually exceeded local capacity on those weekends. Housewives, including my grandmother, put their houses up for rent. They went to the beach every Friday afternoon to seek their own customers.

Visitors paraded their cars around town and drove aimlessly along the usually deserted roads. Cars and motorcycles, rarely seen on weekdays, appeared out of nowhere. Bumper-to-bumper traffic was common, especially on beach-front roads. Drivers fought for the right of way as they negotiated the narrow streets amidst heavy traffic. Yells, screams, and laughter were heard everywhere. The beach suddenly became crowded, noisy, and bright with light and sounds. Spicy braised shrimp, boiled clams, and especially salty roasted crabs were sold by vendors, along with the ubiquitous roasted dried squids that were consumed with a lot of hot hoisin sauce. Loud music could be heard hundreds of yards away.

After the lively Friday and Saturday nights, peace descended on the town once again as one by one, the "strangers" packed up and departed on Sunday morning, leaving behind tons of garbage. It was time for grandmother to clean up the house, put everything back in order, and get ready for next week's guests.

MY MEMORIES OF MY CHILDHOOD IN Vũng Tàu, and of my grandmother and her home, are still very strong. Like other Vietnamese women, she enjoyed chewing betel leaves and areca nuts mixed with a little tobacco. During social gatherings, as guests chatted about their families and businesses, she would offer them betel leaves and areca nuts. The mixture was supposed to give them an "aphrodisiac" feeling. They then spat the red liquid in a jar—or sometimes on the ground, leaving a residue that, when stepped on, stuck to the soles of shoes like gel.

I still remember the townhouse she lived in. Years later, she moved to the house at the orchard and rented out the townhouse to week-enders from Sài Gòn. The townhouse, though, was the first of a row of seven one-story brick houses. It was divided into three almost equal sections: a family room, a bedroom, and a kitchen area with a bath-room. The front door opened directly into the family room, which contained a hutch, a dining table, and a five-foot-tall altar made of fine wood and engraved with lacquered designs.

On top of the altar in the townhouse was the picture of a hand-some man I wished I knew: my grandfather. He'd passed away before I'd had the chance to meet him, shortly after they had purchased the longan orchard. There was a brass candle holder on either side of his photo, in front of which sat an incense holder, a gong, and a brass plate with fruit offerings. Once a week, my grandmother bought bananas, mangoes, or whatever other fruit was in season, lit up incense, beat the gong a few times, bowed many times in front of the picture, and mumbled prayers. I understood that this was "ancestor worship," a means through which the living conveyed their respects and debt to the deceased and kept their lost loved one's soul happy in the other world (*bên kia thế giới*). In return, the appeased soul would protect the family from wandering souls and disasters. If a soul was not cared for properly through that worship, it could become an angry ghost who could in turn harm the family.

The whole family slept in the middle room on three large five-by-seven-foot dark brown divans. We didn't have mattresses for the three-foot-high platforms. Instead, the hard wooden surface was our bed. The wood remained cool, and therefore very inviting, during the hot summer weather. In the winter, however, the divan was cold and unfriendly. At night, each person spread out a straw mat and hung up a mosquito net, which had to be folded back and taken down each morning. Without exception, everyone had to go through the same routine every day. Going to bed thus was a monotonous routine—but a necessary one. The buzzing, blood-thirsty mosquitoes that came into the house at night were so hungry that they would dart at any surface of unprotected skin, leaving sharp, painful mosquito bites that swelled into raised and painful lesions and could lead to severe medical conditions like malaria or dengue fever.

When we had guests, we let them use our divans and we slept on cots or at the farm.

The back room of the townhouse consisted of a bathroom, kitchen, and dining room that led to a small, enclosed backyard, where there was an outhouse for personal needs. Cooking was done with charcoal or wood. Smoke sometimes filled up the kitchen area and darkened its walls. Since refrigeration was not used at the time, my grandmother, like other housewives, went to the market almost every day to get fresh fruit and vegetables.

This is the life in the countryside in 1950s Việt Nam that I remember. A simple life where one could live in a brick house with electricity and sometimes running water, while just half a mile away someone else lived in a straw hut and used well water and oil lamps.

MY STAY AT THE FARM ALLOWED me a unique perspective on country living. Since there was no running water at the farm, rainwater was collected during the rainy season and stored in huge earthen jars that sat on the side of the house. During the dry season, workers were hired to carry water from the nearby well to fill up the jars. (Because the water sat idle for a long time, it served as an ideal ground for mosquito breeding.) Geckos—up to seven inches long— crawled on the walls at night and made their presence felt by making their characteristic noise: *Cắt Kè ... Cắt Kè ... Cắt Kè ...* Outside, hens warned us they had laid their eggs with their *Cù Tác ... Cù Tác ... Cù Tác ...* calls. Then, I knew that it was time to run out and collect the fresh eggs.

The orchards had about forty to fifty longan trees, as well as a few guava and papaya trees. The twenty- to thirty-foot-tall longan trees produced flowers in the spring, and then small longans that needed to be covered until they reached maturity. Ladders were used to reach the outermost branches, where the clusters were the most difficult to cover. Workers peeled back the proximal branches and carefully shoved the clusters of longans into straw bags. They then tied the necks of the bags to prevent bats from eating the fruits.

Bats came out at dusk, making rapid circles over the trees before dropping onto their targets. They loved the juicy longans and could wipe out a whole tree in a couple of nights, thereby greatly diminishing the harvest. For two to three weeks, the workers moved quickly to prevent the hungry bats from stealing the fruit. Once the fruits were safely covered, everyone rested for two to three months while they matured.

At the end of the summer, the air was filled with the fruity aromas of ripe longans. Grandmother would check whether they were ready for harvest, undoing the straw tie and widening the neck of the bag before carefully pulling back the clusters, making sure not to pull on the fruits themselves. At harvest time, workers broke the branches holding the bags and carefully passed them down to Grandma. She opened the heavily loaded bags, pulled out the ripe longans, and with great care set them aside. I remember the excitement of her voice, the happy *aahs* that escaped from her lips at the sight of the golden longans. She handled them with extreme gentleness, as longans attached to their stalks were more valuable than loose ones.

Ripe fruits were covered with a thin yellow-pinkish skin, which once peeled back let a sweet, fruity liquid flow out. The trick was to catch the juice before it spilled all over your shirt. You then dropped the fruit in your mouth and used your tongue to peel the succulent, soft, velvety meat from its brown seed. Once that was done, it was time to spit out the seed and enjoy the succulent meat.

I loved the longans' sweet, juicy taste and could never resist the temptation to sample them, although oversampling did result in indigestion or stomach cramps.

During the harvest, wholesale buyers came to the orchard to bargain for a fair price. They bought copious quantities of fruits and took them to the market for resale. Within two to three weeks, the harvest was completed, and it was time to clean up. The straw bags were left to dry in the sun and then stored away so they could be reused the next season.

ONE TIME I VISITED THE ĐÌNH, a large communal hall about two and a half miles from the orchard close to the back beach. Four gilded dragons, one in each corner, decorated the carved roofs of this community center where all the county's activities took place. A whale that had beached itself and died the night before gave the villagers an occasion to celebrate since it was unusual, even unheard of, for a whale to beach itself so close to the village.

According to traditions borrowed from the Chams centuries ago, villages would pay their last respects to the Cá Ông (King of the Fish) so that the spirits inhabiting the fish would not hurt fishermen. The Chams, a Hindu civilization, had flourished in present-day central Việt Nam between the 7th and 18th centuries CE. The Vietnamese had adapted this foreign tradition and made it their own. Not as adept in seafaring as the Chams, they did so hoping whales would protect their fishermen from the perils of the sea. The Chams also left behind huge stone and brick shrines—temples to their gods—along the coastline of central Việt Nam, which today serve as tourist attractions.

Monks dressed in saffron robes presided over the unprecedented ceremony. There were the usual fruit offerings, flowers, and food, but they all seemed to be more abundant than usual. I stood there in awe, looking at the large plates of plump grapefruits, tropical green oranges, juicy longans, purple mangosteens, and spiny and suspiciously smelly durians. My eyes opened wide at the view of the graceful white lotuses, yellow-golden chrysanthemums, and deep red gladioli that were carefully arranged in gigantic earthen vases. A haze of lingering smoke emanated from the hundreds of lit incense sticks and candles. The villagers had brought in homemade sticky rice cakes, along with a variety of vegetarian dishes, as offerings to Buddha and the spirit of the Cá Ông. Food and drinks would be served later.

The whale looked so huge that I was afraid of getting close to it. Although it was dead, it still looked frightening, with its large hazy eyes and its massive weight resting on a row of tables set up in the middle of the đình. I'd never seen such a huge fish. I wondered how the tiny villagers could have transported such a huge mammal from the beach to this place, especially through the narrow, winding country roads. Nor did I know how they would dispose of the fish. The entire town must have mobilized to lift the whale off the beach.

I found out years later that they disposed of the flesh after that night but kept the whale's skeleton stored in huge glass cases in the Lang Cá Ông (Shrine of the Whale). Vũng Tàu was henceforth able to boast of having one of the few shrines dedicated to the "cult of the whale," a place visitors could visit to revere this savior of fishermen.

ON ANOTHER OCCASION, HÁT BỘI, TRADITIONAL Vietnamese musical plays during which classic themes (good versus evil, saints versus demons) were rehashed, were performed at the đình. Characters with superhuman features engaged in fantastic adventures, trying to prove their moral superiority over evil creatures or devious people. Actors and actresses dressed in traditional, multicolored costumes carried swords and spears with flags sticking out of pockets sewn to their backs. The heavy makeup they wore not only indicated the role they played but also conveyed their emotions. A strong and valiant character always had his face painted in red, and had dark black eyelashes and a long, silky beard. To the rhythm of traditional musical instruments such as cymbals, gongs, tambourines, and flutes, the actors would retell familiar stories while gesticulating and moving around. Each gesture or facial expression was symbolic and full of historical meaning.

These musical plays were magical and grandiose and drew audiences from near and far. I remember how fascinated I was by the display of colorful costumes, the facial expressions, and the armaments and movements of the actors and actresses. I especially loved the plays in which the good characters won over the evil ones.

After I saw the first play, I asked my grandmother to take me to see another one. I still think of these experiences fondly, although it was difficult to be away from my family. I wonder now whether as a child I was drawn to those characters because in my mind they reflected South Việt Nam—the Việt Nam of my childhood, the one I hoped would one day triumph over all those who had tried to conquer it.

CHRISTINA
Vũng Tàu & Phú Quốc Island | 2003

AFTER LEAVING SÀI GÒN, WE TOOK a boat to Vũng Tàu, where we attended the wedding of an English teacher we knew from Hà Nội. He was originally from the U.K., and his wife-to-be was Vietnamese. I had only met the couple briefly, but they were kind enough to let Mai and I attend their large wedding.

In the brief time I'd lived in Việt Nam, I'd met several foreigners who were married to Vietnamese women. Some Vietnamese families might have found it difficult to accept a foreigner; others likely felt that marrying a foreigner might provide better opportunities for their daughter and their future grandchildren. I'd heard a handful of Vietnamese women say that foreign men treated them better than local Vietnamese men, who often didn't help at all at home since it wasn't considered their responsibility. Every morning, I noticed crowds of Vietnamese men sipping coffee and smoking cigarettes while the women were off at the market buying food for the rest of the family.

Since arriving in Hà Nội I hadn't focused on my romantic life. I had shared with Thi at one point that maybe Thomas would turn out to be the love of my life—but Thomas was gay, so that was not an option. I went out three or four times a week and met a few people, including interesting men from around the world. But I didn't want a relationship.

I *had* developed a crush, or rather an infatuation, with another American man, Sam, who worked for the U.S. government in Hà Nội. I saw him at the first HIV/AIDS Policy Forum meeting that I attended and was instantaneously awestruck. When I mentioned him to Thanh, she admitted to me that she had a crush on him too. Sam had that kind of effect on people, especially women. He was handsome and articulate, and prior to living in Việt Nam he was on a fellowship in Cambodia for a year. He'd also traveled extensively around the world, and I thought he was one of the most well-rounded and interesting men I'd ever met.

At the meeting when I first saw him, he charmed everyone around him, including our Vietnamese colleagues and counterparts. When I later began to see him around town, there was an added air of mystery around him because he was often alone; he seemed elusive, intriguing.

Slowly, we became friends. I admired him even more as I got to know him. He was also creative and artistic. He painted and designed his own furniture, and had even renovated parts of his home himself.

My Vietnamese friends often asked me when I was going to get married, or if I had a boyfriend back in the States. I couldn't explain that it simply wasn't a priority for me then, even though I wasn't quite sure what was ultimately guiding me. Unlike my twenty-something year old peers, the search for myself and for the fragments of my past seemed to take primacy in my life—not the corporate ladder, not the relationship, but a deeper understanding of my family's history.

WE ONLY STAYED IN VŨNG TÀU for a few days, but I could understand why my father recalled it so fondly—how the slow southern charm lingered in his memories. We rented bicycles to ride around town, and sat by the beach drinking fresh juice and smelling the aromatic seafood being cooked at nearby restaurants. There were bars along the beach, too, and I saw how easy it would be to spend hours simply sitting there, talking, and enjoying the crashing of the waves.

One evening when we left the hotel, there was a motorbike accident just outside of our hotel. Two young men walking by checked out the accident, and one said to the other Vietnamese, "Không chết"— *Not dead*. With that, they simply continued walking.

I wondered if this attitude stemmed from how much death Vietnamese people had seen in their lives. Those young men who walked by had grown up after the Việt Nam War, but maybe the war—the countless wars, really—that had ravaged the country over the centuries was so much a part of their history and understanding of life that they had a different understanding death than I, as an American, did.

AFTER WE LEFT VŨNG TÀU, OUR next destination was Phú Quốc, which we heard was a beautiful island paradise. The problem was that it was Tết, a time when many expats living in Việt Nam escaped the cities for the beach destinations like Phú Quốc.

All flights from Sài Gòn to Phú Quốc were booked, so we had to take a bus to Rạch Giá, and then a boat. Years before—in 1975, according to what I'd read in *The Pink Lotus*—my father had taken a bus to Rạch Giá and then to Vũng Tàu before the fall of Sài Gòn. He eventually escaped through the island, which was now being developed as a travel destination.

Mai made all the arrangements and wasn't happy about it; by that point in the trip, she was feeling quite frustrated that she bore the responsibility of coordinating all our travel plans, since neither Stephen nor I spoke Vietnamese well. When we reached the island and found a rather cheap accommodation right away, however, all of our concerns seemed to dissipate. Phú Quốc was indeed an island paradise.

Peaceful—that's the best word I could use to describe it. Time seemed to move so slowly there.

We hired a xe ôm driver to take us to the village to go to the market and buy fresh fruits. The drive on the dirt road was long on a motorbike, but seeing the ocean in the distance made it go by quickly.

The air was so fresh on the island, unlike the polluted air in Hà Nội and Sài Gòn, so full of motorbike exhaust fumes. We sat for hours at the beach, daydreaming and reading. One evening we went to one of the nicer bungalow resort restaurants for fresh seafood.

Mai fell in love with Phú Quốc, and she began to think about asking her parents to invest in land there. She envisioned creating their own bungalow resort as an investment. (In just a few years that dream would become a reality, and Mai would spend a portion of the year there, managing the resort.)

The irony of history dawned on me while I was there—just how different my experiences in Phú Quốc, and Việt Nam in general, were from my father's. I was sure that when he was briefly stationed there he could still feel the peace of the environment; on that little island, he must have felt miles away from the fighting. Yet at the same time, there was so much uncertainty in his life. I thought that his memories of Phú Quốc must weigh heavily on his mind. It was here, after all, that he'd taken his last steps in his motherland and his first steps toward freedom. For me, in contrast, it was quite simply an island paradise with no baggage attached to it. It also dawned on me that I was almost the same age as him when he was drafted in the army, how privileged my life had been compared to his. I didn't know if I had my father's strength within me, or how I would have fared in his situation.

Maybe I would never know his story in depth, but I could intuit that our views and relationship to Việt Nam were divergent and full of contrasts. Our love for Việt Nam—in all its contours, shapes, and textures—must be different as well.

NGHĨA
Vũng Tàu | 1950s

GROWING UP, I LIVED IN TWO worlds: one of Vietnamese tradition, one the remnants of French colonialism. These two worlds coexisted uneasily in the late 1950s before finally giving way to a predominantly Vietnamese society.

The Europeans came to Southeast Asia looking for spices, commerce, and an access route to China as early as the 16th century. Others used the occasion to proselytize and teach Catholicism. At first, the Vietnamese kings and emperors looked away and tolerated them, albeit with some apprehension. Believing they were the sons of Heaven and in their mandate as emperors, they did not feel threatened by the infidels. However, as the influence of the priests grew, uneasiness turned into suspicion, then fear. At the urging of the mandarins (high court officials), the kings shut down all doors and contacts, trying to keep foreign influence at bay. The self-imposed isolation kept them away from modern technological advances that could have helped improve the welfare of their people. This economic and cultural stagnation soon led to the downfall of the feudal monarchy in the face of foreign invasion.

Dating back from the period of the French colonization, Vietnamese towns were divided into two areas. The European center included the town's market, the main stores, and, about half a mile away, the church, the secondary school, the convent, and various villas that served as housing for French officials. While buildings in the European section were built of bricks, the indigenous areas, which surrounded the European section, consisted of wooden or thatch houses.

While living in Vũng Tàu, I could see the dichotomy of the Vietnamese tradition and French colonialism. I first attended a grammar school that was managed by a French schoolmistress—a relic of French colonization.

One rainy day in October, my grandmother unexpectedly showed up at the school with a raincoat for me. The teacher called me over to pick it up. Although thankful for her gesture, I was embarrassed because of all the parents, it had to be my own grandmother who showed up with a raincoat. I did not know how to deal with the situation and mumbled something the teacher could not understand. A big and loud "Thank you, Grandma," might have helped. Instead, I uttered shy, soft words that did not satisfy my teacher; she sent me to the back room to sit for the rest of the day.

As I was not adventurous, I had not explored the back area of the building before that day. I knew vaguely that there was a storage area, but I'd never understood its real use. There, to my surprise, I found other students who were also "serving time" for various reasons. Amazingly, I ended up spending an interesting day in the back room and enjoyed school more than I ever had before. The teacher was always in the front room, busy taking care of the "good students," and rarely set foot in the back room, so there was no one to discipline us. We made airplanes out of paper and threw them in the air. We were free to do anything we wished, except make noise.

When I came home from school that day, I noticed a beautiful young lady sitting in the living room of the townhouse. She was busy polishing her nails. Since I did not know what this stranger was doing in the house, I went to the back room and asked grandma about her. She told me the lady was taking a few days off while waiting for her husband, who she said was a cab driver, to pick her up. She was so beautiful; I couldn't imagine her being the wife of a cab driver.

For a few days, I had a wonderful time with her. The lady, despite not being my mother, was nice and thoughtful enough to take me to the market and buy me some toys, the delight of any child. She took me to the front beach, about a mile and a half from home, where I swam in the warm waters while she read magazines on the shore.

I missed the lady a lot when she left. It was only later that I realized what I missed was my real mother, who was in Sài Gòn taking care of my siblings, my aunt, and my uncle. I also didn't understand until much later that I was involved in a family "swap," designed so that my aunt and uncle could study in Sài Gòn. I never fully grasped why my mother chose me to go, but in retrospect, I am glad that she did; I'm happy I got the opportunity to experience Vũng Tàu and the bucolic countryside. But in moments like those, after our kind visitor left, I was reminded of how much I missed my mother. I would one day understand that it was a similar longing to what one felt for the motherland—I could create another home in a different country, but there could only ever be one homeland.

THE FOLLOWING YEAR, I WENT TO study with the sisters at the St. Bethany convent. As in any Catholic institution, the beginning and the end of the day were devoted to prayers. The sisters were good teachers and I enjoyed studying with them, but I always thought they were best at making money. Since they knew very well that students could not resist sweet temptations, they brought out all kinds of candies and cookies to sell to students during recess. We all rushed out of the classrooms to buy the sweets and gorge ourselves on them. The sisters also sold books, pencils, and papers, and other supplies. From my youthful perspective, it looked as if they were making a lot of money.

During the fall season (although South Việt Nam had but two seasons—rainy and dry), leaves would fall and cover the whole school ground. I did not know why they did not hire workers to rake the leaves—perhaps they could not afford it or maybe they did not want to—but they asked the students to volunteer to help with this chore.

Later, we would be rewarded for our good deeds. After class began, we would line up in front of the sister and, one by one, would name our own prize: My friend Tâm asked for forty points. The sister dutifully marked down the number in a big black register book. Because I did more work, I thought I deserved a bigger mark and settled for asking for eighty points. The sister dutifully wrote down the number. We then returned to our seats, happy about having done a good deed, while at the same time earning extra points that would be added to our marks and could raise our overall standing in the class. And so every morning, we came back and volunteered for our work. This may explain why the sisters' schoolyard was always the cleanest in the neighborhood.

During lunch recess from noon to 2 p.m., we walked home to eat our lunch and to take a nap. Someone beat a gong at 1:55 p.m. to advise children and employees to either return to schools or offices. The tropical weather was so hot (air-conditioning was not available at that time) in Việt Nam that the long siesta was necessary. During these recesses, I sometimes stayed back and waddled in a small puddle of water in the back of the school or looked for crickets in the bushes. There was nothing like the freedom to roam around and search for the unknown. When I arrived late for lunch, I sustained a barrage of questions from my grandmother, and got occasional spanks in the butt if I did not give her the right answer.

At the end of the school year, each family had to contribute to the commencement in order to obtain our award. This came in forms of books, crayons, pens, and so on, which were presented at a special ceremony. Students, parents, and other relatives crowded together in a gathering hall. Following the usual speeches, students whose names were called came to the podium to receive their rewards. Those were quaint times, and memories of simple living in the countryside.

CHRISTINA
Hà Nội | 2003

A FEW WEEKS AFTER I RETURNED to Hà Nội, David's house-mate, Ali, a Canadian girl I'd also met on my trip, called me and said that a room would be available in her place in Sài Gòn in early spring.

"If you want the room, it's yours," she said.

Without even thinking about it, I said yes.

She told me where the house was located—between District 1 and 3 on a street called Võ Thị Sáu, in a prime location close to the city center. (District 1 was one of the main shopping districts that comprised the downtown area, and was the equivalent to Hoàn Kiếm District in Hà Nội.). I later learned that the street was named after a woman, who was a Vietnamese revolutionary and guerrilla fighter who fought against the South Vietnamese government and its allies during the Việt Nam War. The house had five bedrooms, each with its own en suite bathroom, and like our place in Hà Nội the rooms were occupied by recent college graduates who were on a similar quest for adventure, or something they had yet to discover in their lives that might be found in Việt Nam.

I didn't know what I was going to do in Sài Gòn, but I felt a pull, a strong desire within me to live there.

While I appreciated Hà Nội and had started to create a broad social network there, its small-town nature felt overly quaint to me. I was still in a place of expansion and exploration, and in Hà Nội I felt constrained. Only later would I realize that this would be a pattern throughout my twenties—not knowing when to stay or go, and so simply deciding to leave.

Through my internship, I learned that UNICEF was going to hire an international advertising agency to work on a campaign with them to help empower the youth of Việt Nam. I made the connection that this was work that could both satisfy my desire to create social change and felt offered the excitement I craved, since it would be with an international agency and visible throughout the country.

Similar to how I arrived in Hà Nội, I began to reach out to all the international agencies in Sài Gòn that I could find online. I emailed the managing director directly and explained my interest in communications—specifically in the area of raising awareness about issues like HIV/AIDS.

Much to my surprise, I received positive responses from the agencies; they said they wanted to meet me when I moved South. I was an appealing candidate because I was a native English speaker and was already based in Việt Nam, so my potential employers would not have to pay additional relocation fees.

One managing director—Lan, a local Vietnamese woman who'd worked her way up the ranks at an international advertising agency—impressed me the most. When we spoke on the phone, she had this strength and composure that I immediately admired. I felt she would be an ideal role model and source of inspiration as a businesswoman in Việt Nam. She told me a small bit of her history—that she'd been educated in Russia and then came back to Việt Nam. I learned later that when Bill Clinton traveled through Việt Nam, she was one of the few female business leaders he wanted to meet.

She said she would hire me to work as an account executive for $500 dollars a month. That was more than I was currently making, since my internship was unpaid, and it would cover all my housing and food. I thought it was a great deal, so I agreed.

"I plan to move to Sài Gòn in a few months," I told her. "I can start then."

A MONTH LATER, MY FATHER AND Alice visited me in Thailand, despite my request that they make the additional one-hour flight and venture to Việt Nam. We met in Bangkok, explored the city and night markets, then spent a few days in Phuket, a popular beach town. We took a day trip to Phang Nga Bay, a beautiful seascape of limestone rock formations jutting out of emerald water that attracted several tourists and was also the filming site for one of the James Bond movies.

Despite his efforts to visit the side of the world where I was living, I still felt a distance from my father, an anger underneath the surface that I didn't know how to express. I was cold toward him, despite his attempts to cultivate more warmth between us. I didn't recognize then that I, too, needed to show up differently in order for us to break out of our old patterns. It wouldn't be until much later that I would recognize that I had long tried to make him fill a role that wasn't his. I wanted him to take the space of my mother—something he could never do.

On the boat filled with ten or so tourists, each wearing our padded orange life jackets, Alice turned around and said to me, "This must be like Hạ Long Bay in Việt Nam."

"It does resemble Hạ Long Bay," I said, having recently spent two days on a junk boat there.

Throughout the first days of the trip, Alice made numerous comparisons between Việt Nam and Thailand: the food, the weather, and the people. It was as if she could not see Thailand for what it was but only in contrast to Việt Nam. I wanted to ask my father and Alice: if they truly longed for Việt Nam, as they seemed to, why had they settled for a trip to Thailand?

"I went to visit Phú Quốc," I told them, thinking that this would evoke a response from my father. "It's beautiful—still rather barren and underdeveloped, but they seem to have plans to build more bungalow-style resorts there."

"That's great," my father said.

I thought this was the opening. This would be the moment when he would finally share with me all about his harrowing departure from Việt Nam; the well of emotions buried deep within him. Instead, once again, he said nothing.

I tried another entry point. I told them about my other news—that I planned to move to Sài Gòn and had found a job there at an advertising agency.

"You were right about the South being different, Dad," I told him. "It's so vibrant and energizing."

This was the moment that I would feel his approval. I imagined he would smile, pat me on the back, maybe even embrace me, and say that he was proud of me. He would exhale, feeling a relief that I had decided to explore the part of the country where my family was actually from. I was going to live in Sài Gòn, his hometown; I effectively had turned my back on the North and chosen the South. Wouldn't he be thrilled?

Instead, all he could muster was, "Oh, that's good, Christina."

Once more, I longed for my father to say more than a few words.

NGHĨA

Vũng Tàu | 1950s

IN THAT PROVINCIAL ATMOSPHERE, BESIDES COUNTRYSIDE life and French education, I was also exposed to two major religions: Buddhism and Catholicism. Had I been brought up in busy Sài Gòn, that influence would not have been significant, but the simple and relaxed pace of life in Vũng Tàu brought people closer to religion.

While Catholicism had been brought into Việt Nam by the French recently, Buddhism had been present in our country since the second century CE. Buddhism had permeated Asian society the same way Christianity had become the main religion in Europe or America. Coming from India and China, it spread into Việt Nam in the second to the sixth centuries CE and reached the height of its glory between the 7th and 14th centuries CE. Although not all southern Vietnamese practiced strict Buddhism, they did all tend to follow a Buddhist code of living, which explains why southern Vietnamese were known to be benevolent, compassionate, and peaceful.

During the day, I prayed to Jesus and the Virgin Mary at the sisters' school, but at night I donned a brown robe to say prayers to Buddha. I remember the routine: *Praise the Lord* or *Ave Maria* songs in the morning, then *Nam Mô A Di Đà Phật* incantations at night. Melodious songs and hymns in the morning were followed by monotonous recitations of Buddhist texts in the evenings. That was enough to give any youngster a split personality, although I moved from one religion to another without difficulty. I had no problem talking to a Buddhist nun one minute and a Catholic sister the next; to me, they were both good people.

I recited these verses like a bird because I did not at the time understand their meaning. I was therefore repulsed by their stiffness and routine. I only realized later that they were the foundations of my upbringing and would help me in my search for peace of mind and meaning of life. More than the reciting of incomprehensible texts and monotonous incantations, these hours of prayers were lessons in turning inward and looking at another dimension in life. This was my introduction to spirituality, without which my life would never have reached its full potential and meaning.

GRANDMOTHER HAD A LARGE PRAYER ROOM at her orchard house with a three-foot-tall Buddha sitting at the top of the altar. This was her "sacred" area that I used to walk into with awe, apprehension, and respect. The bronze statue's eternal smile inspired not only peace but also, for a youngster like me, a sense of power, mystery, and force. I could feel there was something more in the air than just a simple statue. Grandmother insisted that everyone, usually my two aunts and I, be present at the nightly prayer session before the Buddha. It was usually one hour long but could take up to two hours, especially during certain Buddhist occasions. No exceptions were allowed, as Saturday and Sundays were also prayer days, and I dreaded these long prayer sessions.

Worshipers donned brown gowns (saffron robes were reserved for monks). The worst thing I remember about these nightly sessions was that I had to wear one of these brown gowns, which were infrequently washed; the pungent acid odor of the sweat from all worshipers who had worn it before clung to it. Only swarms of mosquitoes were attracted to this odor. I almost became sick every time I had the robe on.

Grandmother began her nightly session by lighting up candles and incense. Slowly, in a reverent tone, she began reciting: *Nam Mô A Di Đà Phật . . . Nam Mô A Di Đà Phật . . .* while beating on the gong. The rhythmic pounding of the wooden stick on the gong induced relaxation and peace in the quiet evening. Occasionally, she hit a bronze bell that gave a clear, sharp, and metallic sound: *Bong . . . Bong . . .* The sound disrupted the peacefulness of the night and marked the signal for everyone to bow down. Recitations went on and on, interrupted only by another bell sound.

Soothed by these monotonous incantations, I usually fell asleep in the middle of the long and "challenging" prayer sessions. Neither the incantations nor the bell sounds could disturb my nap. My aunts would wake me up, but soon I fell asleep again and was brought to bed.

ON ONE OCCASION, I WENT WITH my grandmother to see her adviser who lived on top of the Bà Rịa Mountain. Since there was no road to the top, we had to climb steep slopes through narrow mountain trails that accommodated only one person at a time. These trails were not designed for visitors but rather for monks, who wanted to live in seclusion, and were rugged and barely passable. Some steps were as short as a child's foot, others as tall as a foot and a half. Others were missing or even nonexistent. Time and traffic had taken its toll on them.

By the time we reached the summit, I was so exhausted that all I wanted to do was to sit down on the porch and rest my cramped legs. I looked at the rugged but peaceful hills that spread all the way to the horizon while grandmother talked to her advisor. I was impressed by the ascetic and simple life these monks led, far away from the corrupting ways of modern society.

Visitors came to ask monks' advice on all kinds of things, including affairs of the heart, family problems, and questions about religion and afterlife. In return, they offered the monks either goods, fruits, or money. The monks functioned as spiritual guides, advisors, and occasionally fortune tellers. They were learned men who spent all their time studying, thinking, and dispensing their wisdom to laypeople. I never knew what the monk said to my grandmother, but I certainly appreciated the journey—despite my sore legs.

THE LOCAL PAGODA IN VŨNG TÀU, near the back beach, housed many Buddhist monks, apprentices, and nuns. It was an expansive one-story complex with lodgings, kitchens, working areas, and a larger gathering hall located at one end of a lotus pond. A ten-foot-tall bronze Buddha statue presided over the main hall, along with numerous smaller statues of all sizes and from different countries. There were even a few Indian Buddha statues with twelve arms, six on each side. Each Buddha statue had its own particular gaze: peaceful for some, stern for others. A soft and permanent smile graced the face of some statues, while others remained stone-faced and tight-lipped.

An overall air of mystery, majesty, and power permeated the praying area and caused guests to enter the hall with awe and respect. The dim lighting in there, partly due to the absence of windows, only increased the hall's mystical feel. Incense and hundreds of candles were lit during the main celebrations. Swirls of dense incense smoke gracefully floated around the statues, suspended in limbo, while emanating celestial aromas. Offerings of bananas, oranges, pineapples, and durians were prominently displayed on the altar, along with a multitude of flowers. Monks sang prayers and intermittently hit gongs and bells during these celebrations—which, like prayer time at my grandmother's, could last a long time.

I was too young to be interested in these celebrations. I was bored. One day, I joined the apprentice monks behind the pagoda close to the lotus pond. We jumped into one of the canoes anchored on the shoreline and paddled around the pond, admiring the thousands of green lotus leaves floating on the surface of the water and their beautiful pink flowers, some in full bloom. Nothing instilled an image of peacefulness and permanency like these green lotus leaves—sitting still on the water's surface, impervious and unsinkable. It was no wonder why people had always painted Buddha sitting and meditating on a lotus leaf.

The apprentice monks told me about how they used lotus flowers to decorate the altars, cooked side dishes from the stems of the flowers, and even ate lotus seeds. The lotus flower thus had multiple uses besides symbolizing the purity and freshness of the soul that even mud could not stain.

Then one of apprentices recited the famous poem:

> *Nothing is more beautiful than the lotus in the pond,*
> *Green leaves, white flowers, amidst yellow stamens*
> *Yellow stamens, white flowers, green leaves,*
> *Close to the mud, yet does not smell muddy at all.*

We paddled slowly, savoring every minute of freedom and peace. We looked at the small fish swimming just below the surface of the limpid water while butterflies and dragonflies swirled around us in complete silence. The occasional barking of a dog in the distance or chirping of birds were the only things that interrupted this quietness. There was nothing more peaceful than taking a ride around the isolated lotus pond: no wind, no ripples, and no noises. The overall atmosphere conveyed an image of serene tranquility that symbolized Việt Nam just emerging from colonialism. It also allowed me to let my thoughts wander; it was a time for recollection and healing. After this first experience, I came back many times, wanting another ride around the pond.

The full circle around the pond took us some time to cover. When it was time to turn around, I begged for another trip, but to no avail. When the canoe had almost reached shore, I jumped into the water, trying to get to the ground first. The bottom of the pond turned out to be deeper than expected, however, and I got all wet. The apprentices started laughing, then brought me inside, helped me take off my clothes to dry, and gave me a snack while I waited.

On another occasion, I was sitting in the front of the boat, and when I leaned forward I saw minnows swimming right under the limpid surface of the water. I dropped the iron chain to see whether it would scare the fish. When I turned around, to my surprise, I found a minnow swimming in a small puddle at the bottom of the boat. I tried to do it again, but this time no new fish got trapped into the boat. I never found out whether it was just a coincidence or whether the chain had forced the fish to get through a small hole at the bottom of the boat.

This was life in Vũng Tàu and South Việt Nam in general as I knew it in the late 1950s. Life was bucolic, tranquil, and simple and the people were happy and benevolent. Life unwound itself before us—lovely and peaceful like the stillness of the pond with its lotus flowers, its minnows, and its absence of ripples. There were no rumors about war or killing. My countrymen and I were lulled into complacency by this peacefulness. In retrospect, this left us unprepared for the fact that this idyllic life could not last forever—that terrible things were on the horizon.

CHRISTINA

Hà Nội | 2003

IN THE YEAR AND HALF THAT I lived in Việt Nam, I straddled two worlds—trying to get a stronger footing in Việt Nam, where I felt half-present, but also considering what my future would look like and whether I was falling behind my peers who were steadily building their lives in the States. I often sought advice about when I should leave Việt Nam by asking my Vietnamese friends and colleagues, in Hà Nội and Sài Gòn, to take me to their fortune tellers—the auspicious individuals who they turned to for advice about love, life, and even business. I found their presence comforting when I wanted to grasp on to some truth.

I learned quickly that Việt Nam at that time did not have a formal system for the practice of psychology or therapy, although foreign psychologists did offer their services. Vietnamese people often sought guidance, and perhaps a sense of solace, from fortune tellers instead. This approach resonated deeply within me.

I ventured to the fortune tellers who were hidden, unknown, and accessible to only those who knew of their whereabouts—those who were not readily available to all people. Before these meetings, I often imagined being greeted by great individuals whose inner radiance would beam from the inside out, whose very presence would be calming and uplifting. Instead, I usually met unassuming people with no noticeably grand presence—those I could have easily passed on the streets without giving them a second glance.

In Hà Nội I once went to see a man who had formerly been an art teacher in Hà Nội. My friend told me that he could predict the future. She drove us across the Red River on the Cầu Long Biên bridge to an area where I rarely journeyed.

When we arrived, she called the man thầy, or teacher. The walls of his house were adorned with paintings by his students, from floor to ceiling, leaving no space uncovered, creating the feeling of an art gallery his home. He sat at a small table, smoking a cigarette, and told me to ask questions. Then he asked me to drop a coin six times while he marked on a notepad the pattern of heads or tails. After reading the pattern, he provided a lengthy response to my question.

I didn't necessarily believe these individuals possessed an ability to accurately predict my future, and in this case the coins appeared to be some form of cover. The teacher didn't say anything specific about my life; instead, he spoke in Vietnamese, while my friend translated:

> Some events are supposed to happen, like destiny, and some
> events we create through our free will. The lines on your
> hands, or your future, change, even subtlety, every three
> months based on your actions, your attitude, and your
> approach to life. Life is a mixture of destiny and free will.

I wondered what my future, and particularly my time in Việt Nam had in store for me. Was I meant to stay longer? Was moving to Sài Gòn the right decision for me? Was it destiny or free will that brought me here in the first place?

THE SEDUCTRESS
OF THE SOUTH

NGHĨA

Sài Gòn | 1950s

THIS IS A STORY OF SÀI GÒN, once known as the "Pearl of the Orient."

Where I took my first steps in life,

Where I biked to school under the canopy of tamarind
trees in early September,

Where I skipped out during intermission to play ball
with classmates,

Where nervously giggling schoolgirls held on to their
nón lá and were dressed in their elegant white áo
dài, the lower ends of which floated in the
winds—an image forever imprinted in my mind,

Where I made friends and met competitors,

Where I was exposed to Vietnamese culture, then
French and American cultures as well, widening
my horizon,

Where I saw the war up close and personal with its
endless killing and mutilating and destruction of
land and properties,

Where many could be wolf to man,

Where a person could be there one day and gone
the following,

Where tragic events, difficulties, and tribulations
were as common as day and night,

Where people accepted suffering as part of their
daily lot,

Where women bravely struggled to raise their
   children alone while their men went to war,

Where everyone hoped and looked for peace each
   spring without seeing it,

Where tears were as common as raindrops,

Where endless suffering and poverty opened my heart
   to the world.

ALTHOUGH IT WAS A LONG TIME ago, I still remember Sài Gòn like it was yesterday. I can imagine myself strolling down Nguyễn Huệ Avenue, sitting on the Bạch Đằng Pier to watch the meandering Sài Gòn River flow lazily through the city, dashing through her narrow and busy streets on my Honda motorcycle, trying to avoid her reckless drivers, and eating phở noodle soup in one of the many restaurants.

Although it is cliche, it is true. Do I remember Sài Gòn? The question is, how could I forget the seductress on the Mekong River? The Sài Gòn I remember was a vibrant city with a rich and complicated past that trapped her citizens like a woman who held her lover captive with her charms. Although the Sài Gòn I knew and loved is an ocean and decades away, I still hold her close to my heart.

I RETURNED TO SÀI GÒN WHEN I was in fourth grade. My aunts and uncle had graduated from high school and moved out, and my mother finally had the house to herself and her five children once again. My uncle went to college, one aunt landed a job in Sài Gòn, and the other went to work in Vũng Tàu. I'd always loved Sài Gòn and I was even more enamored with it upon my return.

To this day, I have fond memories of Sài Gòn—the largest city in Việt Nam and a bustling commercial center. It was a sleepy Cambodian fishing settlement known as Prey Nokor when the Vietnamese settled around it in 1624, and then began to control it in 1698. In the early 1970s, at the height of the American intervention, it boasted almost two million people, although that number could be two or three times higher due to the large influx of refugees that came from the countryside in those years. It was the economic center of South Việt Nam—the eye, the ear, and the heart of the country. Rice harvested from the lush paddy fields of the Mekong Delta, fish and shrimp farm-raised along the banks of the river, rubber from the surrounding plantations, and tea and coffee imported from the central highlands were all shipped to Sài Gòn for trade. Imported goods arrived at the Port of Sài Gòn. Vietnamese commerce began and ended in Sài Gòn.

Remnants of French architecture were apparent in many sections of the city, among them the Opera House (former Congressional Building), the City Hall, the Main Post Office, and Notre Dame Cathedral. Majestic boulevards linked with hundred-year-old trees and dotted with high-rise buildings and chic villas coexisted with small winding alleys lined with corrugated steel–covered shacks and crumbling houses. Sài Gòn was crowded, dirty, and disorganized in some areas, while it was serene, upscale, and almost deserted in other areas. Beautiful women could be seen wearing exotic áo dài—the Vietnamese tunics slit on both sides from the waist down—or tailored European outfits amongst poorly dressed people in multicolored shirts and black pants. Sài Gòn was a city of wide contrasts, a city for the rich and poor that had served at one time as a French provincial city and had, many years earlier, been dubbed the "Pearl of Southeast Asia."

Giant tamarind trees grew on both sides of some streets. They were so huge and had such dense foliage that they provided the perfect shade from the sizzling summer sun. Each September, when I returned to school, I felt like I was biking under a canopy of jungle trees. Even today, the sight of a tamarind immediately brings me back to the school year where I got my first taste of freedom, met my first school friends, and played and competed in many extracurricular activities.

MY REMAINING CHILDHOOD YEARS FLEW BY in Sài Gòn, and very quickly I found myself in high school—one of the most memorable times of my life. I remember the Gia Long School, where beautiful, shy, giggling girls wearing white áo dài could be encountered. I would watch them fondly as they walked down the sidewalks with one hand clutching their books and the other holding on to their nón lá (conical hat), protecting it from the wind that frequently displaced it from their head. The free ends of their áo dàis undulated in the breeze and their thick, black, silky hair fell all the way down to their waists. The áo dài molded tightly against the curvatures of their bodies, accenting their beauty. It has been said that they hid everything but also exposed everything.

The girls wore wooden guốc (clogs) that beat against the pavement with a rhythmic noise: *coc ... coc ... coc ...* I used to marvel at how they could move with such ease and precision in their slippery guốc while holding on to their nón lá and books. With their flowing hair and delicate áo dài floating in the wind, they conveyed an image of the frailty of the Vietnamese in the middle of political storms and war tragedies. This was the picture of yin in the middle of a yang environment.

I often biked down Công Lý Avenue. Eventually, the Presidential Palace would appear on my right. If I turned left in front of the Palace, I ended up on Thống Nhất Avenue. There stood the magnificent Notre Dame Cathedral, the main post office, the American Embassy, and, at the end of the avenue, the Sài Gòn Zoo and the National Museum. Công Lý Avenue led me straight to the International and Majestic Hotels. During the height of the war, these places became favorite gathering areas for American GIs, journalists, and businessmen who exchanged tips or traded news about the war and Sài Gòn politics.

Farther down the road flowed the Sài Gòn River, which brought an array of foreign ships and with them merchandise, tales, and news from abroad in exchange for rice, seafood, rubber, and the local charm of the Jewel of Southeast Asia. My parents used to take us to the Bạch Đằng Pier to watch the huge foreign ships load and unload their merchandise and to look at sampans and rowboats gliding quietly on the dark waters of the river. This was another image of yin (sampans) and yang (ships) at work; Sài Gòn was full of contrasting images.

The river, which must have been clear at its source, had collected all the garbage humans dumped into it along its journey to the sea, and by the time its waters finally arrived in Sài Gòn, they had acquired a dark, sad color that was beyond recognition. Nonetheless, they made their way into the ocean, where they dumped their load and regained their fresh color by mixing with the seawater. Occasionally, the noise of a motorized engine ripped through the air, disturbing the quiet. A few ducks waddled in the frigid waters and quacked relentlessly.

We would sit on the pier under a large umbrella, sipping cold drinks and savoring the light breeze that swept through the area while dreaming about a boat trip to a faraway island. Close by was the Mỹ Cảnh floating restaurant, where people would dine while watching river activities. The exotic location attracted many customers—mostly foreigners. (The Việt Cộng would later take advantage of its popularity to terrorize the population: they blew it up in June 1965, killing 124 people, including 28 Americans.)

I was brought back to reality when sunset rays signaled the time to go home. We then went to the Chợ Cử (Old Market) to have dinner together. There were many indoor restaurants there, along with excellent outdoor dining areas that served dishes from noodles with Peking duck to phở. Meals were washed down with delicious deserts of lychee drinks and xâm bổ lượng, fruity drinks of Chinese origin that people claimed were energy boosters. As in many Asian cities, outdoor dining provided some of the best food in the city in a casual and relaxed atmosphere.

On weekends, while ladies enjoyed shopping, their husbands went to the stadium to watch soccer matches between Saigonese and foreign teams. Soccer was the main sporting attraction in the country, with two of the best teams being "Army" and "Customs." My father sometimes took us to the large Cộng Hòa stadium in Chợ Lớn district to watch these games. A smaller downtown stadium had been torn down because of its inability to accommodate large crowds. We had to arrive early at the stadium, otherwise there would be no good seats left. We pushed and shoved to get in, trying to squeeze through the small gates, and then sat through rain and heat to watch our team play. We returned home either jubilant or depressed, depending on whether our team won or lost—but the experience was always entertaining. Those were simple times, the peaceful remnants of childhood in a city that I hold dear to my heart.

CHRISTINA
Hà Nội | 2003

DURING THE MONTHS I REMAINED IN Hà Nội, I bragged that I was moving to Sài Gòn—the sunny South—and leaving provincial Hà Nội behind. I started to plan my going-away party at Bobby Chinn's, which would take place on International Women's Day. I didn't understand why my perspective on Hà Nội had changed so dramatically after being there for only six months. I wondered why I couldn't hold two coexisting feelings about Việt Nam, and in particular Hà Nội and Sài Gòn at the same time: gratitude for Hà Nội and the life I'd led there for six months, and excitement for a new life I was creating in Sài Gòn. Instead, now that I knew I was going to Sài Gòn, I prioritized my new life there. Perhaps this was a result of the country's history—more specifically, my family's history—with the South; perhaps my deeper roots there were beginning to take hold of my ideas about Việt Nam.

A couple of weeks before I was scheduled to move, I had not heard from Lan, the managing director of the advertising agency. I emailed her and didn't receive a response. At the very least, I thought one of the staff would provide me with more information about the details of the job and the anticipated start date. A week before I was to move, I called the office to speak with her.

When she finally returned my call, she sounded cold and distant.

"I offered you the job, but it couldn't wait a few months for you to come to Sài Gòn, so I had to hire someone else," she told me. "Business doesn't wait a few months."

I was gutted. My plans had fallen through, and I also felt embarrassed that I hadn't moved there immediately. I'd wanted the job, but I'd also wanted to linger in Hà Nội for a little while longer.

I was ashamed to share the news with friends, since I'd boasted about the move. I went to Lenin Park, a park in the southern part of Hà Nội and walked around. I thought about my options: should I just stay, or still try to go? I decided I would move and find another job. I did, after all, still have the list of all the advertising agencies I'd initially contacted, and there were others that had expressed some interest. I decided to reach out to every single one of them once I arrived in Sài Gòn.

ON ONE OF MY LAST EVENINGS in Hà Nội we hosted a party at our house. So many people attended that the party extended to the alley outside our home. Friends from various parts of my life showed up; Thanh and Sam were both there, as well as the people I'd met going out in Hà Nội. Truthfully, I'd spent more time socializing than focusing on my internship or learning Vietnamese. It was, in retrospect, a rather privileged and naive existence but perhaps rather common for a recent college graduate.

As I was cleaning up outside of our house late that night, I saw a light on in the house across the street. It was so small in comparison to our own, yet it had its own simple beauty and charm. I noticed the figure of a young girl moving around in the house. Then she came outside, carrying large pots and hot water. She was setting up her family's phở stall, which opened at 5 or 6 a.m.

I thought to myself how a twelve-year-old girl shouldn't be up at 3 a.m. prepping food for a food stall. She should be resting and getting ready for a long, leisurely day riding bikes with her friends around Hà Nội. She should be sleeping so she could participate in school the following day and have a rested mind, so she could learn things that would stimulate her intellect and brighten her future. I thought about how what we'd spent on alcohol for the party that night was more than her family would make in a month from the food stall. The contrast between her life and mine was so visible, and sad. But I saw in her a quality that I found in most Vietnamese people: the ability to make the most of their situations, their lot in life.

I didn't know what would be in store for me in Sài Gòn, but I did know what I would take away from Hà Nội. In the short time I'd spent there, I'd felt embraced by the Vietnamese people I'd met. They felt so much more in tune with their emotions. My colleagues would often ask me, "Are you sad today, Christina?" And if I was indeed sad, it was something I knew I could express to them. I also didn't recognize that in the six months that I was there I had created a rather diverse social life that included established expats, development workers, and other foreigners who simply arrived in Hà Nội to have fun.

A few months before my departure, I'd purchased a 1969 Vespa from the man who'd helped me find my first apartment that I'd lived in for only nine days. I didn't know how to drive the Vespa. I hadn't even driven a Honda Dream motorbike, and the Vespas seemed more complicated to operate. I also didn't have the dexterity and balance to maneuver through the streets of Hà Nội which were congested with vendors carrying bamboo baskets on their heads, selling balloons or any other gadget that could be sold; crazy young people who sped down the streets on their own motorbikes; old men on bicycles; and people transporting pigs, chicken, mirrors, windows, TVs, and just about anything you could imagine. As one of my friends had commented to me, the best invention the Vietnamese had ever been graced with was the wheel.

When I was brave, I would try to drive my Vespa around my neighborhood. One day, I successfully made it around four times. As I completed my fourth loop, I realized that some of my neighbors had figured out that I was practicing. They stood outside their homes and small businesses, watching me, and when they saw I had some success, they cheered, smiled, laughed, and clapped their hands. That Vespa seemed emblematic of my time in Việt Nam to date—trying something completely unknown and having people cheer me on along the way.

I didn't know what adventure was in store for me in Sài Gòn, but because of what Hà Nội had gifted me—namely a deeper perspective of myself, a connection to a country, and an appreciation for its people—I felt that I had the courage and confidence to take this next step.

NGHĨA
Sài Gòn | 1960s

SÀI GÒN WOULD NOT BE SÀI Gòn without its flower market that opened a few weeks before Tết, the Lunar New Year festival. It was the biggest celebration of the year, based on the lunar calendar. According to Asian customs, everyone was one day older on the Tết holiday, regardless of the month he was born in. This explains why Tết was such a big holiday in Việt Nam. While most people celebrated for three days, those who could afford it would take the whole month off.

Preparations began as early as two or three months prior to the date. My parents would have new outfits custom-made. We shopped for new shoes. This was the busiest time of the year for local tailors, who worked overtime to complete their customers's orders. Each person would have two or three new outfits made and brought in an array of fabrics in all colors—silk, brocade, or just plain expensive fabric. Houses were cleaned, broken doors and windows were fixed. New curtains were made, and all the chandeliers and silver were polished. This was the time to settle all debts, as they could bring bad luck for the upcoming year.

There was fervor in the air. People were on the move. Merchants had the best sales at this time of year. Candles, incense, and firecrackers were sold alongside grapefruits, watermelons, persimmons, oranges, and more. There were rice cakes filled with pork meat called bánh chưng and bánh tét, as well as candies, cakes, sweet dried fruit, soft drinks, and beer.

The flower market took place on Nguyễn Huệ Avenue in downtown Sài Gòn. Ablaze with colors and filled with sweet fragrance, it remained open daily until midnight and closed on Lunar New Year's Eve. The spectacle was even more amazing at night. A rich variety of flowers could be found there: dahlias, yellow chrysanthemums, red cockscombs, red and white poinsettias, yellow *"mai,"* orchids, and kumquat trees. We went from one vendor to another to try to get the best deal possible, as the vendors hawked their products enthusiastically, extolling the beauty and freshness of the flowers and competing for customers' attention. My parents chose a mai, the flower of Tết, and hoped it would bloom during the length of the Tết festival: this would be a sign of good luck for the upcoming year.

Vietnamese people lived based more on their feelings, predictions, and hopes than on the active pursuit of or fight for something concrete. They spent a lot of money on fortune tellers, trying to foresee the future—especially during Tết. Teenagers dressed in their best outfits and promenaded around the marketplace with their friends, wanting to see and be seen. Whole blocks of Nguyễn Huệ Avenue were blocked off to traffic so pedestrians could stroll at their leisure.

Tết was a family affair, and as such family members traveled long distances in order to get home to celebrate together under one roof. At the stroke of midnight, people moved to their front porch to light up firecrackers and watch them blast into the darkness of the sky. Families competed with one another, trying to light up the longest and most expensive chain of firecrackers in their area. The explosions dominated the silence of the night and went on for a long time, filling the air with their sound and smoke.

After the last firework exploded, we went to bed, eagerly awaiting the next three full days of celebration that commemorated the passing of the old year and the welcoming of the new one.

WHEN WE WOKE UP THE NEXT morning, we put on our new outfits and set out to greet our parents. We gathered in the main room while our parents sat in chairs to preside over the ceremony. One by one we came around, bowed, greeted them with "Chúc mừng năm mới" (Happy New Year), and wished them good luck and excellent health for the upcoming year. In return, we received our lì xì (lucky money) in brand-new and good-smelling banknotes placed in tiny envelopes. They were so new and crisp that we held them gingerly in our hands, not daring to fold them.

We then sat down for breakfast. If the mai flowers were blooming yellow gold, if the watermelons were bright red on the inside and tasted juicy and sweet, chances for a good and successful year would be great.

After breakfast, some members of the family went to the pagoda to burn incense and pray for good fortune and health. Others went to church for the same reason. We visited relatives and received more lì xì, a temporary endowment of material riches that rapidly disappeared in games or movie tickets. We loved to watch the "dance of the dragon" performed by acrobats and dancers. One acrobat held a huge dragon head while others carried the dragon's long and colorful tail. There was also a địa, a mythical creature dressed as a fat man with a moonlike face who fanned himself with a paper fan. The acrobats would execute dances to the rhythm and beats of drums and cymbals. The whole procession went from house to house, dancing, contouring, and jumping to the sound of music. They then formed a human pyramid in order to reach a prize, which was often money tied to a pole and placed at the level of the first-floor balcony.

All stores and offices were closed during this three-day period. Family members spent time rekindling old friendships and enjoying themselves by playing cards and games. It was a special time when we put our worries behind us and simply let things be. We talked and talked in an atmosphere of peace and brotherhood, trying to be nice and to comfort each other; yelling, screaming, and vulgarity were forbidden during this period. Even enemies tried to make amends or at the very least avoided harming each other. We lived in a period of truce, and I wondered at times why we could not prolong that truce for a longer period. Once Tết was over, everyone returned to their usual frame of mind and began yelling and screaming again: the truce was once again broken.

THE OTHER MAJOR CELEBRATION IN VIETNAMESE culture that I remember fondly is Tết Trung Thu (Mid-Autumn or Harvest Festival), which falls around mid-October, according to the lunar calendar. The merchants would sell mooncakes, about six centimeters in size, four of them in each box. Each cake was prepared differently, with unique ingredients: one to four egg yolks, mung bean paste, lotus bean paste, meat, or other ingredients. The more ingredients, the more expensive the boxes could be; they could go up to five dollars each in some cases. In Sài Gòn, the tradition was to give one or two boxes of moon cakes to each of your friends and relatives.

All the stores were lit up with a multitude of lanterns representing either an animal or an object. They were in the shape of fish, elephants, rabbits with furry ears, boats, cars, houses, and so forth, and came in different sizes and colors, with a candle holder inside. Children loved those lanterns, and they would go from one store to the next, looking for the perfect one, before finally choosing. The ones with the fanciest decoration or presentation were, of course, the most expensive.

At night, we lit up the lanterns and went around singing:

> Tết trung thu em rước đèn đi chơi
> Em rước đèn đi khắp phố phường . . .
>
> In mid-autumn, I stroll around with my lit lantern
> Stroll around the neighborhood with my lit lantern . . .

CHRISTINA
Sài Gòn | 2003

WHEN I ARRIVED AT MY NEW home on Võ Thị Sáu, a host of new people awaited me: David and his sister, Kiều; Ali, the Canadian who had initially told me about the house; and Marc, a Swiss man. Ali and Marc both worked for international nonprofits.

When I told my new housemates about how I wasn't going to be working at the advertising agency that I thought would hire me, I saw David's jaw drop open.

"I'm working there now," he told me. "Kiều is working with a PR company linked to Saatchi, and she helped me get this job."

I was shocked. *David* was working there? Was he the one who'd taken the account executive position that I was promised?

From the moment we'd met on my first visit to Sài Gòn, there had always been some tension in my relationship with David. At first, we triggered one another. Later, I came to the realization that we mirrored each other.

"I think you took the job I was supposed to have," I said.

Disappointment overwhelmed me. I thought that agency had the best chance to win the UNICEF campaign, and I really wanted to be a part of that. But I hid my emotions and became even more determined to find another role.

I started visiting the various agencies in town right away. One day, I ended up at another international agency, where a young Canadian was leading the account services team, located a five-minute motorbike ride from my new house. He liked the idea of having a native

English speaker on his team and invited me to come back to meet Hồng Nhung, the managing director.

When I went to her office, I thought she was beautiful and elegant. Not having ever met Lan from the other agency in person, I imagined she would have presented herself in a similar way.

Hồng Nhung told me her impressive story of how she'd begun her advertising career in Việt Nam: "There were some people who wanted to bring advertising to Việt Nam. I started working with them as their assistant. I did everything for them to the best of my ability, and gradually I worked my way up to this position, managing the entire agency plus our media company, too."

I was immediately impressed, and wondered if I would ever have that same level of ambition, if I would ever want to work my way up a corporate ladder. I hadn't wanted to do it in the States at a pharmaceutical company. I didn't know if it would be any different for me working in Sài Gòn.

Hồng Nhung hired me on the spot. I was relieved, and hopeful that I could find a role model and perhaps even a mentor in her.

SÀI GÒN HAD A BEAT THAT I could feel. It pulsated, reverberated, in the evenings when the skies darkened, the streetlights lit up, and the city cooled down. Motorbikes buzzed through the streets and outdoor venues, including restaurants, bars, and coffee shops, always seemed to be bustling. There was an openness to Sài Gòn; it felt like a city that wanted to grow, change, and evolve, unlike Hà Nội which seemed set in its ways and rooted in its history. I once read a description that said Hà Nội was the older, refined aunt, while Sài Gòn was the rambunctious, wild young cousin looking to find its way in the world.

Perhaps because of this wildness, I couldn't quite settle into my life in Sài Gòn. As quickly as I'd wanted to leave Hà Nội I wanted to return. I thought about the charming, picturesque town I had fallen in love with. I thought about how Alice had compared Thailand to Việt Nam during our trip, and how I was now comparing Sài Gòn to

Hà Nội in a similar way. This dissatisfaction was something that lingered in my essence at that age.

I would often text Mai my complaints about Sài Gòn: *I don't think I'll connect with anyone here. I don't feel that Sài Gòn is as interesting as Hà Nội.*

Mai encouraged me to give Sài Gòn a little more time and urged me to befriend David, whom she knew through a mutual friend. She said she found him to be interesting and smart, and that he could be a good friend.

The problem was, I found David to be a bit aloof and unwelcoming. We occasionally chatted about day-to-day occurrences—our Astonian neighbors who were launching a company and smoked weed every evening at around 2 a.m., sending fumes wafting into our home, and the two guards at the gate who slept on a fold-out cot every night and greeted us when we came home early in the morning—but we hadn't really connected. I had gotten into the habit of quickly going in and out of our house, trying to avoid my roommates.

One evening, when I came home, David confronted me on the stairs as I tried to sneak back into my room.

"Hey, can I talk to you?" he asked. "I don't think you are really giving Sài Gòn a chance. You always talk about Hà Nội and your life there, but there's stuff here for you, too."

"I don't know," I said, defensive. "I just like Hà Nội better."

"Well if you like it so much there, you should move back," he shot back.

"Maybe," I said coldly.

"I think we could be really good friends if you wanted," he said. "But it doesn't seem like you want to. You're not doing yourself any favors by being here if you don't want to be."

"I'll figure it out," I snapped. "I don't need you to tell me what you think. I'll be fine."

I didn't want to admit it at the time, but David was right: I wasn't fully there.

Only later would I realize that this was part of the Việt Nam nostalgia—the longing for another moment in one's Việt Nam life, a phenomenon where one could be stuck in another moment that seemed so much better, therefore creating a chasm between the present and the past. In my case, I kept returning to and longing for Hà Nội. As I did, I started to understand my father, who lived and relived his memories of South Việt Nam so intently that the current Việt Nam could not even exist in his mind.

NGHĨA

Sài Gòn | 1960s-70s

WHILE I WAS IN HIGH SCHOOL, war was ongoing in the countryside. In Sài Gòn, students were shielded from the war, living in a protective cocoon. But we knew that the war equation was simple: failure in school almost inevitably equaled military service for male students.

In high school, we took two mandatory examinations: BAC I at the end of our junior year, and BAC II at the end of our senior year. Students who didn't pass the BAC II had to repeat their senior year, and therefore could not move on to university for higher education. One of my friends, Tân, failed his first attempt at the BAC II. He would have had a chance to retake it in a few months, but one day while riding his bicycle home, he was stopped by the military police at a downtown checkpoint (they'd set up checkpoints at certain street corners to stop teenagers, check their IDs, and look for draft dodgers), and because he'd forgotten his identity card at home, he was immediately detained and then transferred to a camp about ten miles outside of Sài Gòn.

When my friends and I heard about the event, we drove to the camp to visit Tân. We spoke to him across a barbed wire fence—him on the inside, us on the outside—and urged him to get out of camp by telling the authorities his status. He had a BAC I degree already and would soon retake the BAC II exam. His family could bring his identity card. But he was so distraught about his failure on the exam that he hadn't mentioned any of this to the authorities. And we couldn't convince him to do so.

He was soon sent to a training camp. He graduated six weeks later, and was immediately transferred to a battalion in central Việt Nam. Five months later, we learned about his death during an encounter with the enemy. He was only nineteen years old.

When we heard the news, we cried a lot. That was all we could do. We sat in silence, holding and comforting each other. There was nothing more we could do against fate. For myself and my friends, the loss of Tân was our first encounter with the reality of war. It was not something distant, or something imagined by the press or the government. It was real, and it would affect all of us directly.

DESPITE MY MOTHER'S OBJECTIONS, AFTER I graduated from high school I applied to medical school.

My mother wanted me to go into pharmacy because it was easier, simpler, and cleaner.

"In medicine, you have to deal with dirty patients, dirty wounds, and dirty areas," she warned me. "And you could contact diseases from patients. There are germs and bacteria everywhere in the hospital."

"But I like medicine better than pharmacy," I told her. "I would rather sit out a year than go into pharmacy."

In Việt Nam, medical training was seven years long and based on the French curriculum, under the auspices of the College of Medicine. Except for our freshman year, when we had to study basic sciences at the College of Science, the remaining years were all taught by medical professors.

The entrance examination was tough, with an acceptance rate of about 10 percent. That summer, while future students from other colleges went on vacation, candidates of the School of Medicine had to return to study for one more exam. I was one of the lucky ones that was accepted into the College of Medicine.

WHILE IN MEDICAL SCHOOL, I BECAME interested in psychology and psychiatry after hearing a lecture on those subjects that caught my attention. I was fascinated: a physician, in theory, could make the diagnosis of schizophrenia based on a few symptoms. The reality of curing a patient was, of course, not that simple; I knew that psychiatric manifestations were in fact the most difficult problems to deal with and to cure, and that was why I was so interested in these fields.

The chairman of the department moved to France, leaving behind a young associate, Dr. Lâm, to teach the specialty. Dr. Lâm was a simple but very systematic and keen clinician, and it's to him that I owe my knowledge of neurology—a field not many physicians then favored, because it was somewhat abstract and most of the time offered almost no cure for the patient. In Việt Nam at that time, we didn't have access to a lot of psychology books, so I wrote to a publisher in France, and they were kind enough to send me chapters of books to read. This was the beginning of me becoming the person I am today: someone who seeks to understand the mind and human psychology. I soon decided, though, that the human mind was incredibly difficult, if not impossible, to cure.

It was during this time that I met my first wife, Lyne, also a medical school student. She was part of a large population of Vietnamese living in Phnom Penh, the capital of Cambodia—mostly merchants or landowners who had been living there for two or three generations but were forced to leave when animosity broke out between South Việt Nam and Cambodia due to the presence of northern troops stationed there. While these Vietnamese spoke the Cambodian language, behaved like citizens, and in some cases even had Cambodian citizenship, they bore the brunt of the Cambodians' anger and were forced to either leave the country or become naturalized citizens. As the discord grew, the Cambodians started to harass the Vietnamese, beating them up and boycotting their businesses. Lyne was the daughter of a Vietnamese merchant whose family, after living in Cambodia for three generations, left Cambodia for Việt Nam to escape the violence.

Lyne was spontaneous and talkative and had an easy-going attitude. While her interest was in linguistics and her goal was to become a translator, her parents, particularly her mother, had pushed her into medicine. She and her brother, along with three other students who had recently come from Cambodia, enrolled in the College of Medicine in Sài Gòn at the same time. I met her there, and a few years later we were married.

WHILE I WAS STILL IN MEDICAL school, the Japanese government, in conjunction with the South Vietnamese government, opened a forty-bed neurosurgical unit, the first of its kind, at the Chợ Rẫy Hospital. The unit had only one "intern" rotating through the service. They decided to offer an "extern" position to assist the intern in his work. With my knowledge of neurology, I easily passed the neurosurgical examination and acquired the extern spot.

After finishing medical school and without undertaking an internship, a medical student could go into general practice; however, he would not receive his diploma until he had successfully presented a thesis for his M.D. degree. The thesis was either a case report about a certain disease, along with a review of the literature, or a review of the clinical cases seen in a service of a hospital. The majority of graduates presented their thesis twelve to eighteen months after graduation, although some physicians were so busy with their practices that it took them longer, maybe five or ten years, to get around to presenting their thesis.

Those wishing to specialize in any specialty, or subspeciality, were required to take an internship that could last an additional two to three years. Every year, only forty interns were selected, by examination, out of each school class of about 160 students. Therefore, the title of "intern" did carry prestige. The interns were the ones who really ran the university hospitals (under the supervision of staff physicians, who also practiced at private hospitals).

After passing my internship examination, I continued working in the neurosurgical unit, which was a referral center for all neurotrauma patients for the whole city of Sài Gòn and neighboring areas. I cared for patients who sustained gunshot wounds to the head, prevalent in war times, as well as for those who'd sustained blunt head injuries from a motorcycle fall or other accident. Motorcyclists didn't wear helmets at that time. In a one-year period, I was able to collect and review 100 cases of intracranial hematomas following blunt injury to the head; these cases later formed the basis for my medical thesis. (The Japanese neurosurgeon who was working at the center wrote his paper about his experience with 700 cases of gunshot wounds to the head during a four-year period. He said he had never witnessed so many cases of trauma during his whole career in peaceful Japan.)

Finally, the inevitable draft time came around, and I had the opportunity to choose Cần Thơ in the Mekong Delta to fulfill my military duty. I did not know what would transpire in the months ahead, nor could I predict that my service would lead me to Phú Quốc after my time in the Mekong Delta, and from there I would leave Việt Nam altogether.

I imagined becoming a doctor in South Việt Nam, not building a life in another country, thousands of miles away from my homeland.

CHRISTINA
Sài Gòn | 2003

SHORTLY AFTER DAVID APPROACHED ME ON the stairs, I realized the impact of his honesty and the importance of that confrontation. I still flew back to Hà Nội every other month, but I tried to find the beauty in Sài Gòn. Even though I couldn't quite figure out how to love Sài Gòn in the same way, I forced myself to go out more often with friends. I realized that I couldn't compare the two—that I had to learn to love the cities as I would learn to love the people in my life: differently, each in their own unique way. I would come to the realization that this search and longing was a part of who I was then. A part of the very reason I'd ended up in Việt Nam.

David and I began chatting on Yahoo! Messenger every day at work. We joked about having the same jobs as account executives for international agencies. We messaged about our love interests: I was still infatuated with Sam in Hà Nội, yet another reflection of my mind's inability to enjoy and appreciate the present. David, on other hand, was having an affair with a charming Vietnamese man, Victor, who was attractive, successful, and kind. Victor had a male partner who lived with him and his family. His family explained the relationship by saying Victor and his partner were just "friends." Being openly gay in Việt Nam was still taboo and culturally unacceptable.

We also gossiped about our colleagues, procrastinated on writing the contact reports after our client meetings, and talked about where we would eat for lunch. I faced problems with my colleagues that I shared with David. It felt like they had unrealistic expectations regarding what I should be able to achieve. They seemed frustrated that I wasn't able to speak Vietnamese, but gave me a hard time when I tried: one day when I had a board of Vietnamese words I didn't know, they mocked me for my Vietnamese elementary-level knowledge. I had a good relationship with the executive team, many of them foreigners, but it felt like there was distance between me and my coworkers, as well as the managers.

Through my conversations with David, bigger questions started to emerge about Việt Nam in general. We wondered how this experience of being a young adult living in Sài Gòn and making $500 compared to what our peers were living back home.

While I enjoyed being a carefree expat in Sài Gòn, going out to dinner for every meal, and out for drinks any night of the week, I knew this wasn't the life that I wanted to live indefinitely. I felt like my life should be more than what it was currently amounting to in Việt Nam. Unlike David, I still hadn't immersed myself completely in the Vietnamese language; I was almost resistant to the culture that was my own, and to mastering the language that would help me forge deeper connections with Vietnamese people.

As expats, we existed in an interesting social space in Việt Nam: while we were not necessarily wealthy, we were wealthy in comparison to many Vietnamese, which gave us a false sense of where we were professionally. We were able to do more in Việt Nam than we would ever have managed to do in the States with our modest salary. We were living in a bubble, and I had to wonder when that bubble would burst.

Life in Sài Gòn had proven to be a mere extension of my social Hà Nội life; it didn't seem that I was adding anything tangible to my life experiences there. To my friends in the States, living abroad looked like a grand adventure, but for me it was tainted with my uncertainty about where the journey would lead next. I thought about my next steps after Việt Nam. I was leaning toward applying to graduate school. David also toyed with the idea of returning home to the States. Neither of us wanted to overstay what was intended to be a brief sojourn in Việt Nam.

David and I often joked about what we would call a book about our experiences in Việt Nam. His book would be called *Trials and Tribulations in a Nation*. Mine would be called *A Love Affair*.

That title encompassed my first experience in Việt Nam, which I had yet to realize would not be my last. My time in both Hà Nội and Sài Gòn was marked with excitement, infatuation, and embracing of something novel and unknown, but it was more of an affair than a lasting love. As quickly as I'd fallen in love with Việt Nam, I fell out of love. It felt rather tumultuous—an accurate representation of many of my relationships at the time—and indicative of my fickle personality. I moved in cycles: one moment feeling overwhelming joy and gratitude for my experiences in Việt Nam, the next feeling frustration and annoyance at honking motorbikes and the general miscommunications that occurred daily. I grew increasingly tired of Việt Nam, and one small thing, like realizing that I was being overcharged for electricity or the internet by my landlord, could set me off.

After a little over a year there, I started to feel that my relationship with Việt Nam was reaching an end point. Vietnamese food—all the new dishes that I hadn't known before arriving in Việt Nam—now seemed quotidian, and the low cost was no longer an added value but rather indicative of the fact I got what I paid for—small, uncomfortable stools and unhygienic street food. The Western restaurants I frequented were always filled with the same expats I saw all over town at cafés, parties, and bars. There was no escape from the small-town feel, particularly in the expat circles, in Sài Gòn any more so than there had been in Hà Nội. Brunch conversations with friends became dull and predictable, always centered on the same topics and people. Friends came and went, moving in one- or two-year cycles, depending on their jobs or fellowships. The revolving door of people felt exhausting.

A handful of brave souls in our circle decided Việt Nam would be their permanent home—that they would find a way to make it work. I envied those people; they were decisive, not living with one foot in and one foot out like I was. But I couldn't fully commit to Việt Nam. I didn't want to. A part of me still felt that I belonged in the States—or perhaps somewhere else, but certainly not in Việt Nam. Maybe that was a symptom of being Việt Kiều, a benefit and a downside of my inherent duality: part of two worlds, two cultures, and, that year, even two cities. From my father's perspective, two very different, yet intricately connected, countries.

NGHĨA
Sài Gòn | 1975

WHEN THE NORTH VIETNAMESE MAJOR AND his army entered Sài
Gòn through its eastern side by the zoo, they could not find the place
where they were headed to take over the country. They had to stop
many times and ask a few passersby for directions.

Once the first tank slammed through the palace gates, however,
the rest was history.

Many North Vietnamese were surprised by what they saw in
Sài Gòn. Their propaganda told them that Sài Gòn was a dead,
small, dirty, and archaic city. What they found was something
different. Despite the war, the "Pearl of the Orient" carried her
age and scars well. She was still respectable in many ways: tall
buildings, magnificent French villas, business offices, and well-
manicured parks and gardens. In many places, though, the effects
of the war were visible. Due to the rapid influx of refugees from
the countryside, slums had been created around the city.
Government buildings were fortified by sandbags, housing had
been destroyed by shelling, and abandoned cars and motorcycles
were strewn about town.

The local population watched in silence as the North Vietnamese
took over. An atmosphere of fear settled over the whole city and its
inhabitants. The roundups began. Politicians, high-level officials,
generals, leaders, all those known for their staunch anti-communist
views, were taken away. Some would be seen again, others would not.
The North Vietnamese began seizing whatever they liked or wanted.

They displaced families in overtake the villas, buildings, homes, and belongings for their officials. Many locals suddenly became homeless and jobless.

Slowly, all Sài Gòn's communities became reorganized. Houses were grouped into cells with a designated communist leader. Many cells formed a section; those sections formed a subdivision; and so on. The communists went house to house, checking on the identities and numbers of inhabitants. They searched every corner of each house, looking for any discrepancies between registered occupants and what they found inside.

People were told that they needed to stay where they were. If they wanted to travel from one district to another, they had to explain the reason for that travel and receive permission from the authorities. Once they were granted approval, they could leave, but the authority at the final destination had to certify the stay and arrival.

The invaders gave themselves new jobs and titles, and also had to learn how to run a big government in a new city. Many communist soldiers had minimal education: some didn't even know how to read or write, and many didn't have a high school diploma. All the positions in the newly formed government were distributed to the loyalists—those who had been members of the Communist Party.

As former neighbors, coworkers, and sometimes friends turned out to be communist sympathizers, an air of mistrust flooded the city. People reported each other's whereabouts, activities, business, and possessions. Soon, people were afraid to confide in one another, because any activity might be construed as opposition to the government or the party. Anybody could end up in jail based on mere suspicion of wrongdoing. If a person was suspected of harboring anticommunist views, the police could knock on the door in the middle of the night and take him away; often, such a person was never to be heard from again. If someone was jobless (or a merchant, and therefore not deemed as contributing to the well-being of society), they were rounded up and deported to new economic zones. Sometimes communities of people living in whole sections of the city were deported without reason.

In this new environment, nothing—especially our future—was certain.

CHRISTINA
Sài Gòn | 2003

ONE MORNING, I RECEIVED AN EMAIL from my Uncle Thái, my mother's older brother, that said I should visit my other uncle in Sài Gòn. I didn't even know that I had an uncle who lived there. I wrote down his phone number and address, then sent him a message saying that I was Lyne's daughter, and I was living and working in Sài Gòn.

When we finally met for coffee at the historic Café Brodard on Nguyễn Huệ Boulevard—where, I'd learned, many foreigners, particularly journalists, had frequented for coffee during the war years—he introduced himself to me as Mohalam, or Uncle Năm. Since he was the fourth child, he was also known as năm, which meant "number five." I'd heard two versions about why the first child was recognized as the number two child—the first was that the parental unit was considered number one, and then each child was given their subsequent place, and the second rationale was that people feared ghosts would go after the first-born, so the Vietnamese would call the eldest, number two.

While I'd had the opportunity to know my mother's other three siblings, who'd visited during the time she was sick, Uncle Năm was a mystery—everything from his name, Mohalam/Năm, to his son's name, Ali.

"I am sorry to hear about your mom," he said to me. "All the siblings were much older than me. I was just a kid when she was a teenager, so I didn't feel like I knew her very well," he said to me as he sipped on his cà phê sữa đá.

Năm had a broad smile and a warm face, but it certainly felt that he was on the outside of the family—maybe he was the black sheep—since I had not heard anything about him prior to being in Việt Nam. I had always noticed a tension between my father and my mother's family, although I never knew the story. There was a distance, a distrust that I could see even as a teenager when my aunts and maternal grandmother visited my mother while she was sick. I later rationalized that infighting within Vietnamese families seemed to be the norm. What else could I expect from Vietnamese people who came from a divided country, fighting within itself.

My uncle and I discovered that we both loved sweets and were tempted by the desserts at Brodard. I explained to him what I was doing in Sài Gòn, and how I'd landed in Việt Nam.

He then proceeded to tell me about his own story. "I was all over the world," he said, "and got into some trouble. I went to stay in Switzerland with Solange for a bit when I was in my late teens, but I was always trying to leave. I went to France, married a woman and had two girls. We divorced, and I ended up in Việt Nam; now I have a child here with my second wife."

He told me that he had various odd jobs—some sort of finishing company, a partnership in a women's clothing company, and a language school in Việt Nam. He also worked on charity projects in Cambodia, and as he mentioned, was devoted to the church and his faith.

In between all these stories, he always laughed and had a big smile on his face, which made me feel both happy and uncomfortable at the same time. Mostly, though, I was excited to have a blood relative in Sài Gòn, making me feel more at home.

WHEN I ARRIVED BACK AT MY place, I immediately walked up the stairs to David's room. I was so excited to have just met a family member that I couldn't contain myself.

"I just met my uncle, David," I exclaimed. "He has a strange name, Mohalam, and his son is called Ali."

David's eyes widened. "Wait—I've met this guy before!" His response was like the time when we'd realized that he was now working at the job I wanted in Sài Gòn.

"How's that possible?" I asked, "There are millions of people in Sài Gòn. There's no way you met my uncle before me."

"No, I did," he insisted. "I've even been over to his house. My mom met him on a plane, and then introduced us when we arrived here."

"You met his wife, Thi, and son, Ali?" I asked.

"Yes, that's them. I wouldn't forget a name like Ali, because it's so unusual for a Vietnamese kid."

We were both shocked by the fact that out of the many people in Sài Gòn, my roommate and good friend would have met my uncle before I did. David explained that his mother sat next to my uncle on a flight in the States, and when she explained that her children were moving to Sài Gòn, they exchanged numbers so David and his sister could connect when they arrived. We viewed this coincidence as a testament to our friendship—one of the countless ways in which we were connected.

ONE EVENING, UNCLE NĂM DROVE ME around the city and showed me where their family had lived when my mother was in medical school. Because he was so much younger than the other siblings, he didn't remember many details. He said my brother—my parents' first child, the one who had passed away—was charming and chubby, and that everyone loved him. He'd heard bits and pieces of my father's story, too, including the fact that my grandfather had another family somewhere in Sài Gòn. He also recalled everyone saying that my father didn't speak much.

"He was a very quiet man. But your mother had a lot of energy and was very talkative. She was kind, too, and always wanted to help other people."

I knew so little about what my mother had experienced before she passed—she never disclosed any information about her upbringing in Cambodia and her life in Việt Nam. My uncle mentioned that she had been a champion ping-pong player in Cambodia; that was such a contrast to the woman I'd known as my mother, who would never even play ping-pong with me, even though we had a table in the basement. My mother had also feared the ocean, and whenever we'd gone on vacation to the beach, she'd refused to get in the water with us.

I now understood that there had been another side of my mother, a woman I'd never known. After talking with my uncle, whenever I sat in a nice cafe in Sài Gòn and a group of Vietnamese women walked in—impeccably dressed, hair and makeup perfect—I wondered if my mom, who was also quite fashionable, would have been one of those women. Had she been happier in Việt Nam? I thought about all the small towns we'd lived in, with their majority white populations, and remembered how, when we lived in Illinois for one year, she finally met a friend—a Korean woman who she grew very close to. Would she have been more comfortable, more content, with all Vietnamese friends who she could speak to in her language, whose culture was her own? These were the questions for which I would have answers, and that knowledge gnawed at me.

When I was sick as a child, my mother used to sing a song whose melody was lodged in the back of my mind. Instead of the words, she'd sing my name: Ti-na-ti-ti-na-ti-na Ti-na-ti-ti-na-ti-na

She never told me the name of the song, but one day, I heard it again in a cafe in Sài Gòn. I couldn't decipher the words in the café's loud atmosphere, but even in the background, I knew it was the same song my mother used to sing to me. Immediately, I understood that she was there with me—that the song was a sign of her presence. I could feel that she was proud of me for venturing to a foreign land, for trying to uncover pieces of her story and our family history, and, importantly, seeking to understand our family better.

NGHĨA

Sài Gòn | 1980s

BEFORE THE FALL OF SÀI GÒN, my mother had two goals for her life: to raise her children and to travel abroad. She enrolled all of her children in private school, which was a difficult and costly decision for her. When my father's salary as a custom's officer would not suffice, she attended night school and eventually became a nurse. Then, she opened a private business, which brought additional income to our family. When this did not prove to be sufficient for the needs of our large family, she sold our house and moved us into a smaller one.

Under the communist regime, my mother's business flourished, and after a few years she opened a small store that sold only rice and non-perishable items. Someone once asked her why she didn't sell anything besides these items. She explained that this was only a side business for her, and she sold items that were easy for her to get a hold of. As with many of my mother's decisions, this ended up being a wise one, since rice had long been a main staple for Vietnamese people, and in times of war or scarcity, the Vietnamese relied upon steamed rice, dry fish, vegetables, and salted duck eggs to fill their stomach; they could subsist on this food regimen for months at a time.

After the fall of Sài Gòn, there was so much uncertainty under the communist government; all this was complicated by the mid-night roundups, the transfer of people to new economic zones, and the reeducation camps. The economy suffered tremendously; many of the communist loyalists who filled the positions in the newly formed government lacked the experience or knowledge to perform well in their new jobs. Meanwhile, the brain drain and the capital loss following the escape of more than a million people to other countries further handicapped the economy. Food prices increased dramatically, along with inflation.

Some merchants benefited more than other people and made significant profits when prices fluctuated. People, especially merchants, turned to gold, which became the standard currency of business. If a person wanted to escape to go abroad, the down payment had to be made in gold. Many Vietnamese people saw this coming and traded their paper money into gold early on.

In addition to the pressures my mother faced managing a business within a shifting economy, my younger brothers were still within draft age. One of my brothers and his girlfriend attempted to escape through Vũng Tàu, a route that my mother advised them against. She had to bail them out, and was overwhelmed with fears that my brother would be sent to Cambodia. Thankfully, my brother had not actually spoken out publicly against the communist government, and my mother's connections in Vũng Tàu were able to get him released after a few weeks.

Despite all these external factors, my mother's business flourished. With her profits, she bought gold and started saving. The eldest of my younger three brothers was working as a pediatrician at the local hospital. She advised him to stay there as long as possible in order to remain out of sight of the local officials. The two younger ones were doing secretarial work for a company while studying part time.

Wanting to protect them, my mother started attending monthly sectional, or neighborhood, meetings on their behalf.

One day one of the officers asked, "Why are you here at all of these meetings? Where are your children?"

"They are studying at school," she responded. "The classes are so hard that they don't have time for the meetings. And after school, the government has meetings for them too. I'm here to substitute for them."

"Do they know that they need to take turns mounting guard at their housing section at night?" he demanded. "This is an important duty for youngsters."

"What does it entail?" she asked.

"They need to keep watch at night so that no strangers are allowed in the neighborhood."

"I will gladly take their place," she said.

"Fine," he agreed. "This will be done on a rotating basis. You can bring a chair or lounge chair out to the front of your house and keep watch."

The neighbors were all uncertain about who they were watching. There were enough police officers to cordon off the entire city if needed, and young people were so scared of house checks and the midnight roundups that they would rather hide somewhere than run around and disturb the neighborhood. But my mother kept quiet about all this. Based on the schedule distributed by the officers, she took her turn observing the local area, making her strongest effort to keep her children out of the spotlight so that nobody would notice them and subsequently draft them. She was also wise enough to befriend the officials and bring them gifts, actions that certainly helped protect her family further.

EVEN AS MY MOTHER MANAGED ALL these aspects of her life and protecting her children, she was, as throughout her life, slowly creating a plan for her family. She inquired and connected with local officials to obtain special exit visas to get herself and my younger brothers out of Việt Nam. It was difficult, of course, because of their ages, and she faced numerous hurdles—but she persisted, and eventually overcame the situation. She obtained the visas so that she and my brothers could leave Việt Nam. She waited patiently for the green light from the local government.

It happened suddenly: my mother was told that she had twenty-four hours to buy plane tickets and fly out of the country. She turned over her house to the government and flew out as fast as she could—first to Thailand, and then to Los Angeles. She and my brothers settled down in Southern California in the early '80s, and like many Vietnamese refugees, they went through a difficult adjustment period, but ultimately, they were happy that they were finally free and did not have to live with the continuous worries of the military draft and life under a badly run communist government.

Finally, I thought to myself, my entire family was out of that communist country.

CHRISTINA
Sài Gòn | 2003

THE LAST FORTUNE TELLER I VISITED, a few months before I left Việt Nam, was in an obscure location in Sài Gòn's District 3. Cô Hoa, my friend's aunt, owned a street food stall serving one dish—com sườn bì chả trứng (Vietnamese broken rice with grilled pork chops, shredded pork skin, and pork-egg custard)—on the bustling street of Nguyễn Trãi in District 3. She had told us about a famous fortune teller she knew, who was so well-known and trusted that she limited each person to a single visit. I was thrilled when she offered to take us there one day.

Cô Hoa led us through the meandering alley of homes with corrugated metal roofs to a house I never could have found on my own. We passed through the front gate, already left ajar, and walked by three motorbikes parked in the front of the house. A man who sat in front of the TV, seemed to know immediately why we were there, and pointed us to the makeshift stairs in the back of the room.

Three women sat in a row on the floor, waiting for the fortune teller. The looks on their faces told me that they clung to the idea that this woman held the key to their futures—the promise of success, health, and lasting love.

The fortune teller, dressed in a long white robe, seemed at most only five years older than me. She sat in a wooden chair in the middle of the room, which was painted in a soothing turquoise color—a contrast to the bright red lamps sitting on the altar that spanned the entire length of one of the walls. The smell of incense lingered in the

CHRISTINA VÕ & NGHĨA M. VÕ

air, mixed with the anticipation of the guests. The golden Buddha, with its deeply content expression, seemed to be staring at us from the altar.

I knew I was there seeking guidance, almost permission, to leave Sài Gòn. So much had happened in the past few months: I applied and was accepted into a graduate program at the London School of Economics which would encompass many of my interests, including the ability to use communications for social change through public campaigns. The advertising agency I worked for eventually won the pitch to work for a national communications campaign led by UNICEF to empower Vietnamese youth. I worked tirelessly on the campaign and felt passionate about what we were trying to achieve, but as with most projects in a developing country, I started to realize that we would forever be plagued with delays.

I started to feel my time in Việt Nam was ending. It felt very black-and-white: suddenly this experience in Việt Nam was over in my mind. There were only so many dinners and coffee dates that I could plan with friends, and I realized that while my life felt free and easy in Việt Nam, too much anything could be detrimental. I felt it was time to be a little more serious about my life and career.

There had also been dramatic changes in my father's life. He had recently sent me and my sister an email:

> Girls,
>
> Alice and I are no longer together. She is no longer part of the family. Do not share any information with her. Do not write to her if she writes to you.
>
> Dad

Soon, one came from Alice:

> I want to tell you my side of the story. Your father and I have had problems for a long time. We never had a normal relationship. We never lived in the same city and we don't really communicate.

Immediately after I heard the news, I went to David's room to talk to share with him the news.

"I never felt close to Alice," I explained, "but I was comforted knowing that she was a part of my father's life. Then he wouldn't be alone."

"Maybe now's the time for you to be there for your father," he said.

I knew there was truth to his statement, but I wasn't prepared to believe that I could emotionally support my father. After all, there were so many times when I'd felt he hadn't been there for me.

Over the next few days, the emails flew back and forth, at first full of pain and anger, and then gradually into resolution, both trying to find some peace in the situation. Alice explained that just as my father had not been available for us, he had not been present for her, either. My father shared that he and Alice had shared many good moments and years together, but he'd had so much on his mind throughout their relationship—from my mother's death to his work to being a single parent to two teenage daughters—that he hadn't nurtured their bond. His perspective shifted after his initial communication, and he encouraged us to continue to stay in touch with her. He wrote: *You can learn from her, and she could be a role model for you.*

This was a turning point in my father's life. He had already endured so much pain in his life, but there was something about his divorce from Alice that was clearly triggering something deep within him. It would only be years later, when I endured a massive heartache of my own, that I would understand that some endings are portals to deeper wounds we need to face in this life, and after the pain passes, we learn to be grateful to the people who have opened those portals for us—providing us another lens through which to view our past.

WHEN IT WAS MY TURN FOR a reading, I sat before the fortune teller. She looked strong and forceful. Her face caked with powder, reminding me of a young Vietnamese teenager who was trying makeup for the first time. She looked at me with piercing eyes, then shut them, chanted some indecipherable prayers, and exhaled a long, resounding hum that permeated the small room. I held my breath, hoping that she would share with me insight on my own life, and my father's too.

My friend took down notes as cô Hoa sat behind me and translated the main points of the fortune teller's words:

> Her mother is already dead. She died too early.
>
> She's not living close to her family, and she will always be far from home.
>
> She should focus on work, not love. Love will always be complicated for her.
>
> If she focuses on her work first, love will fall into place.
>
> Her life gets better after she turns thirty because she'll understand herself better.

Then she added, "She'll always come back to Viet Nam. And I'll let her speak to me again because I know she will always return."

I donated 50,000 VND. After placing the money in a jar on the altar, I nodded at the woman, who gave me a knowing smile. I looked at the shiny lights, the jumble of items on the altar, and told myself that she was wrong. I believed that I had lived out my Việt Nam experience, that I had learned enough there.

I thought once I left, I would never return to Việt Nam—not to live, at least—ever again.

REEDUCATION | REPATRIATION

CHRISTINA

Virginia | 2004

AFTER MY FATHER AND ALICE OFFICIALLY divorced, he moved to northern Virginia, about forty-five miles outside of Washington, D.C. It was difficult to watch him leave behind his medical practice in Indiana and start anew, rebuilding his life at such a late stage in yet another state.

I spent the summer in the States with him before heading to London for graduate school. When I asked my father why he chose Virginia, he responded that a Vietnamese woman he'd met at a conference had encouraged him to move there. I imagined them talking on the phone, heard her saying, "Nhiều người Việt sống ở Virginia"—*Many people live here in Virginia*—and gently nudging him to consider her suggestion. Maybe he told her about Alice, the divorce, and starting somewhere new. Maybe he emailed her about all of it, as he did me and my sister. Maybe he said nothing.

Perhaps she saw in him the need to reconnect to his roots, to live alongside people who could understand his history because theirs was similar—forced to leave the country they loved, the place they called home, not knowing when or if they would ever return.

I could not imagine this fate for myself, as my decisions to leave the places I'd lived in had always been made by choice, based on a longing to live someplace else. I could always go home, always return to the country where I was born.

IN VIRGINIA, MY FATHER REPEATED A familiar pattern, one I recognized from my nomadic childhood. Everywhere we went—Connecticut, New York, Utah, Tennessee, Illinois, Indiana—we always rented first before buying a place. It took me a long time to recognize that on some level, as an adult, I was recreating these patterns.

When I visited, he was renting a small apartment behind a generic shopping plaza with a grocery store and a few chain restaurants. It was difficult for me to see my father living in an apartment, uncertain about his future; he'd moved from a 3,000-square-foot home in Indiana to a generic apartment complex with six indistinguishable buildings full of people who knew nothing about each other—sharing only a parking lot, a pool, and a gym.

He told me that he was going to see if he liked it in the area before buying a house. He stored most of his belongings, and took only what was necessary to fill the small apartment. A wicker couch that had been in our sunroom. Our kitchen table. A desk. A twin bed for each of the bedrooms. A lamp for each room. He'd set up a room for me with a few personal items he'd hand-selected and the white down comforter that I had used throughout college.

I was so unaccustomed to seeing my father living in a small space. It was unsettling—uncomfortable. I always pictured my father living in houses that were too large for him to manage on his own, with extra rooms that he only entered to vacuum or clean. That was the image I felt comfortable with, and comforted by: my father, protected by empty space. His patio at the new apartment was a three-by-three-foot square of concrete with a few small plants and a lawn chair facing the parking lot. I wondered if he sat there throughout the day, pondering his life and what his future might hold. I wondered if he longed for company.

On his desk, I noticed a brochure for a meditation retreat in the Rocky Mountains. I wondered if he'd attended, or if he was considering it. When I was younger, looking through the items on my father's desk was how I got to know him. In addition to his stacks of medical books and papers, he always had self-help books lying around, and a small green box filled with notecards and inspirational quotes scribbled on it. I knew, even then, that my father was searching for something deeper—that he was trying to craft a meaningful life.

DURING THE TIME I STAYED WITH my father, we took walks together on wooded trails near his apartment—something we had never done with each other in the past. He walked briskly in front of me as I followed behind him at a more leisurely pace.

He turned around during one of these walks and asked, "Do you meditate, Christina?"

"No, Dad, I don't," I said. "But it seems like a good idea."

"It's easy," he said. "Just look at anything, even a rose, and stare at it for fifteen minutes. As long as you can. Don't think about anything. And try to do it as long as you can."

I nodded, and we continued on.

At the end of the walk, he asked another question that surprised me: "Is there anything you want to know about your mom?"

"No," I said firmly, although that was not true. I did want to know about my mom. I wanted to know about him, too—but for some reason, I couldn't engage in this conversation with him. Not yet.

During our time together, he suggested that I consider moving to the D.C. area after I completed my degree, and reminded me that there were a lot of international organizations there that I could work for. I responded to him coldly, "I don't want to live in DC."

I was too young and too self-absorbed to see that my father was extending an olive branch, that this was his way of trying to be closer to me. And, more importantly, he asked me for something—to support him, which I had also never done in my life. I was more comfortable with the two of us remaining like two islands: sharing an ocean, but never connecting.

NGHĨA

Hartford, Connecticut | 1977–1988

IN 1977, I FINALLY MOVED TO a bigger city for my medical training. So much had changed in the two years since I arrived in America. It wouldn't be until the spring of 1976 when I would meet Lyne at JFK Airport. She was thinner than before but still appeared to have her spontaneous nature. Emotionally, she had changed since I had last seen her. I wondered whether her world had been altered so much in such a short period of time that she could not cope with the new reality.

In just eighteen months, she had witnessed the communist take-over, been evicted from her home, suffered the loss of our first child and her identity, escaped from Việt Nam, and experienced the trauma of monstrous new challenges—first in France, and now in America.

In Việt Nam, Lyne had often been upset, but never told me what had bothered her. Was it the communists, or was it the way her family treated her in Việt Nam? At times, she seemed angrier at her family. Here, she would have to learn new ideas, new ways of thinking, as well as a new culture. It was overwhelming. She was afraid.

She enrolled in a local college but did not feel like studying any-more. She just wanted to stay at home. She befriended an old couple, the Donaldsons, through the church and took English classes with them. Slowly, she opened up to them, and she felt happier because she was able to mix with a few people in the community and enjoy their friendship. I was so focused on my training, yet I did my best to sup-port her as she assimilated in the new country. Starting a family seemed to be one way to give her life meaning: in 1977, our second child and first daughter was born, followed by the birth of Christina in 1979. Our children seemed to provide a sense of structure for her, while I worked on continuing to build my medical career.

THERE WERE TWO RESIDENCY PROGRAMS IN the city: one in a 600-bed hospital and another in an 800-bed hospital. Attempts to merge the two programs had been met with resistance from private physicians in the two hospitals.

At our orientation, I was surprised by what the chief resident shared with us.

"You will take calls every third night, and one full weekend every third week," he announced. "The junior residents stay in the hospital while on call, but the senior residents can take calls from home."

One resident inquired about whether we had a day off after we were on call.

"There will be no off-call period," he responded. "What that means is that if you're on call during the two-day weekend, you will continue to work on Monday until 5 or 6 p.m."

"But that means we will have worked for a total of fifty-eight to sixty hours straight," the resident commented.

"Yes, that's correct." The chief resident shrugged. "We did it, so you guys should be able to handle it too."

"What is our daily schedule?" another resident asked.

"In the morning, you must see your patients first, then head to the operating room at 8 a.m. sharp, where you will be assigned to specific cases. As a junior-level medical professional, you will assist with holding retractors during major surgical cases and will have limited opportunities to observe the surgical field."

"How long do the cases last?" the resident asked.

"Some are two or three hours long, others up to five or six hours. One lasted eighteen hours."

"And we have to hold the retractors for the entire time?" he asked.

"Every surgical resident has to go through this period," the chief resident said. "You have to learn to hold still, sometimes not even move a single muscle—not even breathe—during critical moments. Otherwise, you'll hear the senior staff yelling. At the end of the day, all your muscles and your backs will be sore. But you will have to see your patients and do a few more meetings before heading home if you are not on call."

The first few weeks were the most difficult to adjust to. The junior residents had to do all the scut work: patient histories and physicals, take care of patients, give all the intravenous medications, and answer all the calls. Since medications were given at different hours for each patient, a resident could be called at 2 a.m. to give one patient his or her medication, and then called back an hour later to administer another medication to another patient.

These were the most sleepless nights in my life. Some mornings, I felt so tired that I could only give the senior residents or patients blank stares, with my mind a thousand miles away.

IN JANUARY 1978, THE CHIEF RESIDENT told me to come to the hospital at 6 a.m. It was still dark and there were already three feet of snow on the ground. It kept falling steadily. I wondered whether I should go, but I knew I had no choice.

The streets were empty, the hospital corridors even quieter than usual.

When I saw the chief resident, he simply said, "Do your rounds. I'll see you later."

The other resident who was with me couldn't believe it. "Why didn't he do rounds with us?" he asked in disgust.

"I don't know why we're here at 6 a.m.," I responded.

We completed our rounds, went to the operating room, and kept working until 6 p.m. The chief did not show up until an hour later, at 7 p.m.

"It is dark outside and still snowing," the other resident said to me.

"We put in our thirteen-hour shift and we never realize what's happening outside," I said.

He shook his head. "I told you—we are living in a world of our own, in a world that our families and other people have no idea about."

When we left the hospital, snow covered the ground in piles that reached up to five feet in some areas. All the cars in the parking lot were buried. Thankfully, the residents's accommodations were right across the street, so we didn't have to go far to get home.

The storm was coined "The Blizzard of 1978." The city's transportation department was overwhelmed; snow tractors couldn't keep up with the pace of the snowfall.

A few days later, everything went back to normal, and the Blizzard of 1978 became nothing more than a memory. And my fellow residents and I had our work cut out for us in the years that followed. Rain or shine, snowstorm or not, we had patients to take care of. One patient would need insulin regulated. Another would require surgery. Another one would need his dressing changed, and another would have to be sent to the radiology department for more x-rays. The list went on and on.

After my first few weeks, I understood what the term "resident" really meant—that we were the ones who were expected to live at the hospital. We were called upon when anything went wrong with the patient, or if the staff physicians were in transit, or even just in their offices, and something needed to be done for a patient.

It's no wonder that in the early seventies, many surgical residency programs would not accept married candidates. They knew too well that married candidates would find it difficult to dedicate themselves to the grueling training system. They also knew that surgical residents had the highest divorce rate of any other specialty.

Five years of total dedication to the system proved to be too much for many residents. Broken families, bad tempers, and alcoholism were all possible repercussions of the training. Scars from those years could follow graduating residents for the rest of their lives. But the ones who made it were probably the best and most qualified physicians that the system could produce.

ONE DAY ABOUT SEVENTEEN MONTHS INTO my training, one of the attending physicians said to me, "Well, I understand that you'll be staying with us for a few more years."

"I'm not sure I know what you mean," I said.

"We had a vote the other day," he said. "I can't tell you any more than that. Someone will let you know."

I was puzzled but I didn't ask any more questions. That night, I was unable to sleep; I couldn't stop thinking about what he might have meant. Was he saying what I thought he was saying?

The five-year program was a pyramidal system, with a total of sixteen residents. Five residents were chosen for each of the first two years, then it dropped down to two for each of the last three years. If a resident was cut from the program after the second year, he either had to change his specialty or repeat the second year at another surgical residency program.

A few weeks later, the announcement was made: I would advance to the third year of the hospital's residency program. The second position was reserved for an outsider who came from another hospital. Of the four of my cohorts who were cut, two went into orthopedics, one into another surgical specialty, and the fourth into emergency medicine.

I could not be happier. I finally made it and would graduate from a program. I didn't have to look for another position, nor did I have to move.

CHRISTINA
San Francisco | 2005

AFTER COMPLETING GRADUATE SCHOOL, MY PATH would continue to be nomadic. Despite my father's request, I did not end up in Washington, D.C. I didn't recognize the commonality my father and I shared: although he was in the States and I was bouncing around abroad in my twenties, we were both trying to find our place in the world, somewhere to call home.

Initially, I had set my sights on New York. I secured an apartment in Brooklyn and paid the deposit. I even shipped some of my belongings to David's place in Brooklyn, where he'd been living since leaving Sài Gòn.

Then, in Chapel Hill, I reconnected with Thomas, who had just left Hà Nội. He was supposed to move to Los Angeles with his ex-boyfriend. Suddenly, California felt more open and exciting to me than New York. I told Thomas I had always dreamed of living in San Francisco, and he had an idea: why not move together to San Francisco? I said yes immediately.

Some other friends I'd met in Việt Nam had also landed in the Bay Area after moving back to the States. They had stable jobs and seemed to have an easier time repatriating than I did. I wasn't quite there yet, still resisting that corporate ladder and whatever I deemed to be a "traditional" path, and yet a part of me wanted to try to build a stable life in a U.S. city.

AFTER LIVING IN SAN FRANCISCO FOR six months, working on freelance communication projects, I discovered the extensive

Vietnamese community in San Jose, one of the largest in the U.S. I would take the Caltrain to San Jose, then the bus to one of the local nonprofits that planned the Vietnamese American National Gala (VANG), a yearly celebration to honor the achievements of Vietnamese Americans. The head of that organization was a Vietnamese man whose last name—chosen by his family when they became U.S. citizens—was Hubris, as in, "exaggerated pride or self-confidence."

I'd met other Vietnamese professionals, like Sara, a savvy lawyer who seemed to navigate being both Vietnamese and American without issue. She was deeply committed to the Vietnamese community—had even created a non-profit organization, Creating Opportunities in Việt Nam (COVN), that celebrated Vietnamese artists and raised funds to support women in Việt Nam—her way of giving back to her homeland.

I also became acquainted with Kim, a woman my age but had immigrated to the U.S. when she was thirteen years old. When we met, we were both in our mid-twenties and she still lived with her family—something I could not understand.

I believed that it would benefit Kim to live in San Francisco—to be away from her family for a bit, but still be close enough to visit them weekly. I couldn't understand why she wanted to live at home with her entire nuclear family: an older sister who was two years older than her and her parents. Whenever I went to her house, she set up the small guest room in the basement and kept me at a distance from her family. I wondered if I spoke Vietnamese if she'd do the same.

"Don't you want more freedom?" I asked her one day. "We could even find an apartment and live in the city together."

"That would be fun," she said. "But I don't want to live away from my family."

I was relieved, to be honest. Even though I'd suggested we live together, I knew that if we did, I would feel claustrophobic. Kim and I might've had similar hearts, but we were undeniably cut from different cloths.

She often asked me about my own family, and initially I disclosed very little about where my father and sister lived and why I was not close to them. Over time, however, I shared more about my family, and I found the way she asked about my father quite endearing.

"He's alone, Christina," she would say to me. "You should talk to him more; you are his family."

On some level, I knew she was right, but it was difficult for me to communicate more with my father, when my past attempts had so often been met with silence.

THAT YEAR, THE VANG GALA TOOK place at the Westin St. Francis in downtown San Francisco. The theme was "Bridging Endless Possibilities." The emcee, Betty Nguyen—a CNN news anchor at that time, and a former inventor and engineer with Texas Instruments—was honored with the Golden Torch Award for her significant contribution to the Vietnamese American community.

It was a spectacle: a black-tie event that Mr. Hubris promoted as the Vietnamese American community's version of the Oscars. As I watched the parade of Vietnamese people walk through the door in their fancy attire, I felt entirely out of place.

Many of the award recipients that night mentioned the hardships they'd overcome to build a life here—the difficulties and the losses that they suffered—but they mainly focused on their accomplishments and how far they'd come. Pride and hubris filled the room. The people on stage represented a specific part of the Vietnamese American community—those who had "made it."

Later, I asked my father what he thought about VANG and the event I attended. He simply said, "There are many types of Vietnamese in the States, Christina."

NINE MONTHS INTO LIVING IN SAN Francisco, I was working full time as an account executive for a San Francisco-based advertising agency that focused on creating campaigns for the Asian American community. It was yet another attempt to find my footing as a Vietnamese American in the U.S.—but it still didn't satisfy the lack I felt. No matter how involved I was with the organizations that were connected to Việt Nam, I remained fixated on the idea of going back. Slowly, I started to realize that these other communities didn't really fit me. It was being in Việt Nam that was important to me.

At one of the COVN events, I met a Vietnamese photographer and spoke to him of my passion and longing for Việt Nam.

"Why don't you just go live there again?" he asked matter-of-factly. "You're young. You seem to want to be there. You'll have plenty of time to settle down in the future."

One morning, I awoke to an email from the UNICEF headquarters in New York. Avian influenza outbreaks were happening throughout Asia, and the United Nations were ramping up their efforts to support countries in the region. The human resources officer had emailed me to see if I wanted to be considered for a communication consultancy with UNICEF's Việt Nam country office since UNICEF would take the lead on behavior change communication campaigns.

I enthusiastically responded "yes," and after two interviews, a written test, and a lot of paperwork, I found myself heading back to Việt Nam—this time as an expat with a salary and benefits, exactly the type of person I had so admired the first time I ventured to Hà Nội.

NGHĨA
Sài Gòn | Late 1970s

AFTER THE FALL OF SÀI GÒN, any male who had anything to do with the South Vietnamese government, whether he was a former soldier, government official, doctor, teacher, etc., was asked to report to certain locations in the city or county. They were told to bring food and clothing for a few days; after days of reeducation, the communique said, they would be returned to their families.

Many of the men were rightfully concerned about what would happen to their families if they left. Some considered not showing up and hiding forever. However, being a no-show had its obvious repercussions, since the communists would eventually find them, then strip the person of his identity, legal residence, and social status.

Some men decided to hide. They became homeless and vanished into the depths of society, or went to the countryside to escape abroad. The majority, though, showed up for reeducation camps. They were separated based on their background: unlisted soldiers, low-level officials, teachers, business professionals, etc. Those individuals who did not seem to present much opposition to the communist government were placed in one group. Those who had been a threat to the communists, including the secret police, CIA collaborators, green berets, and staunch anticommunists, were placed in a separate group. They were dealt with more harshly.

All the men were hauled away in convoys of covered military trucks. No one knew exactly where. The back of the truck was covered so nobody would know what was going on. A lot of people died of suffocation en route to their destinations, but the communists did not appear to care.

Even the military personnel were triaged: lower-ranking personnel went to local camps, while higher-ranking officials were sent a thousand miles away to camps in the North, close to the Chinese border.

Some of my friends were sent to the southwestern region, close to the Cambodian border—an arid area where only palm trees could grow. They were told that they had to turn that barren land into the rice basket of the country by cutting down the trees and bushes and cultivating the land. The rules in the camps were simple: do what you were told, and as long as your health and sanity held up, you would survive. These men, who had until recently been the heroes and leaders of their communities, felt betrayed, broken, and confused. In these camps, many of them would cry for the first time in their lives.

One friend sent to such a camp was Dr. Cường, a reserved person who rarely spoke his mind. He was stationed with me in Cần Thơ, and while I lived in military quarters to save money, he was lucky enough to live with extended family in town. He was married five months prior to the fall of Sài Gòn, and when I was sent to Phú Quốc, his superiors kept him in Cần Thơ.

A few days after the fall of Sài Gòn, Cường turned himself in to the communists and ended up in the same camp as Dr. Phú, who had also been practicing at the military hospital in Cần Thơ. They slept in the same hut and shared the same work schedule and workload. The two vowed to support each other through these times. They relied on one another to keep their spirits high, and found a common interest in music. While in medical school, Cường had taken some time off to play with his band, and he was known as "Mr. Harmonica" since he played that instrument so well. It had taken him ten years to finish medical school instead of seven—a fact that he was proud of in private, since he'd been able to satisfy his passion for music and finish his medical training at the same time. Phú shared Cường's love for the guitar, and they vowed to each other that when they got out of the camp, they would form a band and travel around the country.

In the camp, the two doctors were constantly reminded that they were in a re-education camp, and at the mercy of their jailers. Every day, they were forced to denounce their old, "corrupt" government and sing praise of "Uncle Hồ." They had to denounce themselves as supporters of the old regime, and to renounce their allegiance to the free world.

At the end of the day, they retired to straw huts, and while the days seemed long and filled with a fight against nature—the weather, the soil, the heat—at night, these men had to face themselves and the countless questions that ran through their mind: *What happened to my family? When will this forced labor end? Will I survive this camp?*

PHÚ AND CƯỜNG ENTERTAINED THEMSELVES AS much as they could at the camp. They were stripped to the minimum physically and mentally, but not spiritually.

One day, Phú tied a thread to a rod, fashioned a hook at one end, and went fishing in the creek that ran through the middle of the camp. He was so involved in his fishing that he crossed a bridge to the other side of the creek, not noticing the small sign forbidding any prisoner to cross the bridge. Although the two sides belonged to the same camp, the jailers took offense.

One of the guards yelled, "Stop right away."

"Yes, cadre," Phú replied.

"Do you know what you were doing?" the guard asked.

"No, cadre."

"Did you see the sign over there?" the guard demanded. "It says 'no trespassing.' Do you understand what no trespassing means?"

CHRISTINA VÕ & NGHĨA M. VÕ

"I was so busy fishing that I didn't see it," Phú replied honestly. "I'm sorry, cadre."

"You'll be punished for not obeying the law."

The guard took him, beat him, and left him naked for the entire day. His flesh was bruised and hurt from the beating. His skin was burned by the sun. His lips were cracked and sore from thirst. His throat was hoarse from crying. His whole body was worn out by the ordeal. His head pounded with anger at the stupid jailer.

After that day, Phú lost his interest in fishing.

Cường was homesick, and so fond of his new wife that he decided to craft a comb to help him remember her. Because he had limited access to materials, he slowly fashioned the comb with what he had, and at the end of it, he carved a picture of his wife. He kept it in his pocket, determined to one day give it to her as a testament of his love for her. Somehow, the jailers found out about the comb. They asked to see it, and then asked Cường to carve a picture of Uncle Hồ.

"I would do anything for you," Cường told them, thinking quickly, "but I don't think I can in this case. Uncle Hồ is such an important official that I could not degrade him by carving his face on a piece of wood."

That answer satisfied the jailers. Cường didn't have a problem carving Uncle Hồ's picture, of course; he just knew that if the carving did not put Uncle Hồ in his best light, or if the jailers did not like the carving, they could take him out and shoot him. Many prisoners had lost their lives for simpler things, and he did not want to put his life at risk.

The jailers left him alone, but did not forget about the incident. He would be the last person to leave the camp.

IMMEDIATELY AFTER THE TAKEOVER, THE GOVERNMENT initiated land reforms whereby they basically took land away from major landowners and redistributed it in small parcels to common people, who were told to farm the land and give the harvest back to the government. In turn, the government paid them a certain amount of money. For many reasons, this program failed. The workers were not actual owners of the land, but rather caretakers or renters. Many of these workers were former soldiers or city dwellers—people lacking agricultural knowledge, not to mention the proper equipment. Furthermore, since they couldn't keep a fair share of the products, they didn't have incentive to work hard or tend to the land as carefully as needed.

During this time, a lot of people went hungry.

Meanwhile, the practice of religion was forbidden. All reunions, even religious gatherings, were prohibited. Churches and pagodas were closed. Anybody who dared go against the rules was deemed subversive and thrown into jail. These were difficult years under the communist regime—a time when former sympathizers began to realize the ineptitude of their new government.

With the economy in shambles and the per-capita income of postwar Việt Nam among the lowest in the world, the communist government began to soften its stance. Gradually, they realized the mistakes they were making, and they opened a small crack in the door of free enterprise. They placed a hold on the land reform, and started, slowly, to send the prisoners home.

But it took years. Physicians were jailed, on average, for two-and-a-half to three years—a long time for many of them who were in the prime years of their life, and a much longer period than the two to three days suggested by the original propaganda. The ordeal left them drained. Many had lost weight and become walking skeletons, weakened by hard labor, malnutrition, and disease acquired in the camps. They looked like scarecrows in shredded clothes, not the dignified men they'd been before their imprisonment.

Upon their release, all prisoners were given a certificate stating that the people's tribunal had found them guilty of crimes against the state, but they were fully re-educated and rehabilitated, and could go back to society to serve their new country. Many of the prisoners, however, claimed that they never went before a tribunal and were never formally charged with any crimes.

Numerous prisoners struggled to reintegrate into society after spending such a long time in the camps. Many kept a low profile for some time after the release, only to plan an escape or departure from Việt Nam. Often, they were permanently changed by the trauma; some had nervous breakdowns.

Certain released prisoners looked at their survival as a personal achievement. They had survived the worst camps, the guards, the mistreatment, the weather, the hardship, and the malnutrition. They felt if they could make it in these camps, they could survive anywhere. They were alive, they were free, and they were reunited with their families.

Frequently, the prisoners—who had lived in the open-air camps for so long—became claustrophobic when they finally arrived home. They could not get used to being confined with the four walls of their houses. Cường slept on the roof of his house for a few weeks before becoming accustomed to sleeping within four walls again.

Many people were left behind during this time. The poorest of all were the disabled South Vietnamese veterans, who, since they'd fought on the wrong side of the war, were shunned by the communists and could not work or even obtain decent medical treatment. These men who had fought for the freedom of their families, friends, and country became the neglected ones, surviving as much as they could as peddlers or beggars, or with the help of their families.

The other segment of the population that was ostracized by the Vietnamese people in these years were the Amerasians, who stood out in the crowd because of the color of their skin or their Caucasian traits. They were the product of the GIs and Vietnamese women, and they were called bụi đời, or "dust of life," by the communist propaganda. Left behind by the departing soldiers, many were not accepted by the Vietnamese community because they reminded the local people what the Americans had done to their country. They were neglected by the government, which made it difficult for them to go to school.

In reality, there were many Vietnamese people who, after the war, would feel like the dust of life. Much damage had been done to Việt Nam, and there was a lot of repairing, rebuilding, and reconciliation to do.

CHRISTINA

Hà Nội | 2006

HÀ NỘI FELT ODDLY FAMILIAR AND unfamiliar at once on my return. There were glimpses of modernity and change underneath the traditional veneer the city tried to maintain. New high-rises had popped up throughout the city, mixing in with the old French colonial style buildings, since I'd last been there. A few KFCs had opened throughout town, offering an option of white rice as a side dish instead of French fries. The fast-food chain targeted the middle-income Vietnamese and the youth who craved Western food. By that time, McDonald's had also made its way to Việt Nam, as had coffee shop chains that felt like copies of Starbucks.

I was surprised how West Lake, the area of town where Lara's aunt lived, had evolved. In two years, it had become a flourishing expat neighborhood with a plethora of stores and restaurants, a posh wine bar, and a specialty grocery store that stocked everything from Swedish crackers to Oreo cookies. I discovered a wide range of restaurants, from Thai to Indian to traditional American fare, all catering to the growing expat population. Bobby Chinn's, the restaurant near Hoàn Kiếm Lake where I used to hang out with friends during my first stint in Hà Nội, had also moved to that area. And there were plans in the works to complete a major construction project: building a road around West Lake and connecting the two sides of Hà Nội. The once-abandoned Sheraton hotel had finally been completed, and in a few short months it would accommodate George W. Bush and his staff when they attended the Asia-Pacific

Economic Cooperation (APEC) forum, to be hosted—for the first time—in Hà Nội.

I had kept the SIM card I'd used in Việt Nam before, which contained my entire address book from two years previous, making it easy for me to reconnect with friends who had stayed in Hà Nội. I relied on them to support me through the transition and help me set up the basics of my life.

Since I'd been hired from the States, I was officially an expat who had been sent to Hà Nội—no more working for free. UNICEF had arranged one-month temporary accommodation for me near the office so that I would have time to search for an apartment on my own. I was making a U.S. salary and living in Việt Nam, an accomplishment of which I was proud. I no longer needed to share a house with three or four others. I upgraded my motorbike rental from a Honda Wave to a Mio Scooter, which was easier to drive to work, especially when wearing professional attire.

A week after my arrival, I emailed my old Việt Nam friends—the ones no longer living there—and told them about how everything had changed in Hà Nội. How many coffee shops with wifi had popped up around the city. How they would hardly recognize some areas.

I beamed about the apartment I rented: a place in the south part of town that I found through a UNICEF colleague. It had tall ceilings and dark wood floors, and it was the perfect size for one person, with one bedroom and one living room and a cute little patio. I also shared an entrance with the family who lived upstairs, which made me feel more comfortable, safer.

My new neighborhood, close to Lenin Park and only a five-minute motorbike ride from my office, was perfect. I'd always been intrigued by that part of town, which had an artistic feel about it with its shaded streets and the trendy cafes targeting Vietnamese youth. At the same time, it was right around the corner from a movie theater—the first one in town to play films in English with Vietnamese subtitles—and walking distance from one of the KFCs.

Not long after moving into my new place, I ran into my friend Minh's xe ôm driver, Thăng—the one who would take him to class every single day when he lived there. Thăng sweetly asked me about Minh, and if I could bring him fruit when I returned to the States. I didn't want to break the news to him that the States was a big place—nothing like Hà Nội, where you could deliver fruit to all your friends, where you could find everyone easily on the same corner, or the same neighborhood, where you'd left them a few years earlier.

I DIDN'T COMMUNICATE DIRECTLY WITH MY new landlords but rather with their nephew, Đất, a fast-talking Vietnamese businessman who always seemed ready to make a deal and prided himself on his ability to find solutions for all his customers.

He dressed casually, in faded jeans and polo shirts, and was average height for a Vietnamese man. He wore his straight black hair longer than most Vietnamese men and combed it over to the side.

In his enterprising fashion, Đất had refurbished his aunt and uncle's building and created apartments targeting expats, mainly Japanese expats. Unlike many other landlords in Hà Nội, he quickly picked up what foreigners wanted in a rental home—no fluorescent lighting, a kitchen with new appliances, and modern furniture, even if it was cheaply made. He'd found a way to affordably design appealing homes that he could rent out quickly and maximize his profits.

"Just tell me whatever you want—I can find for you," he said to me in his imperfect English.

He was baffled about why I would take the apartment I chose and not take one of the apartments he had renovated upstairs. "Come see the other apartments I have upstairs," he said to me. "They are much nicer, newer. You'll like those better."

But I liked my smaller, older apartment. I found the faded dark wood floors and worn-down vintage armoires and television stands attractive; I wanted to sand them down and paint them to give them a vintage feel. I asked him about old furniture stores, wanting to find more furniture that I could do the same with.

"Buy new furniture, Tuyết," he insisted. "No Vietnamese person wants the old things. They want new things. And you want old furniture? It's so ugly."

"It's called charm," I tried to explain to him.

When my whole apartment was finished—furnished with a mixture of the old pieces left over from Đất's family and a few contemporary pieces, including a modern white couch that I had made and different-size lacquered cubes that my friend had made for me—and Đất came to see it, he finally understood the vision I'd been working toward.

"At first I think you crazy. "But now I understand. I know what you mean by that—charm."

While I could see that Việt Nam was becoming modernized and I appreciated the ways that Hà Nội was developing, I yearned for the charming Hà Nội I'd known when I moved there for my internship. I could understand that this was a delicate balance, very much like my apartment: finding the sweet spot between the modern and the traditional, the conveniences and the charm.

RETURNING TO HÀ NỘI FELT LIKE a natural progression, career-wise—from being an intern at UNDP to a position as a communications officer at UNICEF. My new colleagues, some of whom I knew from UNDP, greeted me warmly. I even knew one of the two other members of the team I'd be working on: our national communications officer, Phương. I'd met her before when she worked with my former roommates at the Việt Nam News.

"Welcome back, chị Tuyết," one colleague in the unit said to me.

I didn't know if I had met him before, so I gave him a quizzical look, and said, "Did we use to work together?"

"Yes, I remember when you were here before," he said with a broad smile. "I thought that you might come back."

I had received similar responses from others throughout the office who had heard about my return. Some of their compliments touched me: one said I had impressed him the first time he met me, and he hoped that I would continue to work for the United Nations.

It was as if they knew better than I did that Việt Nam, and Hà Nội in particular, was still a large part of my path.

I returned as *chị*, meaning older sister, whereas the last time I was in Hà Nội I had more frequently been addressed as *em*, the younger sister. I felt that being *chị* suited me this time around, and I was ready for what Việt Nam had in store for me.

I still loved the way my name sounded in Vietnamese, especially with the newness of being a *chị. Chị Tuyết*—there was a gentleness in the way it was pronounced that was so different from the way non-native Vietnamese speakers said my name.

I'd often told people that my middle name meant "snow," but was corrected by my colleague, who informed me that my full Vietnamese name referred to the glistening part, or the sparkles, in the snow.

I FREQUENTLY RAN INTO FRIENDS AND acquaintances from my previous time in Hà Nội. I bumped into Sam (my former crush), as I was walking into an Italian restaurant with a bag of pillows from a local store. I had always admired him professionally for his focus and commitment to his work, but also creatively: he designed his own furniture, acted in plays put on by an expatriate group, and had painted murals on the walls of his house. I finally felt like I was on a solid path, but I hadn't yet begun to explore my creative side. I didn't even feel like I had any creative passions.

When he saw me, we spoke briefly about my work and the past few years.

"You've grown up," he said.

Those words, coming from him, meant a lot to me. Deep down, I understood that my interest in him reflected what I desired to become: a creative, successful professional.

I wanted to believe that I had changed, and that this time around, Việt Nam would be a deeper, richer experience—not the fleeting love affair it had been before.

WHAT I APPRECIATED ABOUT LIVING IN Hà Nội (and maybe this is one of the reasons I returned), was that my Vietnamese friends and colleagues treated me like family. They knew that I ventured to Việt Nam alone, so they offered support whenever they could. When I was sick, my Vietnamese colleagues would text me and ask if I wanted them to bring me soup. In the States, especially in a city like San Francisco, even my closest friends didn't offer to bring me food when I wasn't feeling well. If I managed to see a good friend once a month there, it seemed like an achievement. In Hà Nội, I saw my friends constantly. I felt nourished by these connections that made me feel I was living beyond the surface level.

My Vietnamese teacher, cô Yên, felt more like an aunt than a teacher. She would come to the office for a one-hour lesson during lunch, but often allowed me to eschew the Vietnamese lesson in favor of asking her advice. I still, unfortunately, didn't have the drive to completely tackle the Vietnamese language.

"You know some of the other Việt Kiều," cô Yên said one day. "They didn't speak Vietnamese growing up either. But they focus, they study, and they get better. You could be good but you don't want to."

I knew she was right. There was a reluctance within me to study Vietnamese, although I knew I had more natural ability than those who had not grown up hearing it in the background of their homes.

Cô Yên had firm opinions about everything we spoke about, from jobs to romance. I shared with her all my ideas for short stories, arriving at our lessons with character sketches rather than my completed Vietnamese homework.

"I'd like to write about this year in Việt Nam," I told her.

"You can do it, but then you have to pay close attention to the people around you," she responded. "You are not meant to be in an office, Christina. You should find something different because this type of work takes away from your personality."

Every week, she also asked me about my father.

"Have you spoken to your dad?"

"We don't speak that much," I'd say with a shrug. "I told you that already."

"But he's alone and you're his daughter," she'd press. "You should go be with him. I think that if he comes back to Việt Nam that he'll feel better, he'll feel complete again. He has a hole in his heart because he lost Việt Nam."

I knew she was right; he did have a hole in his heart, one that I didn't fully understand. But I started to recognize the hole I had within my own heart and was busy trying to fill it—through my ventures to Việt Nam, through my work, through my own perpetual search. I couldn't help my father with the hole in his heart until I had healed my own.

NGHĨA
Connecticut | 1980

ALTHOUGH I HAD WRITTEN A FEW papers in Việt Nam, I thought that writing an academic paper and having it published in the U.S. would be more difficult than anywhere in the world. One day while I was on call, I took care of a patient who came through the emergency room with cold feet. A mushy material, unlike normal blood clots, was removed from the patient's blood vessels. The foreign substance was later diagnosed as fungal material that had originated from the valves of the patient's heart.

The case was so original that I decided to write it up. I looked for similar cases at the hospital in the past. I went through all the log-books but didn't find any cases like this one. My heart beat faster and faster, as I asked the librarian to look for all published works related to this problem. Worldwide, I found forty-three similar cases; I analyzed the causes, the differences, the presentation, and the treatment of all these cases. Then I developed a summary and started writing a paper.

Around the same time, I received a notification from the Society of University Surgeons advising me about their next meeting and announcing that they were accepting abstract submissions from residents. I followed the printed instructions, typed an abstract, and mailed it in. Six weeks later, much to my surprise, I received a letter notifying me that my abstract had been accepted and informing me of the timing and location of the presentation.

I was stunned. Never before had a resident in my program been invited to present a paper at a national level. I read the letter repeatedly to make sure that I was not dreaming. I put the letter back in its envelope, took it home, and left it on my desk. That night, I pulled out the letter and read it again. Satisfied, I went to sleep.

It took me three days to recognize the importance of that letter. Finally, I brought it to the chief of surgery, who congratulated me and said, "Now is the important part of the project: you need to write the paper up. Bring it to my assistant and he will help you with the presentation."

I followed his instructions. The assistant chief told me that I could either read the presentation from three-by-six-inch notecards, or memorize it. I decided to read the cards, and I reviewed them repeatedly, trying to perfect my speech.

THAT YEAR, THE SOCIETY'S MEETING TOOK place in Hershey, Pennsylvania. I drove by myself through New York State and then to Pennsylvania. I learned that Milton Hershey, the candy maker, had built his factory in that area some 100 years earlier. He'd become so rich that he'd also built a medical center in his name. As I toured the town, I noticed the Hershey Park, the factory, and the streets lined with silver Hershey kiss–shaped streetlights.

The residents's presentations were delivered a day before the main meeting, so there weren't too many guests in the hotel. The eighty to ninety papers were given simultaneously in four different rooms, with ten minutes allocated for each presentation. The topics included basic laboratory research, clinical investigation, and case studies.

When my turn came, I felt my chest tighten and wondered how my findings would be received.

I walked to the podium and started presenting the paper. I flashed the slides, introduced the case, and reviewed the other cases described in the literature. I read the conclusion and thanked the Society for allowing me to present the paper.

There was the usual applause, followed by questions from the audience. After answering each question, I took a deep breath, returned to my seat, and listened to the next paper, feeling satisfied with my work.

By the time I was driving home from Pennsylvania, I'd made up my mind: I would have at least one paper accepted every year. By the end of my training, I had eight published papers to my name—more than any other resident at my institution had ever done.

AFTER FIVE YEARS OF TRAINING, THE end had finally arrived. I applied for a two-year training program in cardiac surgery but was given a spot on a three-year program. That was too long to stay in training and turned it down. Financial factors also figured into the decision. Lyne urged me to go into private practice, since my first-year salary would be two to three times higher than it would be if I remained a resident.

At graduation, I received a plaque listing my name, my years of training, and the name of the hospital. The other graduating resident and myself gave short speeches thanking the program director, the hospital staff, and our wives. The chief of surgery handed me a sketch of my portrait, with the inscription "The Sài Gòn Scholar." In many ways, I felt that I had made it.

I went on to a critical care fellowship in New York, which I commuted to from Connecticut every single day, and wrote and submitted a few more papers during that time.

When that fellowship was done, I headed to Utah for another one-year research fellowship. I had never seen the Rocky Mountains or that part of the country before. The first day I got to explore my new surroundings, I stood in awe of the majestic and colorful landscapes, feeling inspired by how far I'd come—from Việt Nam to this country, which had afforded me so many opportunities.

CHRISTINA
Hà Nội | 2006

THERE WAS SOMETHING DEEPER THAT I was searching for in Việt Nam during my second visit. Four years before, I thought it was about not wanting to be part of corporate America and a longing to understand my family history. But there was more beneath the surface: layers that I was peeling away. This time in Hà Nội I was just two years older than my father when he left for the U.S. Our paths were vastly different: for me, going to Việt Nam was a choice, not something I was forced to do. For my father, he fled the communist regime to begin a life in a new country, leaving behind the motherland. In comparison, I knew that I possessed the privilege of luxury based on the stable life my father had created for us.

The first six months of my job at UNICEF was a constant adrenaline rush—a quite unusual experience working with a UN agency. We had a limited period to spend a significant amount of money the Japanese government had donated to UNICEF in order to implement a national communications campaign raising awareness about prevention methods for the spread of H1N1, or bird flu. It was a complete whirlwind, working with UN agencies and government counterparts to prepare communications materials for the general public, as well as specific audiences like poultry farmers, health workers, teachers, and public health officials.

During that time, our team of four lost our permanent home within a department in the organization when my boss suffered from a stroke. His responsibilities were delegated to management in other departments, and waves of bureaucracy overtook our work: suddenly, the communications we were producing required input and approval from several people.

When my boss returned to the office after his medical leave, he noticed significant changes in me, and I saw them myself. I was burned out from the intense period of work, but I was also deflated by the change in our responsibilities: I felt that as we were becoming less busy, the job increasingly entailed nothing more than writing reports and paper pushing.

"You used to have so much energy for the job, Christina," my boss said. "Now, it just seems like you see a black hole in front of you. You should use your creativity to find solutions to these problems."

I didn't know what, exactly, had changed within me; what I was yearning for; why I wasn't satisfied with my job and life in Hà Nội. It was the same pattern I'd experienced in the past, and I desperately wanted to rid myself of it. It was as if a wave of discontent over-whelmed me and, as my boss had suggested, there was a black hole in front of me. I had achieved what I'd sought: I was an expat in Việt Nam with a good job and benefits. So why didn't I feel satisfied?

FORTUNATELY, I HAD GOOD FRIENDS WHO tried to help me through these times. One such friend was Yoshiko, a Japanese woman who was conducting research for the World Bank and would on occasion spend a few months at a time in Hà Nội. Yoshiko was grounded, content, and focused—the opposite of who I felt I was at the time.

I texted her one morning and asked if we could meet for dim sum at one of the luxury hotels near West Lake.

"I just feel empty inside," I admitted to her as we sat across from one another.

When she probed me further, about what this meant, I said I didn't know. "I just feel . . . disconnected and disengaged," I said, unable to explain any better than that.

Months later, when I went on a trip with Yoshiko and her husband to Hội An in central Việt Nam, an idea occurred to me that I shared with them: I want to write a book about Việt Nam, about my family's story. The idea appeared out of nowhere. I dabbled in writing, specifically I blogged for a while after returning to Hà Nội, and an editor of a Vietnamese magazine in San Jose had expressed interest in publishing my stories about living in Việt Nam as a Vietnamese American—though I'd never actually submitted anything to him. But I did not consider myself a "real" writer.

ANOTHER EXPATRIATE FRIEND AND I SPOKE at length about my desire to discover a different field and explore my creativity. She was ten years older than me and also navigated the delicate balance of a professional and creative life. She mentioned a home furnishings store, Element, near West Lake, and said the Vietnamese owner of the store was incredibly talented and hoped to implement new creative ideas in Hà Nội.

I'd never considered Hà Nội to be bustling with creative energy; there was certainly a palpable sense of forward movement that was pervasive in Việt Nam, but I hadn't seen an abundance of original products and ideas. My ears perked up.

One afternoon, depleted after a day of what had become the monotony of my job, I decided to visit Element. Surprised when I walked in, I saw the mixture of beautifully curated antique items. I had not seen a store quite like it in Hà Nội. A few stores offered modern furniture, or at least copies of items found in Western home magazines that foreigners selected to be copied—something the Vietnamese did quite well. Element, though, was completely unique, with modern lacquer cubes in different colors used as end tables, antiques including old vases and tables, and a modern lamp the owner had made out of a conical hat.

I walked to the back of the store, where a woman—the owner, I assumed—sat in front of a long wooden table. She had chin-length hair and wore a slight frown. Dressed in stylish linen clothes that dwarfed her small frame, she seemed cold and distant, but also in possession of an understated style and confidence that I immediately respected.

"I love your store," I said as I approached her desk. "A friend of mine told me to come here. I'm Christina."

"Hi, I'm Phúc," she introduced herself.

I sat down in the seat in front of her and immediately started talking about the lacquer cubes, which I loved.

"Why don't you try exporting these?" I asked, gesturing to them.

"Yes, I thought about it," she said. "But first, I'm trying to create a space in Hà Nội for people to create. I am opening a design studio and showroom where I can have exhibits."

I nodded enthusiastically. "I think you can do it. It doesn't seem like there's anything like it in Hà Nội."

She mentioned that she was hosting a party to launch her new studio on Sunday, invited me to attend, and handed me a small flyer with the details. I left feeling excited about the new connection I'd made.

WHEN I WENT TO THE EVENT, Phúc was fully in her element. She did not come across as distant or aloof, as she had in her store. She was smiling, laughing, and entertaining everyone in the room. Her studio was also her apartment, and I sensed her creative spirit the second I walked through the door. It was a simple apartment, yet she had divided the open floor plan into different seating areas, decorated with traditional materials that gave the spaces incredible depth. The whole apartment could have easily been photographed for a design magazine.

Many of the people there were staff from the embassies, but there were also local Vietnamese people who seemed to all be creatives of some sort. The Greek Ambassador was there, exhibiting some of his sculptures. She asked me to give the introduction to the event, and while I initially said yes, when it was time for me to speak, I backed out. A timidness arose within me when I entered the space.

Later in the evening, when only a few of Phúc's friends remained at the party and things were winding down, I learned more about her story. She told me that she had no formal design training, but had decided, at the age of thirty, to quit her job at Air France and pursue something truer to her heart.

"I had no choice," she told me. "I felt that I couldn't stay in that office one more day."

What she said resonated with me. I was now in my late twenties, nearly the same age Phúc had been when she ventured off on her own. I was beginning to feel stifled by my job, by the UNICEF offices—the very same feeling I'd had at the beginning of my career at the pharmaceutical company.

Phúc said that she started out at her first store by simply selling items she thought were beautiful. After a while, she began to dabble in clothing design. Eventually, she reached the point where she was now: decorating the homes of expats, building her own home furnishing line, and creating her own aesthetic in a country that had just started to develop an understanding of the term "interior design."

Later, as I started to visit with Phúc after work and got to know her better, I learned she had also defied the traditional ideas of a Vietnamese family. She'd had a daughter with a Vietnamese man who was thirty years older than her, knowing that this man did not want to raise the child with her. Her parents had warned her that it was a bad idea, but she'd kept the child and raised her alone while simultaneously building her business.

I had never met a woman like Phúc—someone who had truly defined and created her own path. I looked forward to the time we could spend together, where I also began to learn more about design and Phúc's vision. In her own designs, she wanted to maintain the essence of what was Vietnamese while adding in the elements of modernity that she found appealing.

Phúc introduced me to a Buddhist community—or sangha—that followed in the Buddhist tradition of Thích Nhất Hạnh, a Buddhist monk born in Việt Nam in 1926 who began practicing at the age of sixteen. He was a tireless advocate for peace and nonviolence and lived in exile in France for most of his life, having been banned from returning to Việt Nam. The community was founded and led by an American woman in her sixties who, five years prior, had packed up her bags and decided to venture to Việt Nam. While visiting, she met a man who insisted that she stay, and she did, ultimately creating a spiritual community following Thích Nhất Hạnh.

Through the sangha, I met other spiritual seekers from around the world: all of us who had for distinct reasons landed in Hà Nội, not only searching for another land to temporarily call home but also a sense of inner peace—a spiritual home so to speak. I quickly realized Phúc was one of the most modern, progressive, and spiritual women I had ever met—not just in Việt Nam, but anywhere. Soon, I was attending the meditation nights at the sangha with her every Tuesday and Thursday evening. I would first stop at her store, and then we would drive together to meet the sangha.

Those evenings, which would end up being some of my fondest memories of living there, helped to silence the incessant thoughts running through my mind about what I was doing and where I was going. I remembered how my father had mentioned meditation to me during my time back in the States; perhaps he, like Phúc, saw this need for me to quiet my mind and see what would emerge from peace. By sitting in meditation regularly, I saw within me that desire to flee and to leave the moment when things started to become uncomfortable, or even boring. My awareness of this pattern grew while I sat but I was not yet sure what to do about it.

Coincidentally, at the sangha, I also bumped into Thanh, whom I'd befriended when I was an intern at UNDP. She had left her job at UNDP and was planning to study human rights in Singapore, which had always been a dream of hers. She was still as strongly opinionated as before; the work at the UN agencies, she said, was more than anything political, though in theory it was about the people. I found myself agreeing with her.

My conversations with Phúc and Thanh reinforced my thoughts that this UNICEF job was no longer right for me—that I needed to pursue something that would light me up inside.

Shortly thereafter, I decided that I couldn't stay at UNICEF, that even if that path offered stability and potentially a unique career, I had to define and create my own future based on what was right and true to me, just like Phúc and Thanh were doing.

The challenge here, of course, was that I didn't yet know what was true to me; I was still in the discovery process. So, for the time being—once again—the only true thing I knew for sure was that I had to leave.

NGHĨA
Tennessee | 1985-1991

AFTER YEARS OF TRAINING, I FINALLY went into practice in the eastern part of Tennessee—an area filled with majestic mountains covered in luxurious vegetation. Compared to the desert and the mountainous flora of Utah, Tennessee seemed like a tropical forest to me. The town where we settled was tucked away against the northern slopes of the mountain range, a continuation of the Appalachian Mountains, and it remained more isolated and rugged and less advanced than many areas in the state. During all seasons, the views of the mountains were magnificent. In spring, the hills were covered with flowering trees, from pink and white dogwoods to purple and pinkish rhododendrons to wild mountain flowers.

I drove with Lyne and my daughters, who were born during my training in Connecticut, to the mountains almost every weekend to appreciate the variety of blooms on display and see Mother Nature under different lights. In the summer, when we passed along the winding roads that curved alongside the mountain, suddenly ascended, then dropped down abruptly, I drank in the views of the small villages in the valley below, as well as the fresh mountain air. Nothing was more beautiful than the fall, when diverse shades and colors dotted the sides of the mountains, the scenery varying depending on the mixture of trees and the speed with which the leaves were changing their colors. I felt a strange sensation while driving beneath a canopy of brown, yellow, red, and green leaves, pierced intermittently by blue sky and golden rays of sunshine. In the winter months, there was an unspeakable eeriness in the air. Roads became deserted and the mountain slopes were covered with white powder. Columns of gray smoke crept from the chimneys down in the valley, making their lazy, serpentine way upward. Tall pine trees, their branches curved under heavy loads of snow, stuck out in the midst of the white scenery. The landscape was majestically peaceful and magical. Life came to a standstill while Nature decided to take a break.

Nature reminded me of where I was in my own life at that time: We had weathered so many seasons by this point that our time in Tennessee was about recollection, renewal, and rebuilding. Worn out by so many years of training, my family and I were finally able to take it easy.

MY NEW WORK WAS RELATIVELY EASY, and the salary was acceptable for a federal job. I spent some time in the academic surgery environment at East Tennessee State University, which was fun because I was able to be with students. We had an opportunity to prepare different topics for discussion, then teach these lessons to students for a period of six to eight weeks. With such a short period of time in surgery, many students couldn't make up their minds about whether or not they wanted to go into the surgical field. Some were repulsed by the long working hours, the regimented schedule, and the endless time holding retractors. (I empathized; I was quite glad that period of my own life was complete.) Others, though, felt that surge of adrenaline when they reached the operating room that had led many of us into the specialty in the first place.

Research was also part of the curriculum and could be conducted on animals or humans. The university provided us with the volume and mixture of patients necessary to pursue this work, making it possible to conduct comparative studies about the efficacy of a certain treatment. Good results were stimulating, but rare. For so many scientists, research yielding inconclusive results proved frustrating.

A struggle accompanied being both a researcher and physician at the same time. Caring for patients required a lot of dedication. I could spend endless hours checking on the progress of patients. But researchers had to work day in and day out as well, in the laboratory and the classroom. I had to strike a delicate balance.

During this time, I did have two of my research submissions funded by the VA Research Advisory Group and the National Institutes of Health (NIH); the latter was a highly competitive grant, with only 10 to 15 percent of the submissions receiving funding.

There is no way to describe my elation when I was first notified that I had won the NIH grant. I felt vindicated as a researcher; my work was being deemed worthy by my peers. It was my reward for all those long hours in the laboratories, clinging to the faint hope that one day my work would be acknowledged. It also meant job security for a few more years.

MEANWHILE, IN CALIFORNIA, MY MOTHER AND brothers went through sometimes difficult times but they were relieved that they no longer had to worry about the "midnight roundup" and my mother constantly reminded them to earn their college degrees and become self-sufficient. I sent my brother Tiến, who had finished medical school before leaving Việt Nam, all the books he needed to take his equivalency test; he also volunteered at the Loma Linda Medical Center in order to become familiar with the medical community.

After obtaining his equivalency degree, Tiến did a residency in pediatrics, which was what he had studied while in Việt Nam. He entered academia, and after a few years went into practice with a major health care organization in California. Eventually, however, feeling shortchanged by the system, he opened his own practice. While the first few years were difficult, he worked nonstop, always making himself available to his patients and referring physicians, and soon his medical practice was flourishing. Throughout that time, my mother and he lived together.

Quảng and Huy, the twins, continued their studies at the local college. Quảng had some of his own worries during that time. His girlfriend, Thu, and her family had also recently escaped Việt Nam, but they had gotten no farther than a camp in Thailand. Quảng didn't have any money to help them out, and during the time in camp, Thu's mother became ill and passed away. The family spent more time in the camp before finally being sponsored to come to the United States. Thu's father became ill on the journey over, however, and died in a hospital in Japan where he was taken for treatment. Both their parents gone, only Thu and her sister arrived in Little Sài Gòn in Southern California. Against my mother's suggestion, Quảng moved out and quit school, saying he wanted to run a private business. He only returned once in a while for visits, and nobody knew where he lived.

Huy went to college, took some time off, and then finally graduated with a dentistry degree, after which he got married and moved out. His wife also studied dentistry and opened her own practice, where Huy ended up working as an office manager.

My family visited them only a few times over the years; we were busy settling into our own lives in the States, on practically the opposite side of the country.

A CHILD OF VIỆT NAM

A CHILD OF VIETNAM

CHRISTINA
Virginia | 2008

I ARRIVED AT DULLES AIRPORT SIX weeks before Christmas, planning to stay with my father for at least a few weeks. I wasn't sure what to expect but I needed a bit of a respite before heading back to Việt Nam once again.

When I decided to leave UNICEF and also Việt Nam the second time, I met a Swedish man who was at the tail end of a research project. He moved to Brussels for a short-term contract, and we started dating long-distance. I ended up visiting him for a month, and while the relationship was imperfect, I landed a job in Geneva, in part to be closer to him. About a month after I arrived there, we broke up, and I found myself wondering what I was doing in Switzerland. I fell in love with another man, someone I worked with; that relationship also failed and left me heartbroken. I imagined this was a similar heartache to what my father felt with Alice, and yet, we were never able to commiserate about our broken hearts.

That was my lowest point in my twenties, when the emptiness I'd experienced in Hà Nội only seemed to expand. I decided to leave Geneva, and I didn't have a real plan, but fortunately landed a short-term consulting contract that would bring me back to Việt Nam once again. By this point, Việt Nam felt more like home than any other place in the world.

One of my tender-hearted ex-colleagues in Geneva, a Japanese woman who knew my story and my relationship with my father, asked why I didn't use this opportunity, this moment in which I didn't have a tangible plan, to spend time with my father. "You never know when you'll have this chance again," she said. I saw her point which prompted me to make the decision to spend a month at his home in Northern Virginia.

When I wrote to my father, asking if I could stay with him, I didn't explain the context or the reasons behind my decision to leave Geneva, or to come see him. He didn't ask questions; he simply responded, *You're always welcome to come home, for as long as you want.*

At that time, I couldn't see my father for the kind person he was; I only saw the ways in which I felt he had failed me. I blamed him for not being able to help me more, or, rather, save me, from this unknowable sadness. In a sense, I was frustrated with him for a role he could never fill—that of my mother.

THE AIRPORT WAS ALREADY ADORNED WITH holiday décor—fake green wreaths and red bows—and Starbucks, unsurprisingly, had its holiday beverages—peppermint mocha and eggnog latte—clearly displayed on the counter.

For a moment, I thought my father might be late. Then, I saw him in the distance, walking through the gates slowly, wearing a familiar navy-blue hooded sweatshirt and a pair of gray trousers that he'd had for years. He had not changed in this way: I knew he only purchased new clothing out of absolute necessity.

I quickly put together my belongings—shoving a notepad in my purse, shutting my computer and enclosing it in its case—and rose to meet him.

When he approached me, I noticed his visible age—the skin around his face had begun to sag, his gray hair was thinning, and a persistent cough interrupted his speech. He was not the distant parent I'd grown up with; he was now becoming an older man, one who I imagined considered time more carefully.

"So, have you been waiting long?" he asked me with a gentle pat on the shoulder.

"Not long," I said. "Was there a lot of traffic?"

"Yes. It took me a long time to get here."

When we reached the car, my father picked up my two suitcases—the same ones that I'd traveled with for years—to put them in the trunk. As a teenager, after my mother's death, I imagined moving through the world lightly, with just two bags, so as not to be weighed down by roots that might prevent me from leaving whenever I felt like going. I'd been traveling that way ever since.

My father, who looked neither weak nor strong, moved his atlas and small cooler aside, making room for my suitcases. There would come a time, I knew, when he wouldn't even be able to carry my bags for me.

We shared an empty but comfortable silence in the car for a while; then he began talking about the things he deemed important, like where a new road was being built, or the expansion of the metro from Dulles to the center of DC. His attempt at chit-chat. But he never asked me the questions I longed for him to ask—why did you leave, how do you feel, do you need help with anything, who are the people in your life? That wasn't how we communicated.

He pointed out a building where, he said, he'd given a talk about Việt Nam. I wondered what was different now; why could he openly talk about Việt Nam today, when he had declined the invitation by my high school history teacher to speak to our class? Maybe it was because he was now living closer to other Vietnamese Americans. Maybe that was allowing him to recognize a part of himself he'd thought was long since lost. Perhaps he had started to heal, or had already healed, from the losses he'd faced in his life—his son, my mother, Alice, and his biggest loss, Việt Nam.

"Are you hungry?" my father asked. "Do you want to stop and eat Vietnamese food? There's nothing to eat at home."

"Yes, sure," I told him.

We normally stopped at a restaurant off Highway 7 in a shopping plaza where there was a Borders, a Japanese restaurant, and a kids' dance studio. But this time we stopped at a restaurant only about five minutes away from his house.

A Vietnamese woman, who I assumed was in her late forties, greeted us when we walked through the door.

My father spoke to her in Vietnamese, causing her to smile, and showing a softness that I'd never witnessed in him when he spoke English. There was a level of comfort, familiarity, a mutual recognition I noticed when he interacted with a fellow Vietnamese.

He became curious, asking where her family was from, how long she lived in the area and if she owned the restaurant. He charmed her with his questions and attentiveness, intermixed with a subtle distance, which I figured made him even more attractive to this woman.

"Anh, sống ở đây?"—*Do you live here?* —she asked my father.

"Anh ở đấy mấy năm rồi"—*I've been here many years now*—he responded. "Ở đây món ăn gi ngon nhất?"—*Which dish is best here?*

"Anh, phải anh món ăn đặc biệt Huế"—*You should eat one of the Huế specials*—she responded.

She brought two glasses of ice water to the table, looked down, and smiled at my father.

"I'm going to New York after this, then I'll stay a couple weeks with a friend in D.C.," I told him. "My friend Kim is going to come visit too. I'll probably go to Chicago in January. Maybe go see Teresa."

"But why are you going around so much?" he asked. "You should rest."

"Because I want to see my friends and there's nothing to do around your place. I don't know anyone. Do you think you could drive me to my friend's place in D.C.?"

"Sure, just let me know when," he said.

"Have you tried this restaurant before?" I asked him, changing the subject.

"No," he said. "It's too close to home for me to try."

I felt similarly about my life at that moment. I didn't see much value in exploring what was close to home. I felt that everything worth knowing was out there in the world, in places like Việt Nam and Switzerland, and never close to home.

MY FATHER WAS SETTLING WHILE I was still searching for a place to call home. The small town he'd purchased a home in reminded me of the towns I'd grown up in. Towns which, as an adult, I never would have gravitated toward myself. For my father, however, it seemed that the familiar setting—generic shopping plazas, large chain grocery stores, the single street downtown, all within a five-minute drive from where he lived—provided the necessities and the comfort he needed to sustain his life. He didn't seem to need to interact with the town he lived in. We differed in that way—what we sought and needed from our direct environment was quite distinct. That much was clear to me now.

The house my father finally purchased, fifteen minutes away from the apartment he initially rented, didn't resemble a home I would have imagined him buying, or even liking, in the past. The exterior, with its white paneling and forward-facing garage, stood in a row of indistinguishable houses. The interior—or, rather, its contents—did feel oddly like home, though. The white walls, meticulously placed furniture, and unused space created a certain silent ambiance I'd come to identify with home. The furniture reflected different periods in his life—the old pieces we'd shopped for and bought together on our weekend excursions when I was a child in Tennessee alongside the more Asian-looking pieces Alice had purchased. He'd gotten rid of some items during the move, like the paisley couch that used to anchor life in our living room and his large paintings of flowers and sailboats (he said he'd given them to one of his former secretaries).

In the entryway, he'd hung an array of colorful lanterns, all different sizes and shapes, that I'd brought back from Hội An, a picturesque touristy town in central Hà Nội, after my first move to Việt Nam. On the arms of the living room sofa, which I was certain he'd never used, were two white blankets with different-colored squares that my mother had crocheted when she was sick; she'd passed many hours alone, knitting and crocheting, during that time. In the corner of the dining room, next to the window, there was a small table with a few plants on it, and I noticed that there was a piece of flowered paper, with a note written in Alice's handwriting, taped to the side of one of the plants: *If you love something, let it go. If it comes back to you, then it's yours forever. If it doesn't, then it was never yours to begin with.*

That house was a carefully curated space, the culmination of his life, from his years with our family to his time with Alice. He had pared down the items he surrounded himself with. I wondered but didn't dare ask if he had kept the albums of slides he'd kept for so many years—photos he had taken throughout our childhood. Were they hidden somewhere, maybe in a box in the basement? Or had he thrown them out?

In my room, on the second floor in the far corner of the house, he had replaced my old twin-size bed with a queen-size bed. He'd arranged my tennis trophies on the top of the oak dresser, and put the angel figurines given to me by a high school friend's mother after my mom passed away on a small shelf. Whatever leftover clothing I had in the house was neatly put away in the drawers; old prom dresses hung in the closet; and boxes of memories, including love letters, yearbooks, and photos from high school and college, were stacked neatly. A *Miss Sài Gòn* poster that I'd bought when I went to see the show in New York with my college boyfriend hung above my bed.

The only item I removed immediately was my mother's paisley comforter, which I associated with the time she was sick. I scoured the house looking for another one to replace it.

The refrigerator, despite what my father had said to me when we returned from the airport, was just as full as it always was. Tightly tied plastic bags filled with Vietnamese food, usually two bowls of pho and two portions of bún thịt nướng, took over most of the shelf space. He cut up fruit for himself, whatever was in season, put the pieces in containers, and filled a lot of the remaining shelf space with those. He cooked substantial meals for himself now, not what I'd remembered him cooking—the packaged stir-fried noodles and lạp xưởng. Now he seemed more conscious of his health and prepared hearty meals, even pasta dishes, with an array of vegetables. He kept a soup, something simple like tofu and tomato, on the stove, and ate it throughout the day. Whenever he came down to eat, he didn't sit at the table. Instead, he either stood at the counter, staring out of the kitchen window, or sat on a stool at the counter.

I soon learned that a woman I'd never met before bought him Vietnamese food and brought it to him regularly. I wasn't sure if it was the same friend who had advised him to move to Northern Virginia, or if it was another friend he'd made over the years. Whenever she came over, he'd go outside to sit with her in the car, then return with the plastic bags full of Vietnamese food that would sustain us for the week. I knew that he spoke to her every day; even in my previous visits there I'd heard him on the phone, speaking Vietnamese. Her number showed up on the caller ID as a Virginia number, with no name. I saved the number in case a time ever came when I didn't hear from my father. It was comforting to know that someone called him every night to check in on him—that the responsibility was not left to me, which I might have otherwise assumed, even though my father never asked anything of me.

From my bedroom window, I saw his new friend once. She was "điệu," (a Vietnamese term describing someone who puts a lot of attention on their appearance) like my mother, with short black hair that I imagined she curled with rollers every morning. She and my father stood next to one another, chatting, and I realized that she was much shorter and less slender than Alice. She wore a black silk round-neck top with a flowered print and flowing white áo dài pants, as if she'd just returned from a Vietnamese event.

He never introduced me to her or even mentioned her to me while I was there, and still has not to this day—just as we never talk about my mom or Alice, although I'm certain that memories of these women remain in the minds and hearts of both of us.

OVER THE YEARS, I WATCHED MY father incorporate more Vietnamese community into his life, something that he'd mostly lived without in southern Indiana. He began attending reunions with his former medical school classmates and traveling with other Vietnamese friends. Not that he shared any details about these things; I only knew this because of the pictures of him and people who seemed like they were his friends propped up next to the phone in the kitchen. In one photo, they were all dressed up in cocktail attire to celebrate what I believe was the end of a conference. In another image, my father, who never smiled broadly, looked content, maybe even happy.

My father, I started to see, was truly a man of reinvention. He also founded his own nonprofit related to Việt Nam, with a mission to raise awareness about the Vietnamese American experience.

"Many people don't understand us here," he'd once explained to me in a strong, passionate tone uncommon for him. "We work on raising awareness of the Vietnamese American diaspora. What life is like for Vietnamese Americans who now live in the States."

Through the nonprofit, he collaborated with Vietnamese Americans around the country, on essays and anthologies, covering their stories of imprisonment, reeducation, their journey as boat people and how they redefined themselves in their new countries. Occasionally, he asked me to contribute writings about my experiences in Việt Nam. I agreed each time, albeit reluctantly. I was unaccustomed to my father asking for anything from me, even a short story about Việt Nam. In recent years, perhaps as a way to heal, process or simply pass time, he had also begun to write books about Việt Nam, mostly covering its history. The list was exhaustive.

With his nonprofit, he also developed his own annual conference, where he invited speakers from around the country to talk about the Việt Nam War. I'd never observed him work with such passion and conviction.

He never told me the details of what it was like to rebuild his life as a man in his late fifties, and only as I aged would my respect for him deepen. I was too focused on my own personal journey to pay close attention to his. I didn't recognize how similar we were—and not just physically.

Through academic friends of mine, I learned that my father had joined a University of Minnesota Listserv on which professors and students engaged in debates about Vietnamese history and culture.

"Is your father, Nghĩa Võ?" a friend had asked me one time while I was in Việt Nam. We hadn't seen one another in a while and were catching up in Việt Nam.

"Yes," I responded, confused why she would know his name.

"I thought so but wasn't sure," she said. "He makes a lot of comments on our listserv. He has strong opinions."

"But, how much does he write? What does he write?" I asked her curiously.

"A lot—he always writes a lot," she said. "I wouldn't say he has much support from others who are part of the group. He has a certain perspective about what happened in Việt Nam. But I think people respect that he speaks his mind and he represents a certain perspective that's specific to that generation."

I couldn't imagine my father, the quiet man, asserting his opinions. I also feared him being in a space, even virtually, where he was not heard or seen by others. Sadness overtook me as I tried to grasp a part of my father that I had never known, or even explored. While I didn't feel I understood my father completely, I also couldn't bear the thought of him being misunderstood by others.

I ASKED KIM TO FLY TO Virginia from San Jose and visit me at my father's house, in part because I needed someone to help be a buffer with my father, to connect in ways I never could.

When she arrived, she looked around, sat her bags down in the kitchen, and asked, "Does he live here by himself?"

"Yes," I said.

"Your father, he keeps the place so nice, Christina," she marveled. "Look at how he arranged the decorations above the fireplace."

I hadn't paid much attention to my father's placement of items, or the way he'd decorated, beyond noting which objects he'd kept from our old life together and which ones he'd left and packed away. I glanced over at the print of a sailboat above the mantle, below which was printed: Success. There is only one success: to be able to live life in your own way. He'd arranged colorful figurines of sailors, boats, pelicans, and even penguins below it, creating a charming little seascape on the mantle.

"How does he keep the place so clean?" she asked. "And how could he live here by himself? It's so big."

She asked me questions that I hadn't thought to ask myself: *Why would he want to live in a five-bedroom house alone? Why didn't he downsize?*

A few minutes later, my father walked in carrying a small Igloo cooler for the one-and-a-half-hour commute that he made three times a week for his new job helping to review medical grants for a government agency. He put the cooler down next to the door and went back to his car to pick up his dry cleaning and his leftover seafood fettuccini from the previous day's lunch. I imagined he went to a generic seafood restaurant near his office, and I felt sad picturing him sitting at a restaurant alone.

"Dad, this is my friend, Kim," I said to him when he got back to the kitchen.

"Chào bác," she greeted him in Vietnamese. "Bác có khỏe không?"—*Are you doing okay?* She looked up at him in a respectful manner, the way young Vietnamese people are supposed to regard their elders.

"I brought you two different kinds of chả lụa from San Jose," she continued in Vietnamese. "They are supposed to be the best in the city." Her naturally sweet disposition softened even further when she spoke Vietnamese, her native language.

"Oh, thank you. So, girls, did you eat anything?" he asked as he put the beverages that he didn't drink back in the refrigerator.

Soon we were all sitting at the kitchen table, chatting, and I noticed how my father had changed over the years. This version of him, welcoming my visitors and trying to engage, was so unlike how he was when I was in high school, and he would watch me and my friends carefully, without saying a word.

Kim was not afraid of my father, and the fact that she was able to communicate with him in Vietnamese clearly helped him feel more comfortable with her. She kept probing him sweetly, and he was only able to smile in response.

"How's your nonprofit doing?" she asked. "What do you think of how they are trying to name the shopping plaza in San Jose?" She was referring to the ongoing debate about whether to call it Little Sài Gòn.

"Oh, you know what they always say," he said, chuckling. "Two Vietnamese people can work together, but if you put three together, there will always be an argument."

They continued talking in ways I'd never communicated with my father. We didn't have that sort of relationship. I wondered if it would be different if I spoke Vietnamese fluently.

When he left the room, Kim turned to me. "Your dad is so nice!" she exclaimed. "I don't know why you're not close to him."

I needed to see my father through Kim's eyes—through a Vietnamese heart that was not my own.

NGHĨA
Indiana | 1991

AFTER SIX YEARS IN TENNESSEE, WE spent a year in Illinois
and then moved to Ashland, a small town in southern Indiana
surrounded by rolling hills. Although not as dramatic as New
England, the Indian summer there was beautiful. The multicolored leaves engaged in a synchronized fall dance—floating in the
air, swinging back and forth, flipping upside-down, and tumbling
around before gracefully landing on the ground. Most of the
leaves fell at the same speed, although some would dash rapidly
to the ground like students bursting out of the classroom at the
end of the day.

About thirty miles from Ashland, there was a small Amish community. Men and women dressed in black or gray outfits; the men had
long beards and the women had their hair tucked into white linen
bonnets, and you saw them sometimes on their horse carriages, their
primary mode of transportation. I had heard that they were good
builders—exactly what I needed.

I found a man named Abe, a fifty-five-year-old bearded man who
looked older than his age. Had he dressed in red rather than black, he
would have looked like Santa Claus.

When we met, I showed him the plans of the house I wanted
to build.

"This is a Tudor house," I said. "Do you think you could build this?"

"Sure, I can do that at a reasonable price," he responded.

"Do you think it looks too small?" I asked.

"No, and it will be a reasonable price," he said, "but the brick will be special. I will have this plan enlarged and redrawn so we can see the details better."

"When do you think you can have that done?"

"In one or two weeks," he said.

He was mild-mannered but a tough bargainer. After a long bargaining session, the only concession I could extract from him was to lower the proposed price by one or two dollars. I gave up trying to get him to lower it any further; it seemed a fair amount. We parted ways with the agreement that he would let me know when the plans would be ready.

AFTER A FEW WEEKS, I HADN'T heard anything from Abe. I eventually left a message with one of his American contractors, since Abe didn't have his own phone, and he finally showed up a few days later with the preliminary drafts.

The house appeared small on the blueprints, just as I had feared, but Abe assured me that it was large according to his standards. I gave him the go-ahead—only to find out afterward that he was working on two or three houses at one time. He would lock in deals and start the foundation of one house, then begin another project. Some of the homes could be twenty or thirty miles away from each other. If something urgent needed to happen, he might show up consistently for a few days or weeks; then he'd disappear, nowhere to be found, for an extended period of time.

It was Lyne who made sure that Abe and his crew were doing their work. She also went after them to make sure they cleaned up at the end of the day, so the construction area wasn't littered with debris and tools. They loved her, though, because on most days she brought them hot lunches, which they preferred to the cold ones they'd packed hours earlier.

IN ASHLAND AND SURROUNDING AREAS, I met other Vietnamese families whose journeys paralleled ours. We would often meet for friendly gatherings where we would share Vietnamese dishes, our experiences in the U.S., and the difficulties we'd experienced during and after the war.

My friend, Tiên, shared with me how and his brother stayed at a camp in Thailand for three months after escaping from Việt Nam. Upon arriving at the camp, they quickly discovered how poorly organized it was. They also were shocked to learn that the single women there were at risk of being taken away by the camp workers in the middle of the night and raped.

Tiên volunteered as a cook in the camp because he thought it was time he started learning how to cook. He was nineteen years old and knew nothing about how to prepare food. Growing up, he'd relied on his parents for everything, but now he'd been thrust into the greater world—alone with his brother, nobody there to guide him. He knew he had to do something, otherwise they would both end up homeless.

After those few months in Thailand, the two brothers were transferred to Subic Bay Base in the Philippines, where they stayed for another six months, and where he continued to volunteer as a cook. Finally, they were sponsored by church members in Massachusetts to come to the U.S.

They arrived in Boston in the middle of winter. Coming from a camp in a tropical area to a bitterly cold region covered with snow was an eye-opener for them. Eventually, they moved to Texas, where Tiên got work in the oil industry. For a while he partied a lot, but then he realized that without an education, he wouldn't go very far. So he enrolled in a college in Ohio to pursue a degree in engineering. In the mornings he delivered newspapers to earn money, and during the day he attended class. After he graduated, he moved to Ashland and married a Vietnamese medical technologist.

Another friend, Vũ, had been a second lieutenant in the South Vietnamese Air Force. In 1974, he was sent to Alabama for pilot training with helicopters—but after the fall of Sài Gòn, all trainees like him were let go. Suddenly, he had no degree and no specific skills with which to search for a job. He moved to Texas with his friends, and they went to work for a manufacturing company dealing with cooling fibers. While the pay was good, he was so allergic to the fibers that he had to quit. He was then offered a job by a local farmer who promised good pay and free housing above the barn. His job entailed putting on long gloves and sticking his whole arm into a cow's rear end to disimpact it. He only lasted a few days. He eventually enrolled at a college in Missouri, where he studied engineering, before ending up in Indiana.

As I built my life in the U.S. and met more Vietnamese who had immigrated there, I listened in awe to their stories of the trials they faced as they built a life and a home in a new country. I knew one day I would collect those stories—tales of strength and determination to create something new—and share them with the world.

CHRISTINA
Hà Nội | 2010

MY CHILDHOOD WAS NOMADIC. I WAS born in Connecticut, and from there we moved to Utah, Tennessee, and Illinois before finally settling in southern Indiana. I considered Tennessee and Indiana to be the primary homes of my childhood, as I lived in each one for at least six years. I have very few memories of Connecticut. My father once mentioned that my mother opened an Asian restaurant there, but she couldn't even drive so I couldn't imagine how she might have run a restaurant.

Tennessee was the place where we actually nurtured something beautiful—a family life, being connected to the neighborhood, always working on and improving our home. I remember my father planting a white dogwood in front of our house, and the rhododendrons blooming every spring. My father bought us a season pass to Dollywood in Pigeon Forge, Tennessee, and at least a couple weekends a month we would go there and to Gatlinburg to eat pancakes and enjoy the mountain scenery. Life was peaceful, quiet, and we were building something as a family. While we'd lived the same amount of time in southern Indiana, that time felt overshadowed by my mother's illness.

Whenever people asked where I was from and where I'd lived, I would mention all the places. Sometimes they would respond by asking, *Why did you move so much? Was your dad in the military?*

No, I'd say with a shrug. *My father is a doctor.*

It didn't make sense for us to have moved so much, as far as I could see, and my father never explained his reasoning. Perhaps that nomadic existence was baked into me during childhood; perhaps that was what now, in my twenties, was causing me to move from place to place, never staying anywhere for very long. But whatever was driving this unsettled feeling within me, I hoped to one day resolve it. I wanted to find a place that finally felt like home.

THE THIRD AND FINAL TIME I moved to Hà Nội, the city was in the middle of celebrating its 1,000th anniversary on October 10, 2010. Years of preparation went into the ten-day-long spectacle packed full of events. The streets were pristine. There were rumors about street kids being picked up and sent away to the outskirts of town because the government didn't want visitors to get the impression that the city was dirty. Flowers were planted in open green spaces that spelled out *1,000 Năm Thăng Long*, the 1,000th anniversary of the foundation of the capital Thăng Long by the emperor Lý Thái Tổ. Lotus-shaped lights dangled from trees along Điện Biên Phủ. Vendors wearing conical hats descended onto the streets, capitalizing on the opportunity to sell more of their goods, encroaching on any small green or concrete space available to set up shop—offering popcorn, cotton candy, ice cream, bottled green tea, and "I ♥ Hà Nội" T-shirts.

The streets around Hoàn Kiếm Lake were closed off to traffic and packed with people from all over the country who convened for the celebration. Vietnamese youth proudly wore stickers on their cheeks: a red heart with a gold star in the middle, a representation of the Vietnamese flag. Toddlers sat on their father's shoulders and looked up in awe at the multicolored strings of lights above them. I imagined these festivities would linger on in their minds, like the Mid-Autumn Festival and Tết. Perhaps the feelings of pride for their city blossomed inside them during those warm fall nights when they listened to Vietnamese music interspersed with the pre-taped propaganda messages that blared from megaphones: *"Nhà nhà, người người gương mẫu thực hiện nếp sống văn minh để kỷ niệm nghìn năm Thăng Long-Hà Nội"*— *Every household and every person show a good example of a cultured lifestyle to commemorate the 1000th year of Thăng Long-Hà Nội.*

The new images of Hà Nội coexisted in my mind with the images of the Hà Nội I'd first encountered seven years prior. The city had changed, and developed since then; today, it only slightly resembled the charming, almost provincial, city that I remembered from when I'd first arrived in Việt Nam. Many of the beautiful old French colonial buildings—like the one that had housed Au Lac, where I first met Thomas—had been knocked down to make room for more profitable five- or six-story office buildings. I had hoped the city would preserve its beauty, that it would find a way to modernize without sacrificing the traditional—but I understood now that I could not expect Hà Nội to remain the same place I had known in the past.

I asked a good friend in Việt Nam if it was possible to be nostalgic for a place where you were currently living, and she said of course—that for many people in Việt Nam, this nostalgia was a constant part of life. I started to understand that my father's nostalgia for Sài Gòn and South Việt Nam, while dramatically different from my own, was a variant of what I was experiencing.

Since my last sojourn in Hà Nội, Western fashion brands, including Nine West, Aldo, Mango, and French Connection, had popped up in prime locations around town, as had boutiques by Vietnamese fashion designers trying to make their mark. The Vietnamese women I saw around town also appeared more stylish than they had been before, wearing shiny, three-inch heels and colorful, fitted dresses.

Bicycles, once pervasive, now seemed to be used only by old men wearing berets and seemingly stuck in another era. Seas of motorbikes, from Honda Waves to Vespas, now flooded the streets alongside all the new Hondas, Toyotas. And Kias, which honked their meek horns in the sea of vehicles and motorbikes. Traffic jams were common on the streets, which were ill-suited to handle so much moving traffic. Everyone, Vietnamese and foreigners alike, drove quickly, swerving in and out of traffic, ignoring signals, pedestrians, and other vehicles.

ONE MORNING, AFTER I HAD ORDERED a coffee at a new chain opened by an Australian couple, an American man in his fifties handed me his business card. He told me that he was the general manager of a Ford car dealership that had opened across the street. Its floor-to-ceiling windows were lined with polished cars ready to be handed over to new owners.

"I heard you ordering your coffee," he said to me. "We need people like you who speak English well. Let me know if you'd like to work in sales one day."

He'd mistaken me as a local Vietnamese girl who spoke English fluently, someone who could navigate selling foreign products to local Vietnamese. I didn't want to disrupt the image he had formed of me in his mind, so I simply said I would consider his offer.

Hà Nội no longer resembled the place for which I had longed. It was, quite simply, the location where it was easiest for me to set up a life, particularly a temporary one. There was nothing scary, or even novel, about returning to Hà Nội. Once I arrived at Nội Bài Airport, a place which many years before had seemed so foreign to me, I turned on my Nokia phone and immediately regained access to my former world. Once again, I had the same SIM card containing the numbers of friends, housing agents, my tailor, and my former colleagues; everyone was right at my fingertips.

Coincidentally, a handful of my friends had returned to Hà Nội at the same time as me. Mai was there, working on an environmental project, and Minh was there continuing his research, this time for his dissertation. Minh and I decided to live together in the temporary accommodation that he had found, and then I was considering finding a villa where all of us could live together.

Compared to other cities where I had lived, Hà Nội seemed so simple. Phones didn't require long-term contracts, apartment leases could always be broken, rooms were readily available to rent, even motorbikes could be rented with nothing more than a $50 deposit and a copy of your passport.

There was a comfort in returning to this city. Even though the air was more polluted, the streets more cluttered, and the Western influence more pervasive, I knew that I could always return to Hà Nội and find something unknown about myself.

I CALLED MY FORMER LANDLORD'S NEPHEW, Đất, to see if he could help me find a house for me and my friends.

"Yes, Tuyết—hi, Tuyết," he said with his usual enthusiasm. "When did you come back?" Without waiting for an answer, he said, "I'll find you a place. I know what you like now."

I was certain that Đất would be able to find me a new apartment. The last time I was in Hà Nội he'd ridden a worn-down motorbike because he saved the nicest motorbikes he had for renting to his clients, keeping the beat-up one for himself. Now he drove a large, shiny SUV and carried his trusty iPad with him at all times. He'd moved up in the world.

The next day, he called me and asked if I wanted to see a home on Tràng Thi Street. He thought it would be perfect for me and my friends, remembering that I liked places that had a certain level of charm.

When I pulled down the small alley—removed from the noise of Tràng Thi, a busy street running along the south side of Hoàn Kiếm Lake—I recognized the four-story house immediately. With its dark wood–trimmed windows, it stood out from the other homes in the alley, which were all painted in deep golden yellow and hunter green, colors from the French colonial period.

"I've been here before," I told Đất. "I know people who used to live here."

"Really, Tuyết?" His eyes widened. "You know this house?" Đất responded.

A woman in her late sixties with salt-and-pepper hair swept up in a bun came to the gate to meet us. She shuffled her feet slowly, dragging her flip-flops on the ground. I could tell by her features and the way she carried herself that she'd once been a beautiful woman. I imagined that she'd once had a long line of suitors.

"Chào bác, this is Tuyết," Đất said. He turned to me and said, "Bác Nhi used to be a famous actress, and her son is one of the most famous Vietnamese artists."

As bác Nhi opened the gate for us, he lowered his voice to a whisper and said, "Her family is very creative, very famous."

The times I'd been to this house previously flooded my mind. Thomas had lived there after he moved from his house on Trúc Bạch Lake. One time, when I was visiting Hà Nội, I'd slept in the living room area, and I'd been terrified by a rat that dashed across the room and had run upstairs to sleep on the sofa in Thomas's bedroom. When I was working for UNICEF, I'd attended a Thanksgiving party there hosted by another American, Logan, who had built a life in Hà Nội after first arriving as a Fulbright Scholar. He'd learned to speak Vietnamese and continued to work in Việt Nam. I remembered opening Facebook one morning when I was living in Geneva, and was dismayed to see that a memorial page dedicated to Logan had been created. I'd learned from another friend in Việt Nam soon after that he had committed suicide by jumping off a building in Sài Gòn. His death had prompted me and many of my friends who had lived in Việt Nam to reach out to each other. We had all been equally surprised and shocked to learn of this tragedy. It made me realize the importance of friendships in a foreign land; those friends became more like an extension of our families, our lifeblood, when we were miles away from our biological families.

We walked through the first floor into an open space that bác Nhi used as her living room; Đất told me she used it for entertaining and as her storage area. A pile of boxes and an old motorbike collected dust in the corner. There were two large black-and-white portraits of her and her husband hanging above the wicker sofa. A screen door separated her kitchen and bedroom from the common area. I couldn't see into her apartment area, although I was curious about the way this woman lived—alone, oftentimes beneath a group of expatriates. Only a flimsy plastic door, which didn't even lock, separated the ground floor where she lived from the three floors she rented out.

"Bác Nhi will still live at the bottom of the house, even if you rent it," Đất said to me.

"That's fine," I responded, by now accustomed to landlords in Việt Nam living in the same building, even directly above me.

Bác Nhi could afford to live on her own, but she'd grown comfortable in the house on Tràng Thi and said she enjoyed hearing the sounds of friends coming and going above her. I went through the motions of going through the rest of the house with bác Nhi and Đất, but I already knew that this house would be an ideal place for us to rent—much better than anything else on the market.

The part of the house that was available for rent spanned three floors and contained five bedrooms, four full bathrooms, a kitchen, and a living room. It was built, in typical Vietnamese fashion, so that multiple generations of a family could live on separate floors under the same roof. It was spacious and had track lighting in all the rooms and dark wood floors throughout, except for the kitchen, which had terracotta tiles.

Unlike the typical Vietnamese landlords, who seemed to favor cheap solutions and a simple, modern veneer, like shiny wooden floors, which would secure a quick rental, bác Nhi seemed to understand the value of maintaining the essence of her home, of preserving the charm and character at its heart.

"See, this is a good deal," Đất said. "If you don't like the price, I can talk to her son afterward, try to get a better deal for you."

"I think it will work," I told him.

"Her son told me that he rented this house out to Burmese artists when they were doing an artists' retreat," he said. "This house, Tuyết, it has a creative spirit, you see?"

I nodded. "I have to talk to my friends and see what they think."

We thanked bác Nhi, said our good-byes, and left the house.

Đất looked over at me with a big grin as I got on my motorbike and he made his way to his SUV. "Tuyết, I have an idea. If you don't rent the house with your friend, you and I can rent it. We can make it into separate apartments on each floor. You can be the designer and I can be the businessman. You can make it charming, and I can make us money."

Đất's comment made me smile, and while in the past we'd had a rather tenuous relationship, I appreciated his enterprising spirit—a trait I noticed and admired in many Vietnamese people.

NGHĨA
Indiana | 1993

WITH THE HOUSE COMPLETE, WE BEGAN to enjoy our life in Indiana. Lyne especially enjoyed the quiet life. She still hadn't learned to drive and didn't have a job; she dabbled with online interior design courses but was too afraid to complete the final exams. She had made a few new friends, however, including a few French women who were teaching her how to crochet. One of them, Eloise, had met her physician husband when he was working in the U.S. Armed Forces and stationed in France during World War II. When they first met, they couldn't speak to each other well, but slowly that improved. He eventually asked her to marry him and brought her back to Indiana, where she became his nurse. She watched our two daughters like a hawk and was quite strict with them.

In the spring of 1993, Lyne developed a chronic recurrent cough which doctors treated as an allergy. For many months, she received allergy shots without any improvement. While we were on vacation in Tennessee, where we went every summer for one week, she developed severe abdominal cramps. Looking back at her history, she'd had bowel problems for a while that we should have addressed sooner.

We left early from our vacation and brought her to the doctor at home. Upon examining her, they discovered a colonic mass that turned out to be cancerous. She was taken to surgery and underwent resection of the mass, but the cancer had already metastasized to her liver and lungs. She had chemotherapy, which helped her remain stable for a few months, but she developed severe left hip pain due to the metastasis in the hip area. Radiation only slightly eased the pain.

Due to both the radiation and chemotherapy, her appetite markedly decreased during this time. After each chemotherapy treatment, she developed nausea that lasted for two to three days. Everything tasted bitter and she was unable to eat much. She took Ensure Plus as a supplement, trying to keep her weight up, but it tasted awful to her.

We went through a predictable cycle over the next year: Lyne would have two months of chemotherapy and then a few weeks off, and then would have to take daily radiation for another four to five weeks. She slowly went downhill, but all the while she kept on fighting.

DURING THE TIME WHEN LYNE WAS sick, her family came to visit her from Europe and other parts of the States. It had been seventeen years since she'd been in touch with her family. Serendipitously, just after her diagnosis her brother happened to ask one of his physician friends in New Orleans if he knew where to find my brother, who was a pharmacist in New Orleans. A few days later, he received a message on his answering machine with our phone number. The timing could not have been better, since we expected by this point that Lyne had at most eight months to live.

Her first visitors were her sister Margot, brother-in-law Gerard, and mother, who flew in from Paris. Gerard had studied business in France in the late sixties. To supplement his income, he worked at a Chinese restaurant, and after years of being in that environment he became a great cook. Eventually he returned to Việt Nam for a time, and he and Margot met on the flight back to France from Việt Nam. Apparently, Gerard was immediately enamored by Margot, but it took him some time to win her over. They now lived in the center of Paris, in the front of a monastery, where they helped nuns with basic chores. It was by choice that they lived there, as they both had their own careers and investment properties in Paris.

Lyne's brother, Cường, the one who had found our phone number through my brother, also came to visit. He was a neonatologist who had married a flight attendant with whom he had three children in Việt Nam. He was a savvy businessman who moonlighted with an American firm in Sài Gòn and made a decent living while his school-mates were barely making ends meet with their military wages. He shared with Lyne how he'd worked like crazy to support his family when he arrived in the States. He'd had two children with his first wife during his residency, so he had five children to support. For a long time they lived in a small apartment in a poor neighborhood with no sanitation. The turning point for him was when he saw his younger son playing in a polluted creek; it was then that he knew he had to make his life better for his children.

His first wife filed for divorce and walked out of the relationship. He graduated from his program and started a practice in Louisiana; he met his second wife, who was a nurse. They had two children together, and she already had two kids from her first marriage, so together, they had nine children.

Solange, Lyne's youngest sister, also flew in from Switzerland to visit her. She'd left Cambodia when she was eighteen years old and married a Swiss man who took her back to his homeland. She loved Switzerland and the Swiss Alps. For many years, she and her husband had tried to have children, but less than a year after they finally did, her husband died from kidney failure. She'd later met an American man with whom she'd had a second child with, but that marriage had ended in divorce.

While all the visitors were in town, Lyne was an exceptional host. She was overjoyed to be with her family at the end of her life. They cooked food together every day, and the kitchen was filled with laughter and stories. Lyne was delighted to invite her French friends to meet her extended family, and to listen to them speaking to each other in French.

WE MADE ONE MORE ATTEMPT TO save Lyne's life by visiting the MD Anderson Cancer Center in Houston. The original appointment they gave her was for 11 a.m., but we arrived to find out that the meeting was for insurance purposes only. The doctor did not show up until 3 p.m. that day, and gave the verdict within ten minutes.

Nothing could be done.

We took Lyne to eat Vietnamese food after the appointment, and she simply stared out into space, barely eating the phở she had ordered.

WHEN WE RETURNED TO INDIANA, LYNE rapidly went downhill. A week later, she had to check into the hospital for further treatment. Her eldest sister and her brother flew into town to see her during her last days.

One day before she died, she told us she'd had a dream that morning: Two people in white robes had come to her asking if she was ready to go. The older person had said to her in a sweet voice that it was time to go. But she'd asked for one more day to see her family. They'd obliged and said they would be back tomorrow.

She passed away the following night.

HER DEATH WAS TRAGIC FOR OUR family, and its impact would be felt for years to come. At her funeral, I delivered a final tribute to her:

> On behalf of Lyne, I would like to thank all of you, who came from as far as France, Switzerland, California, Louisiana, and Illinois, as well as locally, to pay tribute to a wife, a mother, and a friend.
>
> If I had to write a book about her, I would have entitled it, If Life Was a Cross . . . for God knows how many crosses she had to carry during this journey on earth.
>
> She was born forty-eight years ago in Cambodia from a third generation of Vietnamese who had settled there many years ago. There always was animosity between the Vietnamese and Cambodians. To escape persecution, she had to flee Cambodia in 1972. I first met her at the University of Sài Gòn in 1973, and later on we got married.

In 1975, after the fall of Sài Gòn, she was left stranded in Việt Nam and had to suffer under the communist regime. The loss of her first child at that time added to her suffering. She gathered herself, became a staff physician at the French Grall Hospital, and earned enough money to pay her way out of Việt Nam.

How many people have been persecuted in two different countries like her?

She joined me in the U.S. in 1976. My training led us to Connecticut, New York, and Utah, and she faithfully followed me everywhere without asking any questions. We settled in Tennessee for five years before moving to Ashland, Indiana.

In 1993, she was struck with colon cancer, which is rare among the Asian population. She required two operations before receiving chemotherapy weekly for eight weeks. The medications made her uncomfortable for two or three days following each treatment and she would stabilize for a few days before the next treatment began. She lost her appetite and her weight.

Cancer went into her right hip and caused her to have a tremendous amount of pain. She could barely lift her leg at times. She had to take radiation treatment daily for three weeks. Cancer reached her liver, and she received radiation treatment for two more weeks while still getting her chemotherapy.

The cancer went into her lungs, causing her to cough continuously and to become short of breath. She suffered six more days in the hospital before God took her away. I asked myself: "How much more can a person endure without falling apart?"

Life was a cross. And she carried her cross valiantly and courageously.

She was a good-natured person, one of those rare people who would give her own clothes away if need be. If somebody gave her one thing, she would give him or her tenfold in return. Her mother came from Paris to visit during her illness. Despite her disability and pain, she gladly took a five-hour round-trip to Cincinnati to pick her up first, then drive her back. She would make sure that her mother had her three daily meals. How could anyone do more than that?

Lyne, you are now lying peacefully in front of us. Finally, you do not have to worry about pain, cough, constipation, nausea, loss of appetite—all these physical disabilities that wore you down.

You suffered long and hard enough. You carried all your crosses so valiantly and courageously, and for so long. And for that, I know that God will put you among his angels.

CHRISTINA
Hà Nội | 2010

LIKE EVERY HOME AND ALLEY IN Hà Nội, our villa came with its own cacophony of distinct noises. The construction started at 5:30 a.m. every day—the banging, the drilling, the workers talking in indecipherable Vietnamese in the alley behind our house. The land-lady's cat screeched in the alley in the middle of the night, a harsh sound I found especially disturbing because it sounded like a child calling out for help. The neighbor's bird, which rested in a cage cov-ered in a red T-shirt, greeted people with his distinct call as they neared our front door.

Mai insisted that I rent out the entire top floor of the villa. It was the most spacious room, almost like a studio flat, with its own bath-room. Large enough for its own living room area as well.

"It's like you'll have your own little apartment up there," she kept telling me.

I preferred the smaller room, the one right across from the kitchen and living area. It was quaint and charming and felt more closely connected to the life of the house—which was what I needed at the time. The top room was across the hall from the altar where bác Nhi went daily to burn incense and pay tribute to her ancestors, making me feel closer to the deceased than the living.

Even though I felt comforted by having friends like Mai around, people I had known for years, I felt a distinct distance from everyone. On one level, I was healing from the heartache I had recently endured—but on another, I felt a chapter was coming to an end, and I wasn't quite ready for that to happen. For whatever reason, I needed a little more time to close up this chapter in Hà Nội.

MAI HAD RETURNED TO HÀ NỘI to work on an environmental project. She'd left her job as a corporate lawyer and was helping her parents manage the seventeen-bungalow resort they'd ended up opening on Phú Quốc—exactly what Mai had dreamed about doing the first time we'd visited there. She was also navigating a challenging relationship. We were both on our journeys, so while this was a moment when I'd hoped she could be the "older sister," it quickly became clear that she had too much on her plate to fulfill that role for me.

Mai's father, like mine, had once claimed that he would never return to Việt Nam, but he now taught classes at a law school in Hà Nội. We were all part of an increasing number of Việt Kiềus who were returning to Việt Nam—to work, to contribute, and to connect, or reconnect, with their homeland. Now that Mai was in Việt Nam and running the resort with her parents, she saw them more than she had when they were all living in the States. In Việt Nam, they shared projects and passion, a country that could bridge the divide between them. I longed for that relationship with my own father.

I FELT UNSETTLED IN THE HOUSE on Tràng Thi. I was often ill, and even when I wasn't sick I was cold from the air that blew through the cracks in the windows. I knew that I would only be in Hà Nội for a year this time. I had already started to make plans about returning to San Francisco. I dreamed of a charming apartment in San Francisco—a Victorian or Edwardian building that would be insulated and warm. While San Francisco might be covered in a thick fog, at least it didn't have the pollution that filled Hà Nội's air and made it difficult for me to breathe. For many reasons, leaving Hà Nội before I became too resentful was imperative.

I stayed on the top floor for only a few weeks, and during that time I found every reason not to sleep there: the bed frame was falling apart; the cheap mattress was only a few inches thick and more closely resembled a board rather than a plush mattress; the windows weren't sealed, allowing the pesky mosquitoes and the cold breeze to find their way into the room. That arrangement was creating a fracture in my relationship with Mai. I felt that she wanted me to stay up there to maintain a distance between us, in part so she wouldn't have another challenging relationship to manage. Instead of talking, we emailed our frustrations to each other, even though we were living under the same roof and only thirty steps away from being able to speak in person.

Every evening, I tiptoed down the stairs and crawled into the guest room or lay down on the couch in the living room to sleep. The uneasiness I felt living in Tràng Thi, I believed, would be alleviated if I could only stay on the first floor.

Without even letting Mai know, I moved to the smaller room. Our housekeeper, cô Lộc, helped with the transition. She'd worked for a small group of my Vietnamese American friends and their families in Hà Nội for the past eight years and had grown accustomed to watching us move to different houses in Hà Nội, changing rooms within a house, even leaving Hà Nội and then finding our way back a few years later. Sometimes, she knew more about my friends's lives than I did. She would carefully give updates: "Hôm nay Mai hơi buồn. Tuyệt, nói chuyện với Mai?"—*Today Mai is a bit sad. Have you spoken to her yet?* If she knew one of us was going to a party, she would ask if the others were going as well.

She moved my clothes in large black trash bags and then hung them on the small wrought iron clothes hanger in my new bedroom. She walked up and down the stairs slowly, transferring my belongings methodically. In just a few hours, my room was set up.

CÔ LỘC WAS A STRONG, INDUSTRIOUS woman who refused to get things fixed by someone else until she'd tried doing it herself. She repaired lamps and even tried to fix small plumbing problems before deciding to call the landlord. Her presence comforted us, not only because of her competent logistical support, but because in many ways she'd become a part of our Hà Nội family.

On Wednesday and Saturday mornings, when cô Lộc cleaned our house, I could hear her chopping vegetables, making fried rice or another meal out of our leftovers, in the kitchen. She'd peer inside our refrigerator and prepare a warm meal out of whatever was available. We would wake up to a medley of dishes waiting for us on the kitchen counter.

"Ăn di."—*Eat*—she'd say, pushing the plate of food in front of me.

"But it's too much," I'd respond.

"Một ít thôi; ăn hết."—*It's only a little bit; eat it all.*

When she heard me coughing or sneezing, she'd rush to my room with a cup of trà gừng—tea with freshly sliced ginger, a dash of lemon, and some honey.

"Hôm nay có bị bệnh?"—*Are you sick today?*—she'd ask as she handed me a cup of tea. Instead of addressing me by my Vietnamese name, she often attempted to call me Christina, which ended up sounding like "Tritina."

Sometimes, I sat with cô Lộc at the kitchen island, talking and sharing the coffee I prepared in a French press.

"Do you want some?" I would ask.

"Just a little bit," she would answer timidly.

I later realized that she didn't really like Western coffee but was too polite to tell me.

Cô Lộc saved enough money working as a housekeeper for foreigners to build a house on the outskirts of town. I noticed that she became more "điệu," as the Vietnamese would say, over time, paying more attention to what she was wearing—tighter-fitting, lower-cut tops, high heels and even a little bit of lipstick. A friend told me that she had found a lover, a man who used to work as her xe ôm driver. I quickly understood the reason behind the newfound confidence and the broad smile that she brought with her to the house.

One day, when she saw me comfortably settled in my new room, she asked, "Tại sao Tuyết còn một mình? Tại sao Tuyết chưa có gia đình?"—*Why are you still alone? Why don't you have a family yet?*

My Vietnamese friends and colleagues made similar comments when they ran into me in Hà Nội. "I expected you to come back with a family," they would say to me.

"I want to meet somebody," I said. "I will one day." I couldn't explain to cô Lộc in Vietnamese all that I wanted to tell her.

"Even if sharing a life with someone is complicated," she told me, "it is vui hơn (a lot happier) than living alone."

I nodded in agreement.

I never felt alone living in the house on Tràng Thi, though, with the constant rotation of visitors we received there. Mai's boyfriend visited off and on from New York. Eventually, Mai rented out one of the other bedrooms to a Spanish girl who was working in Việt Nam on a short-term basis. After she left, the two upstairs rooms were rented to two Tasmanian medical students who were training at a local hospital.

FROM MY BEDROOM, I COULD HEAR the steady stream of people moving in and out of the house as they shuttled off to work or went out to meet friends in the evening. Sometimes, our housemates would call my name from the outside if they forgot their keys. Strangers also passed by throughout the day—the man who collected money for the electricity bill, the La Vie salesperson who dropped off bottled water.

I started sitting still, and began writing. I wrote through all my wounds and documented my family's stories. The stories poured out of me. I wrote about my mother's family and what I knew about them. I wrote about watching my mother pass away. I set up a desk right in front of the window, and every morning after I woke up, I sat at it for hours. Through my writing, I began to understand that I had ventured all the way to Việt Nam to connect with my family's roots, and yet I kept distancing myself from my immediate family. I didn't have a specific plan about what, if anything, I would do with my writing. All I knew was that I would write to understand my father, myself, and my Việt Nam.

I also recognized that I didn't need to channel my mother's spirit then; I needed to learn to connect with my family and in particular with my father. I didn't want us to be two distinct islands with a vast ocean between us any longer. I wanted us to know one another.

NGHĨA
Orange County, CA | 1970s–Today

LIFE WAS DIFFICULT FOR THE NEW immigrants in the late 1970s. Besides the language barrier, finding a well-paid job, a lack of familiar food, and the American culture itself presented problems for the refugees. Nothing was more challenging to their eyes than Western culture itself. Where Vietnamese culture was rigid, old, and structured according to Confucian principles, American culture was young, vibrant, noisy, and unabashed.

The sudden and unplanned departure from their native country left the Vietnamese refugees who came to the U.S. unprepared for all these changes. As they stacked up in boats to leave their homeland at a moment's notice to escape the communists, the thought of living in a foreign land may not have even crossed their mind. The vast majority had no idea what their ultimate destination would be, and they certainly had no time to study the languages and foreign cultures they were about to face. The priority was to get out of the country. The rest would be dealt with later on.

As soon as these refugees were released from the camps, they had to work hard to earn a living and become self-sufficient in their new country. They labored day and night, taking on the dirty, low-paying jobs that most people did not want.

One of the areas where many Vietnamese refugees settled was in Orange County, California, close to Los Angeles. Once mostly farmland and orange groves, it was now a sparsely populated town with a few Korean stores alongside empty boulevards. Slowly, the refugees out of Camp Pendleton near San Diego began settling the area, and found the virgin land an ideal place to rebuild their lives. The area where they settled soon became known as "Little Sài Gòn."

Little Sài Gòn has now grown so big that it has its own senior community and parks that are mostly frequented by Asians. Fountain Valley Hospital, as well as other local hospitals, cater to the Vietnamese with medical staff comprised mostly by Vietnamese physicians and nurses. Patients are even served ethnic food. There is a Vietnamese funeral home and cemetery. While the area previously boasted only one mall, Phước Lộc Thọ, now new malls have sprung up everywhere, rapidly changing the landscape.

Shops with Vietnamese signs abound. There's one grocery store chain that has three stores in Little Sài Gòn itself. Fabric stores where shoppers can choose the fabric of their choice and have their áo dàis custom-made in the stores abound. Seafood restaurants offer a variety of menus, including steamed Dungeness crabs, sauteed lobster, fried shrimp, steamed fish, etc. Many Vietnamese medical, dental, and law offices have opened their doors to keep pace with demands.

Over the years, Little Sài Gòn has become a vibrant city, making many refugees feel right at home in the middle of America. It has become a familiar and welcoming place for many South Vietnamese who escaped the communists in their search for freedom. The warm atmosphere I am sure reminds them of the old Sài Gòn, the city where many of them were born or lived in for some time, and the home that they lost forever.

In many ways, Little Sài Gòn has become the cultural and economic center for the Việt Kiều. It is the rallying point and common link for these displaced people, and it represents their fighting spirit and resilience. It is a place where they can display their intelligence, work ethic, dynamism, economic aggressiveness, and scientific and cultural know-how.

At the end of the war, they were chased out of their homeland for cherishing freedom of choice, politics, religion, and commerce. They fought for their lives, hanging on to any kind of floating vessel just to get out of the country. These refugees lost the Sài Gòn and South Việt Nam they loved, but today they have rebuilt a new city—one where freedom is respected and in which their talents can blossom instead of being constrained by communist ideology. The result is a fascinating and vibrant Little Sài Gòn that continues to grow and to serve as a beacon for free Vietnamese people.

At one point, a merchant in Little Sài Gòn plastered pictures of Uncle Hồ and the communist flag on the window of his shop. The Việt Kiều reacted strongly and angrily, boycotting his store, until he took down the pictures and went out of business. Since that time, every store in Little Sài Gòn has flown the South Vietnamese flag: three horizontal stripes against a yellow background. The red stripes represent the bloodshed in defense of the country by people originating from the northern, central, and southern regions of Việt Nam. The yellow color represents their skin color. Orange County, and few other U.S. cities where Việt Kiều live, have passed ordinances recognizing the South Vietnamese flag as the official flag of the Vietnamese.

Little Sài Gòn, a stepchild of the old Sài Gòn, has emerged over the years to represent the exiled homeland of the Việt Kiều—many of whom have spent more time abroad than in the motherland.

CHRISTINA

Hà Nội | 2011

MAI'S MOM, BÁC NGA, STAYED WITH us when she was visiting Hà
Nội and not working on one of their projects in the South. In the past,
Mai had mentioned that their relationship was challenging.

I understood that women's relationships with their mothers
could be difficult, and I also recognized, after having lived in
Việt Nam, that there were expectations that older Vietnamese
women placed on younger women, particularly their family
members. But whenever a friend of mine complained about her
mother, all I could think was, *At least your mother is still alive, and
you have an opportunity to heal your relationship and know her.* I
didn't have that luxury.

One Saturday morning when bác Nga was staying with us, I walked
by Mai's room and saw the mother and daughter duo lying in bed
talking, facing each other as their heads rested on opposite ends of
the bed. Mai sat upright, leaning against the headboard, and bác Nga
lay with her head at the foot of the bed. They were speaking softly to
each other in Vietnamese.

During that same visit, I saw bác Nga sitting in the common room
on a rattan couch. She was grading papers for her husband. The sunlight shone brightly from behind her, hitting the papers and
notebooks on the small table in front of her.

An image of my mother crocheting on our paisley couch crossed
my mind, and I wondered what it would have been like to spend
time with her in Việt Nam. *Would she have come to Việt Nam to visit me?*

Would she have wanted me to live in Hà Nội? Would we have sat on a bed chatting on a Saturday morning?

Bác Nga caught my glance. "I heard from Mai that you were sick," she said. "I bought soup for you from next door." She rose. "Let me get the Tiger Balm for you. Put it behind your ear and your neck. You'll feel better."

She also added finishing touches to the house—handmade, colorful pillowcases with embroidered flowers that she purchased from one of the tourist stores near Hoàn Kiếm Lake.

"See, I bought you some pillowcases for you guys," she said when she came home with them. "I think you can put this one here." Bác Nga placed one of the pillows on the mahogany brown sofa. "You need to have some color in the room."

She walked to the refrigerator and took out a plate of chopped persimmons. "I cut this for you guys, and nobody eats it," she called out. "Why don't you guys eat fruit?"

I felt a pang of envy for Mai. I wished for a mom like this—one who would buy decorations for my home, and bug me to eat more fruit. She didn't know how lucky she was.

LATER IN THE DAY WHEN I ran into Mai, I told her, "You're lucky your mom is here."

"Yeah, she's okay," she said with a shrug. "She's gotten better. There's still a lot we need to work on, but she is so much better than before." Her eyes widened a little as she remembered something. "Oh, Christina, we're going to see that woman I mentioned who can channel ghosts. Do you want to ask her about your mom? Maybe she could talk to her for you? You could ask her questions."

My ears perked up. "Remind me who this woman is?"

Mai told me that the Vietnamese woman they were going to see was known for her ability to channel the souls of the dead, and had become so popular that she was often flown to Cambodia to search for bodies of Cambodians massacred during the Pol Pot Regime. Mai and her mother were planning to hire her to search for bác Nga's mother's grave in a small village in northern Việt Nam.

The thought of channeling my dead mother intrigued me. I was curious about what she would have said about my life, what she would have advised me in the future. But after giving it some thought, I decided against it. I felt my mother would be pleased with how I had chosen to live my life—traveling in search of my story, seeking to understand her better and to uncover parts of my family and myself along the way. My mother was already on this journey with me, so I didn't need to ask her anything else.

My relationship with my father, on the other hand, still was not reconciled. Maybe that was why I felt such a need to live on the main floor of our house, close to the living humans, rather than the landlord's deceased ancestors.

I HAD FIRST MOVED TO HÀ Nội as a twenty-two-year-old; now, nine years later, I was celebrating my thirty-first birthday there. So much had changed, and so much time had passed. This time, though, as I prepared for my next steps—building a life in San Francisco—things felt different. My leaving wasn't about my impatience or unhappiness with Hà Nội; it wasn't about fleeing and not addressing my wounds; it wasn't about fear; it wasn't about running. This time, leaving was about walking toward a different life. I was finally ready to create something stable, and I hoped returning to the U.S. would give me the chance to develop a closer relationship with my father.

On one of my last evenings in Hà Nội, a group of my friends took me to the opening of a new bar. It was a modern venue with concrete walls and floors and wait staff dressed up in overalls as if they were factory workers. Large, abstract paintings created by an up-and-coming artist hung on the walls. As with most bar openings in Hà Nội, the place was packed with a good mixture of foreigners and Vietnamese—but this was a new era for Hà Nội, one that my friends and I no longer seemed to be a part of.

I sat down at an outside table with my friends, and couldn't help but listen to the Vietnamese American girl at the end of the table who was sitting with two French friends. She brimmed with enthusiasm as she told her friends about her connection with Việt Nam.

"My mother is from a small province in the North, my father is from Sài Gòn," she told them. "I just returned from a trip to Sài Gòn, and even though my father is from there, I don't really like it as much. I prefer Hà Nội's charm. It's just so beautiful here."

She seemed so naive to me, but she also reminded me of myself when I first arrived in Hà Nội, so eager to see how life would unfold there. I wanted to interrupt the conversation and make suggestions based on the regrets I had regarding my time there. I wanted to call her em and advise her the way so many Vietnamese women had advised me over the years. *Don't be alone. Find a partner. Create a family. Most importantly, study Vietnamese.*

I bit my tongue. I knew that she'd find her own way through and learn her own lessons in Việt Nam, just as I had. She'd discover her own path, begin to understand her family's history, create some semblance of a relationship with her father. She would incorporate her family's past into her understanding of her identity, and then, when she was ready, she'd find her way back home.

NGHĨA

Everywhere, U.S.A | 1970s–2000s

FOR HOLIDAYS AND SUMMER VACATIONS, I often brought my girls to New Orleans to visit my brother and his family. I thought New Orleans was a colorful and ebullient town with its French Quarter, farmers market, annual Mardi Gras celebration, and Jazz and Heritage Festivals. It was a city of contrasts, with many historical landmarks, and the site of many national conventions and meetings. It was known as the "Big Easy," where one could *"laissez le bon temps rouler"*— *let the good times roll.* Yet even with so much money pouring into the city, it remained poor and crime-ridden.

The South Vietnamese arrived in New Orleans in the latter part of 1975. At that time, the east side of the city was an area of unoccupied and underdeveloped marshland. A section of that area was given to a group of Catholic South Vietnamese to develop. There was no development around, except for a mall that was still under construction.

The Vietnamese who first developed that area were part of a parish of fishermen from South Việt Nam. After escaping their country under the leadership of their local priest, they settled down in the area and started opening stores and building homes. Slowly, it became a small village along Chef Menteur highway and a rallying point for the Vietnamese in Louisiana, southern Alabama, and Mississippi.

After Lyne passed away, through my brother, I was introduced to Alice, a Vietnamese medical student in New Orleans.

Alice's father, Mr. Lê, was a former politician and senator of the South Vietnamese government who'd left Việt Nam on April 29, 1975 by helicopter from the rooftop of the U.S. Embassy in Sài Gòn. The airload—consisting of former ministers, high-ranking officials, and senators—was dropped off on a Navy ship off Vietnamese territorial waters. Along with many other refugees, the former senator first arrived in the famous "Tent City" in Guam. After coming to the U.S. and trying out a few places, he finally decided to settle in New Orleans with his family.

As a former political leader, Mr. Lê, believed that the power of a nation started with its people. In Việt Nam, he could have accepted bribes and become rich, but he'd declined all of them. He believed that if he took the bribe money, he would become dependent and sub-servient to the donor—and once a politician was controlled by the donor he could not be impartial and vote with a clear conscience or in the best interests of his country.

When Mr. Lê landed in New Orleans, like most refugees, he did not have much money. He earned a living by selling fried chicken at a supermarket. The contrast was startling: one day he was a powerful senator, the next he was selling chicken.

He once spoke to Alice about Nguyễn Công Trứ, a high-ranking official in the 18th century who was promoted and demoted seven or eight times in his history. His highest position was that of commander general and his lowest and last position was that of a mere foot sol-dier. Yet Nguyễn Công Trứ never despaired and always performed his responsibilities with the utmost pride. In that same spirit, at the end of a working day, instead of throwing away his leftover pieces of fried chicken, Mr. Lê would give it away to the poor children and homeless people living in his neighborhood.

Alice's father reminded his family that everyone in the family needed to work to pay the bills. While in college, Alice attended classes during the day, then worked from 4 p.m. to midnight as a check-out clerk at a local supermarket. After college, she worked as a computer engineer for NASA and brought home extra income to sup-port the family. She had always dreamed of becoming a doctor, but her family's financial problems dictated that she put financial stability before her passions. Once her family was in a better position, she went back to school, attending night classes while still working full time so that she could fulfill her pre-med requirements. Eventually, she was accepted into medical school.

Mr. Lê, who had also previously been a professor of mathematics at the Naval University of Sài Gòn, eventually earned a position as a math teacher at a local university. He had exquisite people skills and helped scores of college students understand the intricacies of the subject.

During Alice's first year of medical school, her father became ill and was diagnosed with pancreatic cancer. They soon learned that it had already spread to his liver and lungs. The length of time from diagnosis to death was only one month. Although Mr. Lê did not leave his children material belongings, he had given each one of them the privilege of Western education alongside the teachings of traditional Vietnamese wisdom and shared with them the lessons learned from all his rich experiences—as a soldier, a political leader, an artist, and a deep human being—with all his strengths and weaknesses.

Alice and I were in a long-distance relationship for many years while she underwent her training. After years of this, we married. We made it official at a courthouse in Tennessee when we were on a vacation with my youngest daughter, and then we hosted a party in Indiana, where Elvis Phương came to sing. We danced and celebrated.

A few years after we married, we divorced. Although by this point, I had lost many things in my life—my country, my first wife, my son—this divorce was a challenging separation for me. I remembered my history, though, and how the history of my motherland began with the oldest recorded divorce. Maybe there was something about a country so divided from its onset and its descendants fighting against each other, and ultimately ourselves. But one thing I did know about Vietnamese, regardless of whether they were from the North or the South, was that we were resilient. Even after my divorce from Alice, I knew that I would heal, and once again find a way to move forward in life. That determination is what helped me reach this point in my life.

I COULD IMAGINE MY MOTHER IN her sixties at her English classes at a community college. She would be one in a class of twenty or so, including a Buddhist monk and mostly Spanish-speaking students.

I pictured the diminutive but strong woman with her long gray hair tied tightly in a bun on top of her head introducing herself to the class as Daisy, the translation of her Vietnamese name. They would not know that within this Vietnamese woman lived a deep sense of regret that, due to social conditions and the fact that her father died young, she was not able to finish school in Việt Nam. They would never know her long history of strength and resilience; the determination she exhibited throughout her life, the extra burden she faced throughout her childhood in Việt Nam as she was thrust into the limelight, taking care of her family at a young age after the passing of her father. They would never know her fortitude in raising her five boys, to instill in them an understanding of the importance of education.

While in California, she tried to be self-sufficient after four of my siblings graduated from school, and she even took driving lessons in her seventies. She initially failed the test—in fact, she failed many times. Someone told her that private lessons might be more beneficial for her, and after fifty hours of lessons, she finally passed. My mother joked that they were tired of seeing her take the test over and over again.

Before she passed away, we were able to visit her for one last Christmas. Four of her sons and all their children were present. During that time, she had a terrible cough, and about a week after the visit she became sick. The doctors discovered that she had cancerous cells in her pancreas, as well as her liver. She developed severe back pain, and even the pain pills did not take the edge off. She lost her appetite and her weight dropped substantially. I went back a second time to visit her, and just after arriving home from that trip, I found that my mother had been taken back to the hospital. She stayed there for two more weeks before finally passing away.

The night before the funeral, I could not sleep. I knew there was one more thing I needed to do: write her eulogy. I rose from my bed and wrote this:

Looking at my mother, lying in front of us in her eternal resting place,

I remembered that although she was a woman of small stature, she was a strong-willed person with a sharp mind and a bounty of love.

She was born in Ba Ria, a small town in Việt Nam, 77 years ago. Because her father died at a young age, she sacrificed everything to nurture her brother and three sisters to success.

She had a family of five sons. Living with sons only, she confided, was rather difficult for her at times. She did tell me that she could not confide in them as easily as if she had daughters, but she raised them to be successful (one pharmacist, two medical doctors, one dentist, and one businessman), which was a success of her own.

To have five successful daughters-in-law (one pharmacist, one medical doctor, two dentists, and a business manager) was another success of her own.

After the fall of Sài Gòn in 1975, she was left stranded in Việt Nam. She protected her three youngest sons from the communist government and finally brought them to safety in the U.S. That was another achievement of hers.

Later on, when she was struck with cancer, she bravely tolerated the pain caused by cancer and the operation without any lamentations.

Looking at her, I realized that:

No woman had fought so much for her siblings, for her family, and for her children as she did.

No person had sacrificed as much as she did.

No human being had suffered in silence more than she did.

Her life reminds me of Sisyphus in Greek mythology. Sisyphus was once punished by his gods to push a large boulder uphill. As he pushed it uphill, the boulder would roll back down onto him. My mother did not see her role as rolling a boulder uphill, but as carrying her cross to the top of the mountain. As she inched uphill, it would fall down on her, but she never despaired.

Today, she carried her cross uphill to the top of the mountain. She was at the end of her trip and had completed her share in this world.

The lotus in Vietnamese and Buddhist culture symbolize simple beauty, purity, and the elegance of the spirit. If anyone had personified the lotus image in life, it was the simple and remarkable woman who was my mother. She was born in obscurity, but through her will, she left a long-lasting legacy. The odds of her success in life were small. She could have blamed fate, but decided instead to take her chances and work hard to improve her odds.

Throughout my life, I thought about the symbolism of a simple lotus—that blooms through the mud—and whether lying flat in the murky water or dried in a restaurant vase, the lotus is always beautiful. I view all Vietnamese refugees like the lotus flower, within us there is an unprecedented strength of spirit and determination, which is why all over the world, you will see examples of Việt Kiều not only rebuilding their lives, but making a significant contribution to the new countries that they call home.

CHRISTINA
Virginia | 2011

MY FATHER AND I DON'T TALK about Việt Nam. I have realized that we may never understand each other's love for the motherland and we may never speak about Việt Nam. Over the years, what we have learned about each other and our two Việt Nams is through our writing—words we darted back and forth through email.

He sends me his essays and books; I send him sections of a work in progress. His writing is historical—but it is not written from an unbiased lens. In his writing I see a sense of loss, and sometimes a very deep resentment. I, in contrast, write about Hà Nội through an explicitly personal lens, based on the years I lived and worked there. I do not write about the weight of history (while I recognize and sympathize with the suffering it caused millions, including my own family) because, like the 60 percent of the Vietnamese who were born after the war, it does not solely define my understanding of Việt Nam.

When I write about Việt Nam, therefore, it is an attempt to articulate what I gained from the time spent there.

I once read an essay my father wrote for his nonprofit's monthly newsletter, called "The Vietnamese." The statement *Hà Nội is never to be trusted* was repeated at the end of every paragraph.

Does he know that Hà Nội was the very place where I became an adult? I wondered, reading these lines. *Does he know how many Hanoians became not only my friends but also a deep source of support for me?*

Like many of the young Vietnamese growing up in Việt Nam today, war was not the backdrop of my upbringing, and while it deeply

CHRISTINA VÕ & NGHĨA M. VÕ

impacted my family, it is not how I define Việt Nam. I wonder what my father would think if he knew that during my time in Việt Nam, I fell in love with both Hà Nội and Sài Gòn—two very different cities, each with their own charms.

In one of his essays, "On Being Việt Kiều," my father once asserted that "Young Việt Kiều, born and bred abroad, are politically naive and thus more 'history-ignorant' than their elders. Unbiased, they return home in droves, explore the country, see a new world and become a bridge between older generations—those who remained in Việt Nam—and those who had departed."

He likely views me as one of those young, politically naive Việt Kiều. Sometimes, though, when I revert to the role of daughter awaiting my father's approval, I can't help but hope he sees in me— through my writing or other work—the potential to help bridge the generational gap, to understand the history of my elders, and to stay true to my own personal experience of what Việt Nam meant to me.

AFTER LEAVING VIỆT NAM FOR THE third and final time, I visited my father in Virginia. He asked nothing of me, and I asked nothing of him.

I sat with the silence that had at one time plagued me. I set up a work area in the dining room, spending most of my time managing the logistics of my move to San Francisco. Leaning up against the wall nearby, I saw a certificate from the Vietnamese Medical Association, and another one that my father had received from his current workplace.

I would not go back to Việt Nam to live, and while so many thoughts ran through my mind, I couldn't share with my father all that was stirring within me. We barely interacted, and sometimes we wouldn't even pass each other for the entire day; this is also how I remember the years my father and I shared a home after my mother passed away. I heard his coughs and the creaking of his swiveling chair when he worked in his home office, simple sounds reminding me of his presence.

He was working on a book about the history of Sài Gòn. On occasion, I would hear a blast of Vietnamese music—a melodic song with a beautiful woman's voice—which he would quickly turn off. Sometimes he would listen to the entire song. I could never hear the words, and even if I did, I would not be able to decipher them.

We emailed each other to communicate, even though we were under the same roof, only one floor away from each other. He sent me links about emerging Vietnamese American writers, or Việt Kiều, who had made it in the States through business ventures; I sent him information about interesting projects, like artist residencies, that I heard were being launched in Việt Nam.

Our Việt Nams were different—that was abundantly clear.

One day, I received an email from a young friend in Sài Gòn named Giao. She was a brilliant young person who'd grown up in Sài Gòn with a single mother. Her father, who was originally from the North, had passed away when she was a child. We'd bonded over that commonality—a search to uncover and be closer to our fathers, even though mine was still alive. She was putting together one of the first TEDx conferences in Việt Nam, which would bring together some of the leading Vietnamese thinkers in Sài Gòn. I forwarded my father the email that she wrote cleverly from the perspective of Việt Nam to solicit speakers for the forthcoming event.

> My name is Sài Gòn. I've grown up from war, and over the
> past decade my economic growth has been quite compelling,
> compared with other cities in Việt Nam, as well as neigh-
> boring countries—which is accompanied by increasing
> income inequalities, friction between consumption choices,
> difference in cultural identities, and loosened social ties.
>
> However, as a young, dynamic and highly resilient city, I
> know I'm not alone in the midst of those mega-city ques-
> tions. I've seen a diversity of people coming
> here—Vietnamese from all parts of Việt Nam, non-Viet-
> namese who have become my friends, and Việt Kiều who

now understand me more than I do. Most of them meet the
ongoing dream of development. They carry it out using their
own expertise, be it architecture, education, social work,
media, or music . . .

Within five minutes, my father emailed me a response to pass on to her.

It is about time.

My name is also Sài Gòn, a pseudonym for all the Việt Kiều.
It is true that they know the city like the back of their hand
because they lived in it throughout the war, grew up there
and escaped when it fell.

Sài Gòn is not the city that many people cried about
because they lost it,

it is about an idea of freedom,

it is about the birth of an idea,

which grew up from the swamps of the Mekong Delta to
become the guiding light for the South Vietnamese.

It began in 1698 when the Việt took it over from the Khmers,
Before that it was a Cham city, called Baigur
It had seen many wars, rebellions, carnages
But it always rebounded anew,
because the idea was there and is still there.

It is about freedom, commerce.

Sài Gòn

I was struck by the beauty of the exchange between the two of them, between two very different generations.

WHEN I VISIT MY FATHER TODAY, I sneak into his office—just as I did when I was a kid. I look at the books on his bookshelf, most of which are lined with history books about the war—*The Vietnamese*

Gulag, Hearts of Sorrow, South Wind Changing, The Perfect War. There are a few shelves with neatly arranged self-help books about love, intimacy, spirituality, meditation, and death.

He has images taped on the wall above his desk—a small picture of the Virgin Mary with her hands raised in prayer, a sun setting behind an ocean, a lotus flower, and a palm tree on a pristine beach. I still stare at the quotes he has taped to his wall—from Mother Teresa, Antoine de St. Exupery, Nguyễn An Ninh (a radical of great importance to the Vietnamese Revolution in the '20s and '30s), and others.

We don't know each other's Việt Nam. We have a different love for Việt Nam, a different idea of what it represents in our lives. And I may never know the yearning one feels for a country they've lost.

But what we share is a nostalgia for Việt Nam—a quality of longing that exists in many Vietnamese people. For the older generation, it's nostalgia mixed with pain, loss, regret, guilt, love, and resentment. My own nostalgia, and perhaps that of the other Việt Kiều of my generation who have returned to Việt Nam, is different: I long for the Hà Nội I knew ten years ago. My Hà Nội, in a way, is also being lost—to development, to materialism, to overwhelming traffic, to pollution, to so-called progress.

My father spent ten years writing a book about Sài Gòn. He writes passionately about the city that is his muse. "Her free spirit makes her attractive, captivating, and challenging. She is also indomitable, resilient, and unique. Growing by leaps and bounds once left to herself, she is also the seductress on the Mekong, the underestimated nymph that outsiders often misunderstand."

If my father ever returns to Sài Gòn, I think he will be surprised.

If he goes back, he will feel the spirit of the city that lives on in his memories and in his heart. He will find that he can still smell the scent of tamarind in the air; he can still watch boats of all sizes and shapes glide along the Sài Gòn River; he can still eat at the food stalls behind Bến Thành market. During Tết, the flower market still fills Nguyễn Huệ Street, and people still spend hours there searching for the perfect hoa mai. While many of the buildings may have been replaced by large shopping malls, the important ones he remembers biking past as a child still exist.

My father no longer gives me self-help books, as he did when I was a teenager. Now he gives me books about Việt Nam. On one of my trips home, he gave me *Fallen Leaves: Memoirs of a Vietnamese Woman from 1940-1975*, by Nguyễn Thị Thu Làm.

I opened the book to the end and read:

> As for me and the Vietnamese of my generation, there will always be memories of another time and place, another life. I will forever remain an immigrant here. And even when I am happiest, I will remember my beloved Việt Nam and the fate of my people.
>
> I am a child of war; I am a child of Việt Nam.

I'll fold my father's Việt Nam into my own. But will he ever understand mine?

Even if our opinions never change, we can at least find connection through a shared longing for the country we left behind.

He sits upstairs and writes about his Việt Nam, and I sit downstairs and write about mine.

Together, we weave a story that echoes across generations. A narrative of a Vietnamese refugee, uprooted by turmoil, who sows seeds of a new life in the vastness and peacefulness of the United States. It's the tale of a Vietnamese-American who voyages back to Việt Nam, her heart beating with desire to for family and history. It is the saga of a father and a daughter, striving to bridge gaps—of generations, of time and space, and of a shared homeland.

Together, we sculpt a narrative that reaches back into our pasts, reflecting a mutual love for a motherland, intricate and nuanced, that cradled us with the same tenderness of a mother's touch. A homeland that nourished us, shaping us with the same profound influence as our own mothers; another shared thread in our intricate tapestry—mothers who echoed louder in our thoughts than in our day-to-day existence.

Together, we add to the poignant and abiding nostalgia of a homeland that pulses more vibrantly in our memories and our hearts than in our present. Like countless other Vietnamese refugees and Việt Kiều scattered across the world, we inhabit a liminal space—a purgatory of sorts.

My Việt Nam, your Việt Nam—it's here that we nurture an aching longing for a home and a homeland that might, perhaps, only resonate within the confines of the past.

EPILOGUE

NGHĨA

Virginia | 2023

FIFTY YEARS HAVE PASSED SINCE THE Việt Kiều set foot on unfamiliar shores. From the few thousands of refugees who fled Việt Nam before 1975, the community has flourished into a thriving group of three million individuals, many of whom have found their home in the West. In the United States, the Việt Kiều stand as one of the largest refugee populations, their exponential growth a testament to their hard work and perseverance.

Their journey has not been easy, yet their unwavering spirit and determination have driven them to achieve great success, both economically and culturally. This success is due to the tireless efforts of all members of the community, working together toward a brighter future.

The term Việt Kiều was once used by the Hà Nội government to label those who had fled abroad, but over time its meaning has expanded. Today, being Việt Kiều transcends merely living overseas, encompassing the support and love shown by those who have sent back aid to their relatives in Việt Nam and those who have returned home with knowledge and wealth to bolster their country's economy.

Defining Việt Kiều is a complex matter, as its members are a diverse group of individuals with varying experiences and opinions. Generals, soldiers, professionals, and fishermen, young and old, rich and poor, Catholics and Buddhists, all have found a common bond in their South Vietnamese heritage and their shared aspiration for freedom. And among them are the second-generation Vietnamese

Americans, born and raised in the West, who bring their unique perspectives to the definition of being Việt Kiều.

For many older Việt Kiều, their love for their country is tempered by their belief in democracy and freedom, and they vowed never to return unless these values were upheld. However, the younger generation—raised abroad and untainted by political biases—return home in droves, eager to explore their roots and bridge the gap between their elders and those who remained in Việt Nam.

The horrors of war continue to shape the lives of those who experienced it, particularly the men who fought and suffered. The loss of their homeland, rights, and self left them feeling physically, financially, and emotionally destroyed, and it took great strength and resilience to overcome these challenges and become a new breed of Việt Kiều—pioneers and pilgrims who have overcome adversity and remade themselves into resilient, hopeful individuals dedicated to freedom and independence.

Being Việt Kiều is not just a physical state, but a state of mind. It is the willingness to take risks, the ability to reinvent oneself, and a steadfast commitment to freedom and independence. This is the legacy of the Việt Kiều, a testament to their strength and resilience, and a source of inspiration for generations to come.

CHRISTINA

Texas | 2023

I RECENTLY DROVE FROM SANTA FE to Lubbock to attend a conference at Texas Tech University centered on Vietnamese history. This was the second time I participated in the conference with my father; the first one was in Orange County a year prior.

On the five-hour drive, I felt nervous about seeing my father, who will turn 76 years old this year. Every time I see him, I witness a subtle decline in his health, and while I understand that it is a natural part of aging, the thought of losing my father is difficult to bear, despite the distance that has always existed between us.

When I saw him in the lobby, he handed me my room key and smiled. He said he was waiting to talk to one of his friends, so I could go settle into my room.

Ten minutes later, his girlfriend, Giang—the Vietnamese woman who used to call him and bring him food, and yet who he didn't introduce me to until they'd been together for at least seven years—knocked at my door. Over the years, we have become close, and very much like my mother, and in some ways Alice. She's become a conduit to navigate my relationship with my father. She sat in my hotel room and explained his sleep apnea, his difficulty breathing, and how she has encouraged him to talk to me about what will happen if he passes away. She expressed her concern about what she will do if he dies, since they live separately, she is not privy about the details of his private life. She told me that he only recently retired from his research job, having wanted to hold onto for as long as he could, a fact he would never tell me himself.

Truthfully, my father seemed happy at the conference, among peers who also have a passion for Vietnamese history. Many of the attendees he'd met online in forums as they discussed their shared research interests. Years ago, according to Giang, he invited some of them to a Vietnamese conference he organized in Northern Virginia through his non-profit, SACEI. He spoke to a handful of American veterans—individuals who had also been deeply impacted by the war—as if he had known them for years. He smiled warmly when they spoke to him, and laughed gently at their jokes. Within this community, I noticed my father at ease.

This year, his presentation was on "Two Việt Nams," and because of his abiding passion for Việt Nam, I did not have the same fear as I did when hearing him speak years ago at my mother's funeral and at his 25th medical school reunion. By now, I was acutely aware that one of his greatest loves is Việt Nam, and that when one speaks with passion, it is infectious. He began his presentation with a legend—that Việt Nam and its people are the descendants of Lạc Long Quân and the Fairy Âu Cơ. The couple separated and their division bore two separate groups that ultimately became North and South Việt Nam. As I listened to my father's words, it made sense to me that Việt Nam was a country that began with division. That magical land, which inspires great myths and legends, has endured centuries of war and internal conflict. That history and legacy is reflected in my relationship with my father, and perhaps all descendants of Vietnamese. Our father-daughter relationship embodies the duality of Vietnam—we are separated by a divide, and yet somehow, we are still one.

AFTERWORD

IN A RECENT CONVERSATION WITH A friend, after learning about
My Vietnam, Your Vietnam, she posed the intriguing question: "How
did you manage to co-author a book with your father without dis-
cussing it with him?"

I chuckled, responding simply with, "Good question."

However, that question uncovers a remarkable truth about the
creation of this book: we hardly spoke about it. People often find
it hard to believe when I reveal that my father and I hardly
interact with each other. This lack of communication with him
has defined our relationship, and weighed on my heart for most
of my life, influencing all my relationships—particularly my intimate connections with men. Yet, the completion of this book
helped me reach the pinnacle of a long healing journey of that
primary parental bond. By combing through his story, I developed a profound understanding and love for my father, and
ultimately began to understand the way he communicated his
love to me.

The genesis of this book began twenty-five years ago when
my father penned his story, *The Pink Lotus*, self-publishing it a
few years after my mother passed away. Ten years later while I
was living in Việt Nam, the epiphany came to me that I would
one day share his story, though at that time, I had no inkling of
how that would come to fruition, but did not disclose the narrative structure.

Then, in 2022, after completing my first memoir, I realized our stories could intertwine—that one book could tell both his story and mine. I reached out to my father to ask if he still had the original file for *The Pink Lotus*. Unfortunately, he did not, so with the physical copy in hand, I typed his words again, at the same time exploring my writing on Việt Nam and finding ways to weave together the themes of our unique love and experience of the motherland.

While working on the book, I kept my intention to intertwine my Việt Nam experiences with his narrative hidden, and curiously, he never probed. Occasionally, I reached out to clarify details or delve into specific topics that needed to be elaborated upon.

Later, in March 2023, while attending a conference at Texas Tech University with my father, I heard him present his ideas on "Two Việt Nams." As he spoke, my mind spun, recognizing insights that shaped not only the book's introduction but also illuminated our differing perspectives and experiences, and alluded to the historical divisions within the country for hundreds of years.

When the conference ended and while he was en route to his home in Virginia, I texted him, requesting a summary of his talk. I was excited about this epiphany, and my father implicitly understood this.

During the subsequent months, while searching for a publisher, my father remained completely unaware of the book's structure or my writing perspective. Only after securing a publisher, and following meticulous rounds of editing, did I share the full manuscript with him. My fear and apprehension were tangible; I worried he might disagree with the structure or specific content. My primary intention with him reading the full manuscript was to seek his expertise in reviewing the Vietnamese diacritics, given my limited Vietnamese language skills. His reaction, however, was both surprising and reassuring. He carefully reviewed the text in just two days, providing feedback with the grace that has always defined our relationship yet often remained hidden to me.

Along with the revised manuscript, he sent this message:

> Christina,
>
> This is a good book.
>
> Thank you for writing it.
>
> Attached is the revised copy.
>
> Good luck.
>
> Dad

Although he wrote only a few words, they landed straight to my heart. All the worries and fears I had of his disapproval washed away, and I felt his respect for my creative vision. Those succinct lines felt reassuring and soothed my concerns. Most importantly, they reverberated his love.

This undertaking has deepened my admiration and affection for my father. The trust and the way our stories have woven together have underscored my respect for his journey. My youthful experiences in Việt Nam pale in comparison to his profound odyssey, yet they found harmony. His unflagging belief and confidence in my creative process demonstrated his love for me and his faith in my vision.

When I responded to him, I expressed my gratitude for his journey, courage, wisdom, and willingness to share. I feel honored and blessed to have such an intelligent, respectful, kind, thoughtful, and profound father. Although not many words pass between us, the emotion, the care and the concern can be read through these pages.

To this day, my father continues to inspire me to seek deeper understanding and greater purpose.

ABOUT THE AUTHORS

PHOTO BY ELISA CICINELLI

CHRISTINA VO IS A WRITER, WHO currently works in development for Stanford University. She previously worked for international organizations in Vietnam and Switzerland and also ran a floral design business in San Francisco. She is the author of one previous memoir, *The Veil Between Two Worlds* (She Writes Press). Vo resides in Santa Fe, New Mexico.

NGHIA M. VO, A RETIRED PHYSICIAN, is an independent researcher of Vietnamese history and culture. He has written numerous books on Vietnamese culture and works to document Vietnamese-American culture through conferences and publications. His books include *The Vietnamese Boat People* and *Saigon: A History*.

RECENT AND FORTHCOMING BOOKS FROM THREE ROOMS PRESS

FICTION

Lucy Jane Bledsoe
No Stopping Us Now

Rishab Borah
The Door to Inferna

Meagan Brothers
Weird Girl and What's His Name

Christopher Chambers
Scavenger
Standalone

Ebele Chizea
Aquarian Dawn

Ron Dakron
Hello Devilfish!

Robert Duncan
Loudmouth

Michael T. Fournier
Hidden Wheel
Swing State

Kate Gale
Under a Neon Sun

Aaron Hamburger
Nirvana Is Here

William Least Heat-Moon
Celestial Mechanics

Aimee Herman
Everything Grows

Kelly Ann Jacobson
Tink and Wendy
Robin and Her Misfits

Jethro K. Lieberman
Everything Is Jake

Eamon Loingsigh
Light of the Diddicoy
Exile on Bridge Street

John Marshall
The Greenfather

Alvin Orloff
Vulgarian Rhapsody

Micki Janae
Of Blood and Lightning

Aram Saroyan
Still Night in L.A.

Robert Silverberg
The Face of the Waters

Stephen Spotte
Animal Wrongs

Richard Vetere
The Writers Afterlife
Champagne and Cocaine

Jessamyn Violet
Secret Rules to Being a Rockstar

Julia Watts
Quiver
Needlework
Lovesick Blossoms

Gina Yates
Narcissus Nobody

MEMOIR & BIOGRAPHY

Nassrine Azimi and Michel Wasserman
Last Boat to Yokohama: The Life and Legacy of Beate Sirota Gordon

William S. Burroughs & Allen Ginsberg
Don't Hide the Madness:
William S. Burroughs in Conversation with Allen Ginsberg
edited by Steven Taylor

James Carr
BAD: The Autobiography of James Carr

Judy Gumbo
Yippie Girl: Exploits in Protest and Defeating the FBI

Judith Malina
Full Moon Stages: Personal Notes from 50 Years of The Living Theatre

Phil Marcade
Punk Avenue: Inside the New York City Underground, 1972–1982

Jillian Marshall
Japanthem: Counter-Cultural Experiences; Cross-Cultural Remixes

Alvin Orloff
Disasterama! Adventures in the Queer Underground 1977–1997

Nicca Ray
Ray by Ray: A Daughter's Take on the Legend of Nicholas Ray

Stephen Spotte
My Watery Self:
Memoirs of a Marine Scientist

Christina Vo & Nghia M. Vo
My Vietnam, Your Vietnam

PHOTOGRAPHY-MEMOIR

Mike Watt
On & Off Bass

SHORT STORY ANTHOLOGIES

SINGLE AUTHOR

Alien Archives: Stories
by Robert Silverberg

First-Person Singularities: Stories
by Robert Silverberg
with an introduction by John Scalzi

Tales from the Eternal Café: Stories
by Janet Hamill, with an introduction by Patti Smith

Time and Time Again:
Sixteen Trips in Time
by Robert Silverberg

The Unvarnished Gary Phillips:
A Mondo Pulp Collection
by Gary Phillips

Voyagers: Twelve Journeys in Space and Time
by Robert Silverberg

MULTI-AUTHOR

Crime + Music: Twenty Stories of Music-Themed Noir
edited by Jim Fusilli

Dark City Lights: New York Stories
edited by Lawrence Block

The Faking of the President: Twenty Stories of White House Noir
edited by Peter Carlaftes

Florida Happens:
Bouchercon 2018 Anthology
edited by Greg Herren

Have a NYC I, II & III:
New York Short Stories;
edited by Peter Carlaftes
& Kat Georges

No Body, No Crime: Twenty-two Tales of Taylor Swift-Inspired Noir
edited by Alex Segura & Joe Clifford

Songs of My Selfie:
An Anthology of Millennial Stories
edited by Constance Renfrow

The Obama Inheritance:
15 Stories of Conspiracy Noir
edited by Gary Phillips

This Way to the End Times:
Classic and New Stories of the Apocalypse
edited by Robert Silverberg

MIXED MEDIA

John S. Paul
Sign Language: A Painter's Notebook
(photography, poetry and prose)

DADA

Maintenant: A Journal of Contemporary Dada Writing & Art
(annual, since 2008)

HUMOR

Peter Carlaftes
A Year on Facebook

FILM & PLAYS

Israel Horovitz
My Old Lady: Complete Stage Play and Screenplay with an Essay on Adaptation

Peter Carlaftes
Triumph For Rent (3 Plays)
Teatrophy (3 More Plays)

Kat Georges
Three Somebodies:
Plays about Notorious Dissidents

TRANSLATIONS

Thomas Bernhard
On Earth and in Hell
(poems of Thomas Bernhard with English translations by Peter Waugh)

Patrizia Gattaceca
Isula d'Anima / Soul Island

César Vallejo | Gerard Malanga
Malanga Chasing Vallejo

George Wallace
EOS: Abductor of Men
(selected poems in Greek & English)

ESSAYS

Richard Katrovas
Raising Girls in Bohemia:
Meditations of an American Father

Vanessa Baden Kelly
Far Away From Close to Home

Erin Wildermuth (editor)
Womentality

POETRY COLLECTIONS

Hala Alyan
Atrium

Peter Carlaftes
DrunkYard Dog
I Fold with the Hand I Was Dealt
Life in the Past Lane

Thomas Fucaloro
It Starts from the Belly and Blooms

Kat Georges
Our Lady of the Hunger
Awe and Other Words Like Wow

Robert Gibbons
Close to the Tree

Israel Horovitz
Heaven and Other Poems

David Lawton
Sharp Blue Stream

Jane LeCroy
Signature Play

Philip Meersman
This Is Belgian Chocolate

Jane Ormerod
Recreational Vehicles on Fire
Welcome to the Museum of Cattle

Lisa Panepinto
On This Borrowed Bike

George Wallace
Poppin' Johnny

 Three Rooms Press | New York, NY | Current Catalog: www.threeroomspress.com
Three Rooms Press books are distributed by Publishers Group West: www.pgw.com